Fearless Confessions

Fearless Confessions

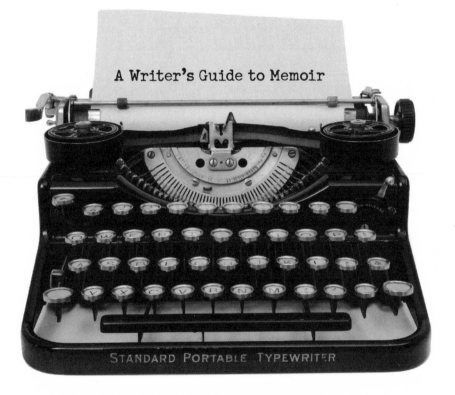

A Writer's Guide to Memoir

Sue William Silverman

The University of Georgia Press
Athens & London

Published by The University of Georgia Press
Athens, Georgia 30602
www.ugapress.org

Designed by April Leidig-Higgins
Set in ArnoPro by Copperline Book Services, Inc.
Printed and bound by Thomson-Shore

The paper in this book meets the guidelines for
permanence and durability of the Committee on
Production Guidelines for Book Longevity of
the Council on Library Resources.

Printed in the United States of America
09 10 11 12 13 P 5 4 3 2 1

Library of Congress Cataloging-in-Publication Data
Silverman, Sue William.
Fearless confessions : a writer's guide to memoir /
Sue William Silverman.
p. cm.
Includes bibliographical references.
ISBN-13: 978-0-8203-3166-9 (pbk. : alk. paper)
ISBN-10: 0-8203-3166-X (pbk. : alk. paper)
1. Autobiography — Authorship. I. Title.
CT25.S53 2009
808'.06692 — dc22 2008050248

British Library Cataloging-in-Publication Data available

Selected portions of chapter 9, "Confessional and (Finally)
Proud of It," appeared, in another form, in the *Writer's Chronicle*,
Special Commemorative Issue, 2002, published by the
Association of Writers and Writing Programs.

for Marc,
with love

with gratitude and thanks to
the Vermont College of Fine Arts,
a haven for writers

In fact, I sometimes think only
autobiography is literature.

VIRGINIA WOOLF

Life must be understood backwards.
[Although] ... it must be lived forwards.

SØREN KIERKEGAARD

Contents

Preface

In *Fearless Confessions*, I invite you to accompany me as I look back at what I learned on my path toward becoming a writer, hoping to assist you with your own journey. When I first began to write, I struggled through numerous false starts and made many mistakes before gradually understanding how to plot and focus a memoir, find an authentic voice, shape imagery into metaphor — all the elements needed to craft raw experience into a fully formed story. *Fearless Confessions* also contains exercises and examples to help you cultivate the courage to send your own words out into the world.

Why the title *Fearless Confessions*? Critics frequently belittle the entire genre of memoir, especially books by women, by labeling memoir "confessional." I initially conceived of this book as a way to redeem the notion of "confessing" for silenced women. Additionally, I've come to realize that the lives of a whole host of us — rebels, dreamers, anyone considered "other," regardless of gender — have been marginalized. Many critics don't yet understand that when we "confess" we seek the *commonality* of our experiences, thus adding to the full range of what it means to be intensely human. Fearlessly writing memoir allows us to understand our own life narratives, as well as to learn from those "others."

The more artfully we write, the more difficult it is to ignore or dismiss our stories. *Fearless Confessions* is intended to help ensure that our voices are heard.

Fearless Confessions

Chapter One

The Longest Paragraph

Y ou should write your own story," Randy, my therapist, says to me.

I've been in therapy about a year. I slouch on the blue couch in Randy's Atlanta office, lean my head back, and stare at the ceiling, nervous to meet his gaze. I put my feet, in red leather Reeboks, on his coffee table. This table, this couch, his office — they're all designed to comfort his clients.

But I don't feel comfortable. I want to say to him: Write about myself? You're the one who must be crazy! Why would I want to write about myself? I want to say to him: I don't have anything to say about myself. Nothing. I don't have any earthly idea how to write about myself . . . I mean, even if I wanted to!

I want to say: No, no, no!

"Well?" he says, waiting.

I glance at him, at his blue eyes — blue — the peaceful color of the couch, of the walls of his office. But as he raises his eyebrows, inquiring, I look away again.

The plant in the corner by the window seems dry, brittle. I want to tell him to water it. Maybe we can spend the session discussing horticulture. I lean forward and retie my left sneaker, even though the knot is perfect. I want to do anything but respond to what surely must be, if not a crazy idea, then clearly an impossible one.

"I don't have anything to say about myself," I answer.

"You sound angry," he says. "Why don't you want to write about yourself?"

He knows I've been trying to write novels for years. So what he really means is: Why don't I stop writing fiction and write a true story?

A true story.

On this day in his office, I'm sure that the official word, *memoir,* isn't in my mind. How could it be? Back then, in the early 1990s, I hardly even knew the title of one.

I want to say: None of my writing teachers ever suggested I write about myself. So why would you? I want to say: Who'd even want to read a story about me?

A story about me.

He means: Why don't I write a story about a woman whose father, when she was growing up, sexually molested her? He means: Why don't I commit to paper secrets I've hidden for years, secrets about both my childhood and my current disarray — that I'm in therapy for sexual addiction and anorexia?

Which means, in my mind, that I'd be writing a story about a woman whose life is embarrassing, humiliating, shameful.

Why would I want to do *that*?

It's true that last week I did write about myself — but only as a therapeutic exercise, and only for Randy to read. I wrote a short, unmailed letter to my father about growing up as his daughter, living in houses that felt like prisons.

That letter I wrote is now in Randy's hand.

"That's all I have to say about myself." I nod toward the letter.

"I know you think that," he says. "But I don't think that's true."

Periodically, over the next few years, Randy continues to say, "Write about yourself." I always respond, "I have nothing to say about myself. Nothing at all."

Now, today, for the first time, he includes a new word, the word *safe*, in his statement. He says that maybe now I'll feel safe enough to write about myself because just last week both my parents died: my mother from lung cancer, my father from a stroke. I am relieved they are dead.

I am sad they are dead. I am angry they are dead, angry because they died without once, even on their deathbeds, acknowledging the incest. They never apologized. Nothing. I also feel stunned to realize that, within six days, I have suddenly become an orphan.

Yet I've always felt like an orphan, anyway, haven't I?

Randy would probably say that if I wrote my story, I'd find out why I always felt like an orphan; I'd also better understand the relief, the sadness, the anger.

I stare at an Ansel Adams photograph hanging on the wall across from me. I see it. I don't see it. Images, snapshots of my childhood seem, for a moment, more real, as if I'm watching a slideshow or leafing through pages of a photograph album.

No one would want to see *these* photographs — photos of me and my father — would they?

I've told Randy facts and feelings about my childhood. I've cried. I've raged. I've also sat in his office silent. Speechless.

But I've never described these snapshots in my head, these images. I've never talked about sensory details, what it sounded like, looked like, to be me, growing up. Maybe it is a narrative comprised of this imagery that must be written.

A book to help me understand my childhood . . . and a book, Randy frequently says, to help other women as well.

But a book sounds too daunting. Maybe something shorter. An essay?

Finally, after years of Randy's urging, I whisper, "Okay, maybe I'll write a *paragraph* about myself. But that's *all* I have to say."

A short paragraph, I want to add, but don't. A very short paragraph. Three sentences. Four at the most. A paragraph just to humor Randy. A short paragraph so he'll stop bugging me. A very short paragraph so he'll see that he's wrong. So he'll understand, once and for all, I have nothing to say.

But even if I did, hypothetically, have something to say about myself, who'd want to read it? Maybe there aren't any other women like me. No one would be interested in my messy life — that story.

No one, except Randy and my husband, even knows my secret.

On that particular day, driving home to Rome, Georgia, from Atlanta, about an hour and a half away, I try to reassure myself: I've written hundreds and hundreds of pages of fiction. Surely I can coerce one small paragraph of nonfiction from myself just to show Randy I tried.

When I arrive home, I change into "professional" clothes to prepare for the evening class I teach at a community college. I wash my face. Apply makeup. All traces of the wrinkled cotton sweatpants and scuffed red Reeboks are removed. I fix my hair so none of my students will suspect that I'm in therapy, will suspect that, at times, I'm a physical and emotional wreck. Any visible residue of a chaotic childhood is rinsed away. I don a skirt, starched shirt, and blazer. To enter a classroom with thirty students, I must appear to be in perfect control, adult.

I sit at my desk while the students bend over their blue books, composing their final in-class essays before summer vacation. Outside the windows of this cinderblock structure, dusk shadows magnolias. A sheen of chartreuse pollen from loblolly pines dusts the windows. Even though it's a beautiful evening, I prefer to be in here. I love being with my students — even knowing most of them would rather be outside.

Ironically, here, they are the ones who believe they have nothing to say, nothing to write. Most of them hate English class, hate to write. Nevertheless, week after week, I encourage them to place sentences on pieces of paper. "You can do it!"

I simplify the indecipherable rules in the *Harbrace College Handbook* into easy-to-follow instructions for them. "This is a comma splice. This is a run-on sentence." Before they can pass English Composition 101, they must successfully complete an essay exam required by the Georgia Board of Regents. All semester I prepare them for it. I want them to do well. I glow when I'm able to convince even one student to not hate English.

I glow brighter when I'm able to convince even one student about the power of language. I felt breathless when Marci changed her major from dental hygiene to English, after an offhand comment I made one day when asked by a student why I liked to teach English.

"I guess because I love words," I replied.

After class, Marci, a timid young woman, waited for the rest of the students to leave the room. Alone, she finally approached me. Quietly, she said, "I didn't know you could love words. I love words, too, but I've never told anyone before." She feared her friends and family would make fun of her. Here in rural north Georgia, she told me, education, reading, writing, weren't valued. This was her secret.

"Oh, yes," I say. "It's fine to love words. And you're a good writer. If you'd like to write extra essays, I'd love to read them."

She turned in an extra essay about a place in the woods where she hid, where she read books, where no one would find her. No one had ever discovered her secret.

On that evening back then, I did not fully comprehend that what I wished for Marci was, in many ways, what Randy wished for me.

Now in the classroom, as my students write, I finish grading their essays from last week, and I read — oh, dear — many abstract thoughts, many wayward sentences. I read, "I loved my grandmother because she was kind and loving." And I write in the margin that I want to know *how* she was kind and loving. "Give concrete examples," I write. "What details and images *show* her kindness? Be specific."

Many of these students are the first in their families to attend an institution of higher learning. Most are either older women or single mothers training to be nurses, dental assistants, something practical. They take this class because it's required. But toward the end of the semester, even as some continue to write about their favorite pet or loving grandmother, others, tentatively, go deeper. One student explores how uncomfortable she feels when entering a store because, as an African American, she believes white shopkeepers watch her, certain she'll shoplift. Another student describes a fishing expedition with her grandfather, urging the material into a more meaningful nature essay than I expected from such a familiar topic. Others write about abusive husbands or boyfriends. Alcoholic fathers. Secret abortions. In tiny letters at the bottom of their essays they write: "Please don't let anyone see this."

Of course I don't.

In the margins of their papers, I praise their courage. And I wonder whether some students trust me with their words because — even as I try to hide all traces of my own past — they sense I haven't always been this in control, this professional. Maybe this is why some share their tentative words, their secrets, with me.

After the semester ends, I'm alone in my house, my husband at work. Next to my computer is a stack of over three hundred pages of my most recent unfinished novel, a novel about child abuse (sort of). But the protagonist isn't quite me; the story isn't quite mine. I riffle the paper. All these chapters, all these pages, all these paragraphs, all these sentences, all these words . . . why do they not say what I want?

I must be stupid.

In fact, my own high school as well as my undergraduate educational background is extremely shoddy — another secret. Which must prove I'm stupid. A failure. I will never be a writer.

I am procrastinating.

I think about Marci, all my students this past semester brave enough to place secret words on pieces of paper, courageous enough to show them to me.

The cursor on my computer blinks.

I type the word "Preface." I write a long paragraph about my father's career, his numerous professional accomplishments. Before I realize it, I'm at the bottom of the page. I've already finished the one paragraph that I promised Randy!

Except I haven't yet said anything about me. A memoir should probably be about me, right? So hurriedly, almost before I realize what I'm writing, my fingers type: "My father is also a child molester. I know, because he sexually molested me."

Yes, this is the truth. This is what happened. I had a father. He had a successful career. But behind closed doors, when no one watched, when no one saw, he sexually molested me.

This is what happened to me.

Straight facts. Unadorned truth. I'm not a fictional character such as those in the novels I write.

"I was born on Southern Avenue in Washington, D.C., in a white, two-story duplex across from a cemetery, and in that house . . ."

I am writing the story of living in that house, writing about a little girl named "Sue." A girl who is me.

I am on page ten or so before I realize: I don't know how to write a memoir.

Up until then, I only wrote and read short stories and novels.

I print out the ten pages and read what I've written. Fact by fact, I've set down what it was like living in that white house on Southern Avenue. I've just completed a scene in which my father is teaching my mother to drive a car for the first time. There I am, a little girl, with my father, mother, and sister in our black Chevy, driving down quiet roads in northern Virginia.

But the inside of the car is not quiet — my angry father is yelling at my scared mother: "Turn the wheel left, shift into third gear, give the accelerator more gas." And because of my father's rage and my mother's temerity, we slide onto the shoulder, roll down a short incline, and end up in someone's front yard. The woman in the house rushes to our car, helps us out, helps me, gently checking for broken bones.

I wrote this scene. I set the facts down on paper. I reread it. And I think to myself: so what? We had a car accident, but who cares? Loads of families have accidents, many much worse than ours. No one, after all, is hurt. Why would anyone care?

There must be more to the story, more to the scene, than this. There must be a reason why I even recall it so vividly.

Then, as if I'm following a whisper — a whisper because I must listen closely, carefully — I write what I now know to be true. I write what I now, years later, understand to be the significance of this scene. Which isn't only the car accident — that's just a straight fact. More significant is this unknown woman who touches me with a hand that's soft and caring. The strange woman gently touches me to determine if I've broken any bones.

Why is it important?

I hear this whisper as I write: Her touch is meaningful because it is so different from my father's touch. This woman is a stranger, yet she touches me more gently, more carefully, than my own father.

I rewrite the scene, crafting all the details to show what I now know to be true about this episode in my own personal history.

Did I know this at the time of the car crash? No, not at all. I was a little girl. I could never have understood this then. It is only now that I, the adult writer, understand.

So a memoir, I realize, is only partially about writing recollected facts of what happened. The other part requires a more authorial observation and understanding of events. This part is written through the viewpoint — and with the insight — of the author sitting at her or his desk trying to figure out what it all means. Crafting this scene, I come to realize that writing memory, writing what we remember, is a creative act. We *interpret* facts about the past in order to reclaim them, make sense of them.

With this realization the words, the sentences, the paragraphs, the pages, the chapters fall out of me. What I was sure would be one paragraph — the story of me and my father in one short, short paragraph — evolved into three hundred pages.

Three hundred pages in three months.

I write as if with a brain fever. I barely stop. I hate when I must pause to eat, to sleep, to shop for groceries. All I want is to return to my room, close the door, and write, write about me and my family from the time I was born in Washington, D.C., until the time I first stumble into Randy's office exhausted, needy, defeated. I write to explore, to decipher who I am, who I was in that family of mine, seeking clues in words and images. I write as if following a path through a forest — a narrow path — but one that goes deep into the discovery of me, of what living with that family of mine meant.

At the end of summer, before the fall semester begins, I present those three hundred pages to Randy. He beams.

WRITING EXERCISES

For some of us, it can be scary to confront our deepest, most intimate secrets — even alone in the privacy of our writing rooms, and even if no one reads what we write. But let's get started, knowing you can proceed at your own pace, as slowly or as quickly as you like.

1. Write a short paragraph about a secret you've never told anyone, except maybe a therapist.

2. Is there a memory that has always haunted you? Write it down. Try to discover why it has such power.

3. Write a letter (not to be mailed) to someone you love or hate, fear or enjoy — but to whom you never told your feelings. Explain the moment that person first made you feel this way.

Chapter Two

Savory Words

The First Bite of Your Story

I begin writing my first novel while living in Texas, several years before moving to Georgia — before therapy with Randy. One afternoon, I simply set up a card table in my apartment in a restored Victorian iron-front building in Galveston's Strand District. I place my portable Smith Corona typewriter on it. I open a ream of cheap, canary yellow paper, certainly a metaphor (I see now) for my lack of self-confidence at the time. As much as I want to write a novel, I'm equally sure I'll fail — uncertain, back then, whether I have a voice with which to write, or any stories to tell. No reason to buy expensive paper if it'll all end up in the trash!

At this point, I've never studied creative writing. I have no clue how to approach a novel. Nevertheless, I type word after word, pages spewing from my typewriter. After a life of never hearing my own authentic voice, I finally sense a thin shred of one. And even though it's a fictional voice, still, it's closer to me, to mine, than the childhood language of lies and denial with which I was raised — pretending we were a perfect family when we weren't.

I write more than a thousand pages before realizing that while maybe I've begun a novel, I don't know how to end one. Without a doubt, I don't know how to artfully craft a beginning, middle, or end. Tenaciously refusing to admit defeat, I arrange to audit an undergraduate creative writing class at the University of Houston.

The professor, an author who recently published his first novel, enters the classroom barefoot with a seagull feather tucked behind his ear. He holds up a magnolia blossom and instructs us to describe the color, the texture, the scent. In my predictable descriptions, the flower is white, the petals are soft, the blossom smells like perfume.

"Unoriginal," the instructor writes in the margin.

Our next assignment is to write one paragraph on any subject using all five senses. Back in my apartment, I type draft after draft about a fictional homeless man who, drunk, spends the night on the Galveston jetty. I cram all five senses onto my page, showing the hapless man awaking to the textures of gritty sand and damp clothes, the scents of seaweed and salt water, the sounds of seagulls cawing and waves lapping. I barely remember the description because the man could be anyone, the jetty anywhere. It could be any day. Only one sentence from the exercise remains with me. As the sun rises on my homeless, hungover man, I write: "Sunrays clanged in his ear."

Okay, it's not a Pulitzer Prize–winning sentence. But after writing it, I finally understand two things. First, in order to be original, writers can use sensory imagery in unexpected ways: the sun doesn't only have to be warm and yellow. "The sun is yellow" or "The rose is red" are descriptive phrases but aren't illuminating or compelling. Sure, you can envision the image of a yellow sun or a red rose in your mind's eye, but I'm sure you'd say to yourself, "So what?"

So what, indeed! For the second thing I learn from the clanging sun is that external images can be slanted (to echo Emily Dickinson) in such a way as to reveal the inner state of a character. If I'd merely written, "The yellow sun shone on the man," the reader might even get the false impression that the man is happy, that this is a pleasant scene. But just the opposite is true. The word "clanged" guides the reader toward understanding the true feeling behind the passage: this man's head aches from too much bourbon and hard luck. His sorry life clangs in his ears.

A few weeks into the semester the barefoot professor is fired for drug possession, or maybe he has a nervous breakdown — I can't remember. I never see him again. Yet he's taught me one of the most valuable lessons of creative writing: how external sensory imagery is crafted — slanted — to create mood and emotion. How different from the speeches I once drafted for politicians when I worked on Capitol Hill, just before moving to Galveston. Bureaucratic communication is primarily nonvisual; it doesn't paint pictures. It's more general, less specific: "This legislation will fix loopholes in tax laws to alleviate the burdens of middle-class taxpayers everywhere." Such vague language actually obscures the physical world — which for lawmakers is often the whole point.

A memoir on middle-class life, on the other hand, would focus on one middle-class taxpayer who once lived in a restored Victorian apartment in Galveston, who typed tentative novels on cheap yellow paper because she didn't want to smudge expensive paper with her uncertain words.

> Craft and slant external details that shed light on the internal emotions of you, the narrator. These images also enhance the atmosphere of the piece.

Don't Just State Your Story — Reveal Your Story

As writers, we must bring readers inside our stories, describe our lives, by writing artful and sensory sentences. If I simply stated, for example, that my father molested me, of course you'd think that's sad, but you might not feel sadness. Wouldn't I be writing to your intellect (like a document) more than to your heart (like a memoir)? You certainly wouldn't know how growing up in my family actually felt, sounded, even smelled and tasted.

Or, if I simply told you that I once struggled with sex addiction, you'd probably think "that's unfortunate." But you wouldn't feel my words, emotionally. You wouldn't hear my own harsh sunlight clang in my ear. To convey the concept of sex addiction, my job as a writer is to imbue this abstraction with concrete details. Here, for example, by describing a seedy motel room where I met a dangerous man, I try to fully reveal the darkness of the addiction: "I feel a damp chill between my shoulder blades . . . How can love be two bodies wrapped in a sheet that's singed by careless cigarettes, here, in a room with plastic curtains, tin ashtrays, stained carpet, artificial air, and a television promoting . . . pornographic movies every hour on the hour."

How do we, as writers, discover these specific details?

Whether you're sitting before your computer figuring out a divorce, taking notes about a recent illness, or worrying about a visit with an estranged mother, reimagine the moment — not exactly as if it's still happening to you — but almost. Enter it deeply enough so that you touch the sensory nerve surrounding the event. To transport the reader into your world, you must submerge yourself into the very world you wish to describe. Since this might sound scary, especially if you're writing about traumatic events, please see chapter 9 for ways to feel safe while doing this. Don't turn off your computer, worried you can't do this. You can! Be gentle with yourself. Patient. One step at a time. Or, one word at a time.

Here's how to start:

When I studied fiction, I was taught to pretend that I was watching a movie, whereby I copied down images I saw in my mind's eye. With a memoir, however, it's as if you're inside the movie, inside your own life, whereby you not only see images, but you taste, smell, hear, and touch the images. You are the movie. (For those of you who have always wanted to be a movie star, here's your chance!) Your life is the celluloid. As you write, select those sensory details that best illuminate you and your world.

I wouldn't, for example, simply state: "I was born in Washington, D.C., where my father worked for the government. Before I was old enough to start school, I wandered around the cemetery across from my house in my favorite red shoes. Most of the other kids, like my sister, were in school. Lonely, I spent a lot of time by myself."

Can you see how flat, informational, and list-like these sentences sound? Why? Because they don't bring you inside the celluloid of my life.

Instead, I need to reveal my experience in a narrative using the senses to create an emotion or a mood that reflects how I feel in this one moment of time:

> Mornings, after my sister leaves for school, I wander past the wrought-iron gate into the cemetery across from my house on Southern Avenue in Washington, D.C. Tombstones, gray and cracked with age, resemble the teeth in my grandmother's mouth. Fallen leaves smell of dust, only a hint of air breathing across autumn. No one passes as I sit beneath a maple, the ground chilly and damp. My red shoes, like a beacon, like an emergency light on a police car, are the brightest splotch of color. But no one sees.

Here, rather than write the abstract word "lonely," as I do in the first example, I rely on external details to convey my internal sense of loneliness and unease: no one sees my emergency. In the context of a larger work, it would be clear this alienation is caused by my absent sister, my preoccupied mother, my sexually abusive father. As I'd proceed with my memoir, additional exterior details of my surroundings would continue to show my emotions as I deepened myself as a "character."

In short, reveal your life. As you write, strive to show your innermost self, not merely to list facts like a résumé. By conveying your story imagistically, you're creating on paper a fully realized world and inviting readers to enter.

> The exterior, atmospheric milieu you're creating through sensory imagery is, in turn, mirroring the interior you.

Here are two more examples to clarify the importance of details to depict interior feelings. Both are written about a trip to Portugal. Consider which one uses slanted imagery to convey a specific mood. Which one draws you deeper into the emotion? Why?

EXAMPLE 1

Portugal is beautiful. The weather is warm; the days are sunny. Every afternoon I sit outside reading or writing letters, with the ocean in the distance. The air smells fresh and sweet. Sometimes, I feel as if I could fall asleep outside in the warm air. I never want to leave. It's so vast and beautiful that I hope this moment lasts forever, that it never ends.

EXAMPLE 2

Drowsy, I recline on the *terraço* of a friend's villa in Sintra, Portugal. Across the valley is another villa, owned by the Rothschilds, and beyond that, the Atlantic Ocean, currents flowing from the Gulf of Cádiz, azure and hot. I am writing an aerogram, the paper supported by a book, Graham Greene's *The End of the Affair*. Beside my lounge an oval table holds a pitcher of ice water. Slices of lemon circle a tray. I place a slice in a goblet, fill it with water, and sip. From the valley rise the spicy scents of eucalyptus and olive, lupine and poppy. Cerise bougainvillea etches whitewashed walls. I drift in sun, in shade from cork trees, sun and shade, pages of the book and the aerogram fluttering against my fingertips.

Do you think (I hope!) that the second example is more evocative? In it, by using slanted details, I hope you feel almost as if you are in Portugal with me, feel this seemingly suspended moment of time. My goal is to convey this abstract sensation of endless time without announcing it to the reader. Details aren't randomly chosen. They're consciously selected.

Which external details reveal you? Whether you write about growing up on a farm in the Midwest or about the disruptions of life caused by a military father, be sure the reader is moved. We write memoir to better understand ourselves, as well as to bring a reader with us on our journeys.

You've all heard the cliché, "A picture is worth a thousand words." But it's also true—maybe more true—that one word is worth a thousand pictures if it's the right word.

The "right" words we seek are those that artistically re-create our worlds, internal and external, on the page, by evoking how those worlds feel, taste, sound, smell, look. In real life we might think to ourselves, *I feel lonely*. Or, *I think I'm in love*. In memoir, however, we translate our abstract feelings ("love," "loneliness") into concrete language. We can, conceivably, write an entire memoir about feeling lonely without once using that word — if all our other words specifically evoke a sense of loneliness. Images aren't merely flat scenery or wallpaper. An image directs the reader to an insight, brings your work to a higher emotional pitch, embodies your persona's feelings and ideas — the emotional and physical habitat in which you dwell.

Move Readers with Active Words

To maintain specificity, use active verbs and specific nouns as much as possible, while, at the same time, avoiding adverbs, adjectives, and variations of "to be." Rather than write, for example, "I was in the living room," you could write, "I slumped on the couch." Rather than write, "I was in love with a cute guy," you could write, "John's hands, the color of cinnamon, stroked my bare shoulders."

That first example about the trip to Portugal is boring because it's generic. But if I overwrote it, relying on too many adjectives and adverbs, it'd be equally bad: "Flowing, rosy red flowers are draped over clean and sparkling whitewashed walls, walls glowing in summery sun. I feel as if I can drift forever in the warm sun, in cool shade from trees, very thin pages of the book, the wrinkled aerogram, fluttering against my fingertips."

Even though this is less generic than that first example, these extra words do not add spice. Do you see how abstract the passage sounds? By crossing out "rosy," "are," "very," "clean," "sparkling," "glowing," and "cool," do you think the passage is cleaner, tighter? Likewise, try replacing the generic words with specific ones: cork trees, not trees; bougainvillea, not flowers. Are there any other words you might revise or discard? Remember, a specific description isn't enough: details must be slanted in order to convey the mood of the scene, your interior state, the atmosphere of the piece.

Following a Sensory Trail

Maybe you already tried writing your story. Maybe you wrote a page or two, or made a few attempts, before giving up. Did your prose sound flat or lifeless? Did it seem as if you were stating your scenes rather than revealing them? Did they seem underdeveloped? If so, then let's recast them in sensory imagery. As you write, consider the milieu in which you live, in which your stories take place. Evoke these settings with taste, touch, smell, sound, and sight until the blank surfaces of paper shimmer with life.

To begin this journey, let's undertake an archaeological dig, probing memories that dwell deep in the senses. Imagine taking off your shoes and walking through your childhood or adolescence or marriage or divorce or whatever area of life you wish to explore. What do you feel? Fresh-mowed grass under the soles of your feet? Sand? Hot pavement? Frigid streets? Open the window of your childhood bedroom. What do you see? What do you smell? Lilacs? Exhaust fumes? An ocean? Icicles and snow?

Follow this trail of senses. Where does it lead you? Where do you go? Write what your heart, your eyes, your nose, your mouth, your ears remember. Follow a path of scents, of sounds, of touch, that leads back in time. By practicing the exercises below (at this point, don't worry about writing a perfect draft), you'll begin to gather these details from your life — images that are sensory — so you can organize and understand them. By examining these exterior imagistic details, you'll also be revealing and discovering inner experience: the authentic "you" with your own personal images that shaped your life. You will then allow readers to feel this world, too. As Picasso said, "If only we could pull out our brains and use only our eyes." I might say that we should write with our ears, our fingers, our taste buds, our noses, and our eyes.

WRITING EXERCISES

1. Using the list below, garner a few specific details to begin submerging yourself in particular moments of time. This is a jumping-off point. After you finish this list, keep writing if you like, as you remember other potent images.

- The item of clothing I recall most vividly from childhood is

  _____.
- When I was ten, I smelled _____ outside my bedroom window.
- That summer when I was _____, I felt _____ beneath the soles of my bare feet.
- The first time I hiked in the woods, I smelled _____.
- My favorite dessert growing up was _____.
- The first time I touched a basketball (baseball, tennis ball, golf ball), I felt _____.
- The noise that scared me the most growing up was _____.
- The noise that pleased me the most growing up was _____.

2. Now that you have these particular details, let's slant them to show a feeling or an idea behind them, one that represents you in that moment. For example, let's say the item of clothing you recall most vividly from childhood is a yellow dress. Now, suppose this dress provides a positive memory. If so, you could write: "When I wore my yellow dress, I felt as if buttercup petals sprinkled from the hem as I skipped to school." Or, on the other hand, if the dress provokes a negative memory, you could write: "The dress cast a pall on my skin, sickly and yellow."

Continue down the list in exercise #1 and rework each sentence to show the emotion you associate with each physical element. The following fill-in-the-blank sentences might help you get started if you're struggling to think of ways to frame your images.

- When I was ten, I smelled _____ outside my bedroom window. Now, the smell reminds me of _____.
- That summer when I was _____, I felt _____ beneath the soles of my bare feet. Now, when I recall this, I _____.

- The first time I hiked in the woods, I smelled _____. Today, when I hike in the woods, I remember _____.
- My favorite dessert growing up was _____, because it tasted like _____.
- The first time I touched a basketball (baseball, tennis ball, golf ball), I felt _____, because _____.
- The noise that scared me the most growing up was _____, because _____.
- The noise that pleased me the most growing up was _____, because _____.

3. Write a paragraph about a "first" (first day of school, date, love, house, pet, etc.). Slant the details to reveal how you felt about this "first" at the time it happened.

4. Write a physical description of yourself. Let the physical "you" reveal the inner "you." Is the outer self in sync with the inner? In conflict?

5. Discover fresh concrete language and images for the following abstract words. For example, you wouldn't want to write that "love is like a red rose." That's a cliché. Instead, in your particular story, maybe love reminds you of sand beneath the soles of your feet. Or maybe love reminds you of flute notes trilling from an open window on a summer morning. Anything! Just be faithful to your own unique story. In your memoir, in your own frame of reference, what concrete images are evoked when you consider abstract words such as

Loss	Love	Happiness	Loneliness	Pain	Fear
Soul	Death	Anger	Danger	Safety	Identity

6. Choose three or four of the images you wrote from the above list and develop them into a scene or paragraph. Let's say, for example, the word "love" does remind you of flute music. Why? What's the connection? This relationship between love and flute music would be interesting to explore. Part of memoir writing is the discovery of the various images that evoke our lives — and why they're important. Maybe you heard a flute play through an open window a few days after you gave birth to your baby. But maybe this sound, in addition to reminding

you of love, also causes you to feel fear: now, you must raise this baby! What are all the things that could go wrong on the journey through life? People are complex, of course, so it makes sense that a new mother could feel love and fear at the same time. Try weaving two emotions such as these together, using the images generated above.

One of my own examples is that I feel both nostalgia and fear whenever I use a Brillo pad to scrub a pan. Why?

The first time I remember using a Brillo pad was in college at a boyfriend's apartment. Paul and I, as well as his roommate and the roommate's girlfriend, had just finished dinner, and the roommate took his girlfriend to his bedroom. As I scrubbed the frying pan with a Brillo pad, I heard the other couple having sex. Meanwhile, Paul sat in the living room smoking dope. Thinking back about this now, I feel nostalgic toward the freedom of the hippie era — the free-love, flower-child, psychedelic decade. At the same time, the unpredictability of drugs scared me: Paul never seemed like the same person when he was high. Plus, I felt scared and slightly disoriented listening to friends engage in sex. I didn't want to hear them. I didn't want to breathe the marijuana smoke drifting from the living room, mixing with the smell of hamburger grease, the metallic scent of the Brillo pad, my hands slick with oily water.

If I developed this into a full-length memoir or memoir essay, I could even twine that moment together with a recent one. I would portray myself nicely settled in a house close to the shore of Lake Michigan, and describe how after dinner, I scrub a pot with a Brillo pad at the kitchen sink, my two cats looking out the screen leading to the patio, the scent of lilac blowing in from the garden. My partner Marc dries the dishes, the television tuned to CNN-News.

By juxtaposing this quiet domesticity with the swirl and unrest of the hippie era, I could show an arc to my life, how my life changed over the years.

A Note on Genre

When I refer to essays in this book, I mean short — less than book-length — pieces of writing that come from personal experience. In other words, a memoir can be a full-length book (typically a minimum of about 150 pages) or a shorter piece of writing (typically anywhere from one page up to about 25 pages). Memoir is one subgenre of the broader genre called creative nonfiction or literary nonfiction. For a fuller exploration of all the forms, please see appendix 1, "The Meandering River: An Overview of the Subgenres of Creative Nonfiction." Since, frequently, forms overlap and definitions blur, much of the information in this book, while specifically geared for memoir writers, is applicable to other forms of literary nonfiction as well.

FOR YOUR READING PLEASURE

In the following memoir essay, "Candy Cigarettes," Anne Panning focuses on sensory images (of taste, smell, touch, sound, sight) to explore the role cigarettes played in her life. Additionally, she skillfully relies almost solely on imagery to examine her relationships with friends and parents, as well as her husband. You might also note Panning's interesting use of the second-person point of view. While it's obvious Panning herself is the "you" in the essay, this technique — which also directly addresses the reader — is a way for readers to more closely identify with the narrator. While it's difficult to sustain this second-person point of view in a long book, you might enjoy trying it in a shorter piece.

CANDY CIGARETTES

While your parents drank in Schmidt's Bar, you and your cousins gathered under buggy streetlights. No one watched you. No one cared. You all ran down a big hill in the dark, holding hands. Then up again. Later, inside the bar, you begged for everything: cashews warmed in white waxed cups, giant pickles like dead babies in brine, Orange Crush in bumpy bottles, candy cigarettes: Marlboro, Winston, Lucky Strike. The cigarettes powdered your lips white. The tips brushed pink with false fire. All of you stood outside the bar, smoking. You knew the positioning well: one arm folded over the stomach. Your other elbow propped upon it: the cigarette swing arm. In. Out. Break to chew. Which always seemed like a failure of sorts: breaking the thing they taught you.

When you were fourteen, you found your mother gasping in bed, blue. I *have* to quit smoking, she said, but I *can't*. You stood there in your cheerleading uniform: twiggy legs, curling iron bangs, eyes squinting through smoke. You were on the edge of everything. You would succeed and supersede, or come down like the rest. You hid the cigarettes for her under the kitchen sink by the Comet. But your father continued, souring up the house. You could hear the grind of his old metal lighter first thing in the morning, last thing at night. He kept the lighter in his pocket, and sometimes, when he took it out, you held it, warm silver square, in your hand. Its heat leaked through. And into you. Your mother quit her two-pack-a-day habit. And lived.

Later, you married a two-pack-a-day smoker. But meeting in a foreign country made this okay. Even expected. Because he was tall and thin and smart — your requirements — you bummed a cigarette off him, though you didn't smoke. Two things made you fall in love. The way his long fingers curled around a coffee cup. The way he held his cigarette so tenderly to ash upon the floor. Unlike some, he was a beautiful smoker. Long-limbed. Dark-eyed. He blew smoke up, then ushered it away from you with cupped hands. He was eager to please. Which pleased you. Cold turkey is the only way, he said years later. And quit one weekend while overhauling the engine of the old Datsun. Sometimes, still, you miss that cloudy haze.

Chapter Three

Writing on Key

A Few Notes about Theme

I recently worked on a memoir essay about a crush I had on a boy in high school, Jamie, whom I dated on and off for a few years. Having written two dark, full-length memoirs, I envisioned this piece as a light-hearted romp of teenage love and angst — something I could probably crank out in a day or two. How difficult could it be to write a simple little love story — and not even a story of true love, but of puppy love? To add a modicum of complication, I included another girl, Kathy, whom my boyfriend also dated. Long story short, he boomeranged back and forth between the two of us for a few years. The theme, I thought, would be about love, or how to survive a love triangle. Nothing to it.

After finishing the first draft, I showed it to my favorite editor, Marc, who also happens to be my partner. (Note to writers: marrying, living with, or befriending an editor is very helpful. If you find one who also likes to cook as well as take care of your cats while you travel, even better!) He read it and, as tactfully as possible, said, "It isn't quite there yet," his way of implying it was a disaster. It sounded, Marc suggested, like a nonfiction equivalent of a Harlequin romance. Very embarrassing.

Draft after draft, week after week, I worked on this essay, attempting to discover what I really wanted to say. If it wasn't about a simple love triangle, what was the theme, the main focus? I tried to craft it into a coming-of-age romance during the cold war. Terrible. I wrote it as a faux comic book with Jamie, Kathy, and me mimicking roles in *Archie*, a popular comic book at that time. Worse than terrible. Each time I confidently thought I'd discovered a way to portray these relationships, Marc said, "It isn't quite there yet."

Very frustrating.

I was on about my gazillionth draft, month seven into the process, when all of a sudden — I have no idea where she came from — my grandmother simply landed on the page. Yes, there she was, smack dab in the essay. I was simply typing along, sentence by terrible sentence, attempting to force Jamie, Kathy, and me into any kind of authentic-sounding essay, when, in my mind's eye, my Russian grandmother, wearing a babushka and black wool stockings, waddled up the suburban street in New Jersey where my family had lived at the time when the essay was set. My grandmother had stayed with us then, but it never occurred to me that this woman who had scared me was part of this essay — an essay that was supposed to be, after all, a simple love story.

In subsequent drafts, I discovered that this relationship with my grandmother was the true focus of the essay. It would never have worked without her presence. She was the linchpin, the one who caused the friction and conflict, the one from whom the theme evolved. My desire to flee her — really flee my own Russian Jewish heritage — was at the heart of the essay. Since I was only one of a handful of Jewish kids in my school, I felt like an outcast, an alien. I wanted to blend with my peers: if I were Christian, Jamie would really love me; if I looked like Christian Kathy, I would be lovable. If I were Christian, I would love myself, or so I felt at that time. If only my grandmother weren't my grandmother!

The essay was ready for liftoff. I'd finally found this clear focus, this theme — a quest for identity — exemplified by a pull between being Jewish and wanting to be magically Christian. Of course I wish I'd discovered my grandmother's presence as soon as I began to write, wish it hadn't taken me months to craft a sixteen-page essay. Still, as writers soon learn, the discoveries we make during revision are a vital part of the writing process.

Discovering the theme at the heart of any piece is crucial. A theme is an abstract concept that represents the underlying meaning, idea, or message of your memoir, whether it's a full-length book or essay. It reflects what the piece is about. The author, however, rarely overtly states the theme directly in the work itself. Instead, it, too, is shown by slanting details, just as we learned in the previous chapter. Slanted details, therefore, not only convey our personas ("persona" refers to the "you" artistically recreated on the page) in a specific moment of time and place, they also impart — over the course of any given work — our otherwise abstract themes.

Revealing a theme is more effective than announcing it. I would never state, for example, "This essay is about my search for identity." That's too generic to engage a reader. It doesn't invite the reader along on my journey of self-discovery. Instead, it's more powerful to explicate our themes by using imagistic, sensory language developed into scenes. Here, for example, are a few sentences about how I dreaded encountering my grandmother, not wanting to be captured by her or by her identity:

> Every morning, I awoke to the arthritic shuffling of my Russian grandmother in her terry cloth slippers. Unable to live alone in her own apartment, she invaded my family with a babushka, black wool stockings, and a gnarled Yiddish tongue — she even cleared her throat in Yiddish. She skulked suburban streets as if still fleeing pogroms, even though she'd long ago immigrated to America. She prowled our neighborhood, trailing the scent of boiled cabbage, as if she, now the pursuer, hoped to capture me, save me from the Christians whom I emulated and desired.

If I've selected the correct sensory details, then hopefully the reader will be able to emotionally feel my plight — feel, in effect, my theme — not just know it intellectually.

The author must know the abstract theme in order to portray a clear, vivid memoir. Even if readers themselves never articulate the theme, they will sense it.

False Starts

Before examining how to establish your theme right on the first page, I'd like for us to look at a way *not* to start, a way that would cause you to lose your focus, and never discover it.

Suppose I say to you, "Listen, let me tell you a story about my life." Are you inwardly groaning? Do you feel a strong urge for a nap? Just think about how you feel when a stranger on an airplane says, upon learning that you are a writer, "Oh, I've had the most amazing and exciting life, and it'd make a great book," and then proceeds to tell you all about it. This does not usually make the time on the flight go quickly.

This conversational story will almost certainly be all over the place, full of disjunctive events, stories, and ideas all crammed and jumbled together. By listening to someone's entire life story, it's virtually impossible to discern a clear, underlying theme. When we simply reminisce about ourselves, we might begin by talking about a sister or brother. Then, the next minute we're describing our cats, maybe even flipping open a wallet full of photographs. Next, we might describe a family outing on Lake Michigan last summer, or a winter storm that knocked out the electricity for a week . . . and on and on.

So even though no one would actually begin a memoir by writing, "This is a story of my life," nevertheless, it can be easy to fall into the trap of giving a sense of an all-inclusive story covering an entire life, thus lacking one defined, unifying, overarching theme.

Let's see what this looks like.

First, a disclaimer: what follows isn't my life, or anyone else's. It is an amalgam of many manuscripts I've encountered over the years as an editor and teacher. This first page of an imaginary memoir shows the kind of beginning you want to avoid, one with free-floating events and ideas that sound too much like an endless, informal conversation. In effect, it has too many themes and story lines, whereas the aim is for any given piece to have just one. As you read along, place a little check mark in the margin every time you think the narrator is introducing a new focus.

According to my parents, there was a terrible blizzard that day in April when I was born, and every day following, too. We lived in the Upper Peninsula of Michigan (what's known as the UP), where it snowed, or could snow, about seven months of the year. It's beautiful and peaceful, though, with snow covering pines (except that loggers are slowly cutting them down). My grandfather, on my father's side, moved here from Sweden, so it probably felt like home to him. In fact, we lived in a community of Swedes, and you can still hear a modified version of the language amongst some of the old-timers, as well as eat Swedish foods in the local café.

But how could my grandfather even notice the weather, one way or the other, since he drank every day, every night. So did my father, who yelled at my two younger brothers and me whenever he came home drunk. Some days he went hunting, and I'm surprised he didn't shoot off his foot — or worse. Conveniently, my grandfather owned a tavern, the family business, which my father inherited, running it for years. My father met my mother in high school, where she was the student council president. My mother's family was from Holland, and she was blond, beautiful, and smart — she got good grades but never had the opportunity to go to college, which is what I knew she wanted. That's because she married young. Well, to be truthful, she got pregnant with me first, then married, right after she and my dad graduated from high school. In fact, growing up, my mother always told me never to get married or have kids. "Don't make the same mistakes as me," she always said.

But even though my mother was smart, she was mean. From all the disappointments she'd had in her life, she took it all out on me. So imagine my fear when I found myself — no, not married — but very much pregnant at seventeen.

I barely knew the baby's father. I certainly didn't love him. In fact, I'd been planning on leaving Michigan as soon as possible and moving to New York City.

Whew! Why do you think the "author" struggles with this piece? You're right: too many story lines, each with its own possible theme. We've got several decades of a family, starting before the narrator was born, condensed and summarized in a few paragraphs. If, as you read, you inserted check marks beside every topic, you probably placed quite a few. I count about nine. Here they are:

- weather (April snowstorm)
- geography and the environment (the UP as a beautiful place to live)
- immigrant story (grandparents left Sweden and Holland to settle in Michigan)
- grandfather (an alcoholic bar owner)
- alcoholism (the way addiction runs through this family, generationally)
- no-good father (an alcoholic, angry drunk)
- disgruntled mother (unfulfilled dreams)
- out-of-wedlock pregnancy (also a generational issue)
- narrator's coming-of-age story (the narrator is pregnant and scared and must now sort out her life within the context of a troubled family).

Why can't you have so many story lines, each with its own theme? Because a memoir isn't about a whole life. It's a slice of a life, an exploration of one aspect of a life. Therefore, you'll want to focus the material around one congruent theme at the memoir's core. The above example wouldn't work as the beginning of a memoir because it's all over the place. Neither the reader, nor the writer, has a clear idea where this book is going.

Let me hasten to add that there is good news about this first page: given the amount of material introduced, there are several memoir essays or full-length books that our faux author could write. Therefore, the author of this particular piece could focus on any one of a number of different aspects of her story, including:

- her love of nature — how living in the wilderness gave her a sense of spiritual and personal power
- her ethnic heritage — how that ethnicity both helped and hindered her quest to find her authentic self

- her family's history of addiction and substance abuse — how that heightened the emotions behind her decision to either stay or leave her home.

But don't you think that what most interests our author, in terms of this memoir, is the pregnancy? Since her energy seems to point in this direction, she could start her story the moment she learns she's pregnant — scared and uncertain about her future. By starting there, with one clear story line, the theme will be clearly established.

Now, once this author discovers her main focus, might another issue play a secondary role? Yes, especially in a long memoir (as opposed to a short essay, where the focus is even tighter). Once this narrator's out-of-wedlock pregnancy is established, she'll probably explore her mother's own out-of-wedlock pregnancy as well. In other words, over the course of a longer work, you probably will want to examine variations on your theme, different events and images to enhance and complicate the central focus. All strands, however, will connect and advance your main theme. The key is to be sure you've got one theme or focus front and center at any given time.

Starting True

Okay, the first draft of our faux memoir got off to a rocky start. In the second draft, let's revise toward a clear beginning. Let's slant details to reveal the theme without overtly stating it. Setting a scene will help us to avoid a common tendency to attempt to summarize an entire life right up front. After all, one of the faults of that failed first draft is that it's an overview of all the issues the author planned to address over the course of many pages. Does the second draft better capture your imagination?

An April mist dampens my cheeks as I race into the front yard, one word hammering my mind: the harsh syllables of *pregnant.* Even though the air is surely warmer than that spring blizzard in which I was born, my skin seems to sense that earlier chill — all the chilly scenes growing up in my home. Barely noticing the kids on bikes, the mothers pushing strollers — *that could be me* — I race down Otter Street toward town, toward Kelly Tires where Adam, the boy I only went out with a few times, works as a mechanic. What'll he do when I tell him? What should I do? I don't even understand why I got so drunk — why I had sex — with a boy I don't love. I didn't mean for any of this to happen.

My rubber-soled shoes slap the sidewalk. Only three in the afternoon but the air hangs dense, heavy, weighting the ends of my hair. My footsteps beat a rhythm, yet I feel as if I'm running to the tune of the same old blues . . . my mother's. I was the one supposed to escape Deep River, move to New York City, become . . . someone. Become *me*.

Before I reach town, without slowing, I veer down Main toward Lake Michigan, which seems to swallow our town whole. Swallow me.

I kneel on the shore. Sand grits beneath my jean-clad knees. There's no end to Lake Michigan. Waves churn on this bitter spring day. Yet I want the sheer power of my dreams of escape to make me strong enough to swim to the other side, as if there *is* another side, another way to live . . . swimming along the shores of Lake Michigan to Lake Huron, down the St. Lawrence Seaway to the Atlantic, to reach Manhattan.

Though this baby — *my* baby — can't possibly yet have a heart, I seem to hear it, like a depth charge, deep under water.

From reading this, what do you think the author is *really* writing about? What's her theme? This opening passage seems to be about the difficulty of escaping her past, the emotional burden of family legacy — exemplified by her pregnancy — which she fears will thwart her dreams, even cause her to lose her identity. Since she's revealed these abstract concepts in a concrete scene, the narrator doesn't have to come right out and say, "I'm afraid I'll never escape the legacy of my parents' mistakes, afraid I'll lose a sense of my own identity if I have this baby. But I'm also scared about not having it. I'm not sure what to do."

The Colors We Choose

I sometimes think of a fiction writer as beginning a novel or short story much as a painter does, with a clean, white canvas. He starts, as it were, with a blank slate and draws or creates characters, plots, and scenes. He picks up a metaphorical paint brush and begins sketching an imaginary world.

A memoirist, on the other hand, gazes at a canvas that's already swirling with color. Whereas a fiction writer crafts images onto that blank canvas, the memoirist decides what to remove from it. She already has a life full of siblings, friends, relatives, jobs, pets, successes, failures, joys, heartbreaks — a life full of many themes. She can seem emotionally solid one day, like an emotional wreck the next. What to do with so many seemingly disparate roles and events? A memoirist must follow one clear, thematically congruent design embedded in the palette of all of life's colors — and erase the rest.

For any given piece, then, a memoirist chooses which events, people, and images from her real life will best portray the theme at the core of any particular story. Even as her life is vast and complicated, she must be selective, eliminating anything that doesn't fit the pattern. Remove all extraneous material from that cluttered canvas. Soon, what remains will be one thematically cohesive picture.

Don't be afraid to discard what doesn't belong in your first memoir. You can always save the material for the next. We all have many stories to tell.

WRITING EXERCISES

When I'm unsure what any piece of writing wants to be about, I'll freewrite, doodle with words, just type and type until I seem to hit on one word, image, or idea that has steam. I feel my pulse quicken when I stumble upon that word or detail that galvanizes any given piece. I certainly felt my heart race when my grandmother suddenly appeared in that essay!

1. Set aside about fifteen minutes and write down every single thing the theme of your memoir might be. Freewrite. Don't judge or second-guess. After, as you review your list, consider which two or three areas have the most energy, either positive or negative. Focus on those as-

pects of an experience that draw you toward it — or else are the hardest, the most difficult, to face. Both have great power and significance. After you've selected these areas, write a paragraph about each. Which topic makes your heart race?

2. Now that you have the theme, make a list of three places (time frames, specific moments, and locations) where the memoir could start. Which one seems to best lend itself to a strong opening scene written with evocative images and sensory detail? Try writing that scene using all five senses — with slanted images, of course, which show your theme.

If you feel as if a lot of your "good stuff" is being left out, try not to worry. There's always a second memoir or essay. Frequently, readers ask me why I wrote two memoirs, why I didn't combine the book about incest with the one about sex addiction. In real life, of course, a connection exists: I struggled with sex addiction because my father sexually molested me. In the artful presentation of life I wanted to create on the page, however, I realized, soon after I began to write *Because I Remember Terror, Father, I Remember You*, that whenever I tried to weave even a hint of the adult sex addiction into the childhood incest, the memoir simply balked. Each issue has a different theme, energy, and voice (see chapter 5 for more details). I couldn't meld them together.

In writing any given memoir, therefore, we have to constantly ask ourselves: does this scene, metaphor, event, or detail reflect my theme? If not, we should save it for later.

FOR YOUR READING PLEASURE

In her memoir essay "Rob Me Again," Katherine Jamieson dynamically sustains her theme from the title itself to the end of the essay. We learn almost no facts about her other than those that highlight the theme: that sometimes fantasy is more enduring than reality; that she's willing to believe her fantasy about the man on the bicycle — at any price. Any other information about her life, anything that doesn't complement this theme, is left out.

ROB ME AGAIN

On a drizzly Sunday evening my first summer in New York City, I was walking in Chelsea when a man rode up beside me on a bike. *I really don't want to bother you,* he began, a baleful look in his brown eyes, *but this ridiculous thing just happened to me.* He explained that the costumes he had designed for a Broadway show had accidentally been locked in his apartment, and he had lost his keys. He just needed to borrow a little money so he could get in touch with his assistants and sort the whole thing out.

The glamour and urgency of the man's dilemma charmed me, and I agreed to lend him the money. We went to a deli where I broke a larger bill by buying a pack of gum I did not want; I laughed and offered him a piece. The man was poised and grateful throughout, assuring me that I was "doing a service for the theater world." I gave him the address of my office in Midtown and he promised me that someone would return the money Monday morning, first thing.

Monday came and went with no rushed assistant appearing at my cubicle, no complimentary front-row tickets, no appreciatory bouquet of flowers for a small but life-saving loan. Tuesday, nothing, and as I returned to my computer terminal each day it began to dawn on me that the biking costume designer might have been a biking crook after all. I did not feel angry, though. My first impression of the man lingered, and I could not separate my subsequent disillusionment from the romantic circumstances under which we had met. I wanted to believe that it was possible for a bored, entry-level employee living in a cramped apartment to brush up against a famous costume designer. For a moment, he had made me feel like I had an important place in the workings of a city where often I felt I had no place at all.

Three years later, in Soho, a light rain was falling, giving everything a washed-out, grayish tinge, as I wended my way from West Broadway to

Broadway. A man rode up beside me on a bike. *I'm so sorry to bother you,* he began breathlessly. I looked at the brown eyes with a yellow, feline cast, the deeply creased face, a short ponytail pulled to the back of his head. It was the same man.

I stared at him, dazed by the coincidence. It dawned on me that I had been granted a rare opportunity to redeem my naiveté from years before. There were people everywhere: I could accuse him loudly of trying to scam me, flag down a police officer. But I did nothing. As he went on and on, animated by the drama of his own fabrication, I felt sad for him, for me. He was so sincere; I did not want to call his bluff. He may not really have been in the theater, but he was a great actor.

About halfway through, a voice broke in: *Don't believe that guy, he practices that story in front of the mirror.* We both turned to face a young, lightly bearded man on the street corner. Something inside me crumpled, and when I looked back at the man, the creases in his face seemed even deeper than before. Perhaps it was just because his cover had been blown, or perhaps it was hearing an outside confirmation that he was lying, a fact that he may have, by this time, forgotten.

Our intimacy had been breached; the story had to end. I looked one last time into the man's wide, bright eyes, pained now, and as he turned his body, lifting up on his bike, I could see a damp spot on his jeans from the rain. For a moment, I wanted to reach out and stop him from going, tell him I still believed his story. I wanted to say, *Don't you remember me? I helped you before, but you forgot to return the money,* and for him to chuckle and tell me that it was all a big mistake, his assistant had come to my office but the doorman wouldn't let him in. I wanted him to tell me something, anything different than that he had robbed me then, and here he was, trying to rob me again.

Chapter Four

Plotting Your Life

P lot is as important in memoir as it is in fiction. In fiction, plot is invented; in nonfiction, it is discovered.

In a novel, you invent each scene, each episode, fabricating all sorts of trouble for your main character in order to thwart her or his wishes and desires. You create antagonists with whom your protagonist engages in conflict. You concoct roadblock after roadblock that your protagonist battles in order to reach the end of her or his plotted journey.

In nonfiction, we scrutinize our lived lives to discover our plots. We select only those significant, relevant details that enhance them. Memoirists erase extraneous people and events from that fully painted canvas of their lives, anything that doesn't reveal the plot. As we erase irrelevant moments, we're highlighting and emphasizing relevant ones, those that best propel our plot forward.

There is, however, an important similarity in terms of plot between these two genres. The novelist John Gardner, in his book *On Becoming a Novelist*, emphasizes the need for immersing the reader in "a vivid and continuous dream." In memoir, plot must likewise engage and mesmerize the reader. While life has down time (say when we lie around channel surfing), a memoir doesn't! As you ponder which events best illuminate your story, try to identify your most acute moments in order to hold the reader's attention. This doesn't necessarily mean a constant flood of blood, sweat, and tears. Rather, what this means is that you, the author, must feel a strong sense of urgency that must be vividly presented to the reader. The events you choose can be life altering in a big way, such as divorce, illness, addiction, birth, the death of a loved one. But these events can also be life altering in smaller ways, such as an irresistible urge to pick early blooming tulips before a spring blizzard. Examine why these tulips are important. What do they mean to you? How do they fit into the overall arc of your life?

Finding the Arc of Your Story

Memoirs that convey a profound sense of depth, self-reflection, and urgency — that continuous dream — implement two distinct plots. These two lines intersect throughout the memoir in order to fully develop the story.

Horizontal Plot

This line resembles a traditional plot in fiction in that it tells your story in terms of action. It represents external events. This plot relates the facts almost as if you're still in that moment, back then, when the events occurred. *Let me tell you what just happened to me!* While your memoir (like a novel) doesn't have to be written chronologically, still, this line shows events unfolding.

And they must unfold causally. That's the essence of plot. Each event is dependent upon what happened before. This narrative of action reveals how one event causes the next, and the next — like pushing the first domino in a line and watching them all tumble, one after the other.

To return to our unwed teenage mother, here's how she might begin to construct her plot: "My period was three weeks late. I feared I was pregnant. I walked five blocks through a cold April drizzle to the drugstore to purchase a home pregnancy test. By the time I reached the store, my frigid hands, trembling with fear, could barely open my wallet to pay for it."

What's the initial spark that causes the action to start? The woman fears she's pregnant. What's the subsequent effect? She buys a home pregnancy test.

When following a causal plot line, be sure to include only relevant details. Other than the trip to the drugstore, what else happened to the woman the morning she awoke and realized her period was three weeks late? Suppose, just as she's about to leave for the drugstore, a FedEx driver pulls up to her house and asks her to sign a receipt for a package. Or suppose, just as she's about to open the door to the drugstore, a friend stops her, reminding her about a math test on Monday. Why doesn't the author include these two events as she recounts the story of this fateful morning? After all, that's how it *really* happened. She doesn't include them because they aren't relevant. These details don't impact the plot line: *I'm pregnant; what will I do about it?*

Selecting plot details is crucial. Weigh each event or image by asking yourself whether it's pertinent to the story you're writing.

Vertical Plot

This line focuses more on the internal journey, plunging the plot into the heart of emotions, thoughts, and insights. This is the thinking and feeling part of the narrative. How do thoughts and emotions evolve over the course of your story? It's a more complex line that enhances the surface plot. The idea of progression, of cause and effect, is as important in the vertical plot line as in the horizontal. One thought or feeling causes the next, and the next, propelling the memoir deeper into your psyche.

To return to our poor unwed-mother author, here is how the two plot lines intersect: "The pregnancy wand turned blue. I was pregnant — and I felt as if I were plunging into an ocean of blue. I'd never resurface. Should I tell the baby's father, this man I barely knew? Should I have the baby? An abortion? Why had I had too much to drink that night? Why had I made the same mistake as my bitter, bitter mother?"

The narrator feels as if she's plunging into an ocean because the wand turned blue. The tangible fact of the wand turning blue (horizontal plot) causes the protagonist to feel as if she's drowning (vertical plot). In the same way that one action prompts another action (horizontal), actions likewise cause (vertical) questions, thoughts, or feelings to occur: *Because I'm pregnant (horizontal), I'm scared (vertical).* This is how the two plot lines work in conjunction with each other. Actions cause other actions; they also result in feelings about any given action.

Are the questions and thoughts in the above passage the only ones the author had that morning? No. Let's say the author worried that a sweater she bought her mother for a gift might be the wrong size. This aside wouldn't be included (just like that FedEx truck stopping at the author's house wasn't included) because it's irrelevant to this particular plot, which is to understand what this pregnancy means, how it'll affect her life, how it might connect to her past and future. Sure, maybe in the first draft this author included musings about the sweater. After all, she really did think about it just as she left for the drugstore. In subsequent drafts, however, the author realizes that this moment doesn't fit. We discover our plots slowly, during the actual writing process.

The vertical plot is crucial. As memoirists delve into their intimate thoughts and feelings, they interpret their lives in a meaningful way.

Motivating Your Plot

While the two plotlines impart *what* happens both in terms of external and internal action, motivation explores *why* something happens. When the author ruminates, say, about why she got drunk, why she had unprotected sex, she's examining the motivation for her actions. Maybe this narrator got drunk because that's how she's observed her alcoholic father dealing with stress. Maybe she had unprotected sex because her mother, her role model, likewise was an unwed teenage mother. Maybe her motivation is a lack of healthy emotional choices. Why does she lack choices?

Motivation is encompassed in both plotlines. In the horizontal plot, it shows why an action takes place: *Why did I get pregnant?* In the vertical plotline, it shows why she feels a particular way about an action: *Why am I scared to be pregnant? Why do I feel as if I'm drowning?* What's the motivation for the fear? Nothing occurs in a vacuum; what makes the protagonist tick?

Why is motivation important? When we read a memoir we want to know more than the facts, more than the surface story. We both read and write memoir to understand the story behind that which appears on the surface. We want to know why events occur. *Why did I do this? What causes me to act in such a way? Why do I feel this way about it?* As memoirist Vivian Gornick says, "What happened to the writer is not what matters; what matters is the large sense that the writer is able to *make* of what happened."

To review: An action or event on the horizontal plotline not only causes another action or event, it also causes a corresponding thought or emotion on the vertical plotline. The braiding of these actions with emotions and thoughts enhances and further propels their respective plotlines: *Because I was drunk, I felt fearless. Because I was fearless, I had unprotected sex. Because of the unprotected sex, I got pregnant. Because I'm pregnant, I'm sad and scared. But why did I get myself in this predicament in the first place?* (The motivation.)

The author discovers the answers to these questions over the course of the memoir. We write to understand what motivates the action in the horizontal plot, which, in turn, deepens the vertical plot. Why do you speed in your car? Why do you have an affair? Why do you hate your sister? Why do you plant a gorgeous spring garden? Why do you let your garden go to seed? Why do you hope your spouse dies in a fiery car crash? Why do you worry that every time your partner leaves the house he or she might not return?

The quest propels the plot. In this journey, this seeking of answers, this desire to understand the meaning and motivation behind the story, you create a sense of movement—a series of external actions and internal explorations—all of which bring the memoir alive.

Thunderous Plots

Your memoir should begin — first sentence, first page — with what I call the it-was-a-dark-and-stormy-night effect.

Okay, you can't *really* use that infamous, melodramatic line for your opening, but, melodrama aside, it's not such a bad beginning. It immediately creates atmosphere and tension.

A plot needs that tension established right off the bat. Whatever your opening words might be, you want to give the feeling of a "dark and stormy night." Not that all memoirs must be dark and stormy. Not at all. Some are gray and drizzling! Others are sunny and languorous, as when I wrote about reclining on a terrace in Portugal. There the tension, albeit subtle, was between my wish that the lush sensory moment would last forever, and my knowledge that a more mundane world would, inevitably, dispel it.

In short, something must be at stake for you, your persona, in the memoir. That you are emotionally, spiritually, and/or physically at risk, to whatever degree, must be conveyed immediately. Who or what are your real-life antagonists? Or, are you mainly battling yourself and your inner demons?

So as you begin to write, ask yourself: What is my "dark and stormy night"? What event in my life best jump-starts my memoir? Where does my real story start? Is there a moment when all hell breaks loose? Why am I beginning my memoir *now*? Our faux memoir might begin when the protagonist fears she's pregnant. Immediately, she's engaged in a dark and stormy night of conflict: *What's at stake if I give birth to the baby? If I don't?* Readers turn pages to find out. Readers want to watch the heroine or hero — *you* — struggle, to cheer you on to victory, to mourn your defeats, to stick by you as you overcome one obstacle after the next.

The possibilities for conflict are endless. Establish this conflict on page one. Any of the following could be a ripe beginning for a memoir: If your spouse or partner just left you. If your loved one was caught sneaking home late at night, rumpled, when s/he was supposed to be at work. If *you're* considering an affair. If you're waiting for test results from your physician. If you just lost a job. If you're about to enter rehab. If you just met a person who will change your life. If you're about to begin college at age fifty and you're scared. If you just realized you've made terrible life choices so all you want, even though you are forty years old, is to run away from home and start over. *Do* you run away? What is at stake for you if you do? If you don't?

Or, what's at stake if you have a baby out of wedlock? What's at stake if you have an abortion? If you put the baby up for adoption? After you make your decision, complicated as it may be, what obstacles prevent you from implementing it? What are the roadblocks you fight through to come out the other side? What is the arc, the plot you follow as you struggle?

Set the plot in motion in the first paragraph with a scene that establishes both the theme and what is at stake, emotionally and/or physically. Don't start the memoir a few pages — or even a paragraph — *before* the real action starts. What just happened to you? What do you want? What will you do to get it? This promise established by your own "dark and stormy night" opening scene must be sustained over the course of an honestly explored experience.

Let's briefly look at two more examples that show how to begin plot at the point of impact.

Let's say you want to write a memoir about starting college at fifty, with a theme focusing on life changes. How can you immediately show this in a concrete scene? You could start the memoir at the moment you enter your first classroom: you notice you're the only one in the room with gray hair. You're old enough to be the professor, yet here you are a freshman. All the other students, waiting for class to begin, are texting friends . . . whereas you don't even know how to send a text message. Doubt floods you: you won't fit in; maybe this is a mistake.

Later, after you establish the opening scene, you could introduce background information about why you decided to attend college now, why you didn't go right after high school.

Or, let's say you want to write a memoir about a rocky marriage, a time when you were considering an affair. One night, after a fight with your husband, you stormed from the house . . .

The punch of the jukebox stuns the soles of my feet as I enter the Moulin Rouge, a bar by the wharves in Galveston. Through a haze of cigarette smoke, I watch a woman in a glittery top slither against a man, his western boots barely moving across the dance floor. That could be me . . . except here I am in frayed tennis shoes, baggy jeans, no makeup. Yet a man sitting at the bar smiles . . .

By beginning the memoir as you enter the bar, at the point of impact (will you or won't you pick up a guy?), you create a more dramatic opening than by starting, say, on just any given day of your marriage. Here, entering a bar, tempted, something is at stake: What happens to you if you have an affair? If you don't? Your inner conflict, your motivation — all the elements of plot — will unfold from this one scene.

The Structure of Plot

Each story must find its own structure, a skeleton that events flesh out. What's the best way to organize *this* story? Chronologically? Or maybe you begin in the middle of things, then use flashbacks to color in the past before moving forward, subsequently switching back and forth between past and present. Or you could both begin and end in the present, framing the story, as if with bookends, with observations from the person you are now. Then, the bulk of the memoir, the middle chapters — about the main event you want to portray — would be written in flashback. This is how I structured *Because I Remember Terror, Father, I Remember You*, which begins in my therapist's office, in the present. The book is then written as if I'm telling him the story of my past, my childhood. In effect, most of the book is a flashback, before I return to a present-time sequence, back in his office, at the end.

My memoir *Love Sick: One Woman's Journey through Sexual Addiction*, on the other hand, employs a chronological structure, beginning the day before I enter rehab. Each subsequent chapter represents one day of my twenty-eight-day stay in rehab, ending the day I leave. Embedded within some of these chapters, however, are flashbacks that portray my out-of-control life before I began therapy, when I was acting out my sexual addiction.

Why begin just as I'm entering rehab? Because the memoir focuses on *recovering* from sex addiction. If, on the other hand, I focused on "how I acted out as a sex addict for years," then I might have begun the memoir when I was in college, say, when I had my first affair with a married man old enough to be my father. In other words, the theme will help determine the structure, how you organize the material.

What are the structural options for our unwed mother's memoir? If the plot is to represent her journey as she decides what to do about the unborn baby, she could begin when she realizes she's pregnant. What conflict does she endure as she makes her decision? What external tension might she encounter with the baby's father, with her parents? What internal conflict plagues her? *Do I or don't I have the baby; do I or don't I move to New York?*

Or, if the theme is how she learns to live as a single mother, the plot could begin *after* the decision, say as the narrator first drives into Manhattan, with the baby in a car seat behind her. In this scenario, what internal and external conflict confronts her as she struggles as a single mother in a strange city?

Once you discover the central concern of your memoir, it'll be easier to determine where the plot begins and how best to structure it. Remember, it's much stronger to begin your story at the point of greatest tension and then provide background information and exposition later, after the plot has a full head of steam. Once you've hooked the reader with a dynamic opening scene, once the stakes are high and the reader wants to turn those pages to know what happens next, then it's all right to take a deep breath, backpedal a bit, and show the reader (through flashback) how you, as narrator, reached this critical juncture in the first place. As you weave together the ways in which your interior life affected external events, and vice versa, you will be constructing the most lasting and universal of plots — not just *what* happens next, but *why*.

Crossing the Finish Line

Even our faux memoir must end at some fixed point in time. Eventually, we have to type "The End." When? Let's consider two different options, since the end of a memoir depends, to a large extent, on the beginning.

First: If the narrator decides to have an abortion, this memoir, as mentioned, could begin as she takes the pregnancy test; then, it could end as she walks, sadder but wiser, from the clinic. The journey, in this case, could show how she breaks with the past and makes choices that differ from her mother's as she leaves the past behind.

Second: Or maybe she decides to have the baby and move to New York anyway. If so, the memoir could end, say, after the first year in the city as she illustrates how she's still been able to overcome the past and not become a bitter woman like her mother. Maybe the memoir ends as she picks up her daughter from day care, holding her first paycheck.

Not only does the end depend on the beginning, it reflects the specific journey you decide to explore. Our unwed and pregnant author, for example, probably wouldn't continue her memoir another ten years or so into the future. Not everything that ultimately happens to her is likely to flow directly from this one occurrence. A rule of thumb is to bring the memoir to its natural outcome or resolution only for the present crisis.

As you write, carefully consider the time frame. The end doesn't need to bring the reader up to your present minute. It can be narrowly circumscribed to cover one year (or less) of your life, or you can follow one clear plot line (and theme) through many years.

The good news is that our lives are rich and complex, providing us enough material for more than one plot, more than one book.

Turning Real Life into Art

I tend to see my real life in a continuous line. I don't separate it in segments whereby each event has a clear, artfully designed beginning, middle, and end. In real life, I don't usually understand the connections between events as they happen. Nor do I daily consider my motivation for behaving in any given way. Rather, I stumble from moment to moment without seeing exactly what I've learned, when I learned it, or where I'm headed.

Remember that car-accident scene I told you about in chapter 1, when my angry father was teaching my timid mother how to drive? At the time of the actual event, all the child-me understood was that our family rolled down an embankment, landed in a woman's front yard, and that no one was seriously hurt.

It was only as a writer, years later, that I understood the meaning of the event: that the woman who helped me, who touched my arms and legs to determine if I had broken bones, was safer than my own father. By discovering this, I understood how this one episode fit into the overall plot and theme of the memoir. It is through writing that we make connections and understand our motivations. This is the process we all undergo while writing memoir: to learn about ourselves. Art, unlike life, offers the possibility of a clearly delineated plot. What we ultimately reveal through this arc is that we are different at the end of our memoirs from who we are at the beginning — more knowledge-able, insightful, wiser.

> The writing process itself is part of the journey. The insights you have while writing aren't things you knew at the time the events happened. It's only through writing about events after they happen—as we craft our memoirs—that we come to understand what they mean. All our lives have plots. We find them through writing.

Discovering your plot is much like following Hansel and Gretel's crumbs through a forest. The crumbs are there, even if you struggle at times, in a dim light, to see them. Just keep searching, writing, follow-ing one crumb (one word) at a time, even though the forest is dark, the trail at times confusing. Don't be afraid to walk into the forest. Don't be afraid to get lost. The loss is temporary. You will find your way out. Don't despair. Keep writing. When exploring a dark, possibly traumatic past, don't hesitate to seek the help of a best friend or therapist — a warm hand to hold yours — as you continue your journey, putting one foot in front of the other along this path that leads into the profound center of your story.

WRITING EXERCISES

1. Let's begin with a reading exercise. Pick up a copy of the memoir you happen to be reading (if you like, please see my recommended reading list in appendix 4) and underline the sections in the first few pages where you think the author is crafting the horizontal plot line. Next, note where the author slides away from recounting the straight facts of the story and develops the plot with thoughts and feelings *about* the action: the vertical plot line.

2. In the previous chapter, you learned how to focus a memoir along one theme, and you practiced writing a beginning. Now, let's extend it. Either revise what you've written (say, for example, if you feel the plot gets off to a slow start and you want to pack more of a punch) and/or continue on using both the horizontal and vertical plot lines.

Let's pause for a moment just to be sure your events and thoughts are following a clear plot pattern. For example, here is how the cause and effect could be delineated for my own car-accident scene:

Horizontal Plot Line
Because my father was in a rage while trying to teach my mother how to drive, we had an accident.

Vertical Plot Line
Because the woman who helped me after the accident had a gentle touch, I came to understand that even a strange woman's touch is safer than my father's. I learned through comparison that my father's touch was scary, not gentle at all.

The car crash causes me to understand ideas of safety and love. This understanding is the effect of the car crash. This symbiotic relationship between the two plot lines is always present when a memoir is well designed.

3. On a piece of scratch paper, just for yourself, write out a few notes about your own plot. Does it follow a cause-and-effect progression? If not, keep tinkering with it until it does.

4. Select one of the main events you plan for your memoir. Make a list of *all* (there's usually more than one) motivating factors for this particular event. Why did you do it? Why did you feel _____ because of it?

FOR YOUR READING PLEASURE

Katy Read's "Scavengers" begins at the point of impact, when the first "scavenger" arrives on moving day. As the essay unwinds, her evocative details enhance the plot's theme, ending with the narrator reflecting upon the concept of possessions. This reflection (vertical plot) gracefully and congruently evolves from all the actions that occur previously, in the horizontal plot.

SCAVENGERS

The first one arrived early that morning: a small, unsmiling man riding an old bike with a wire basket. When he saw us carrying cartons out to the U-Haul trailer, he stopped.

"Got anything you gonna throw away?" He spoke quietly, as if conserving energy. His forehead glistened. The sun hadn't climbed above the roof of our building, but already the air felt like a warm washcloth on my neck.

Mike and I glanced around at the boxes and furniture. Clearly, our stuff wouldn't all fit into the cars and trailer. Here stood someone willing to haul away the excess, saving us a run to Goodwill. But what to jettison?

"Why don't you come back in a few hours," Mike said.

I watched the guy pedal away, wondering whether we had anything he would want. Our furniture was mostly hand-me-downs and rummage-sale finds that could have been replaced, even upgraded, at any decent flea market. We could afford nicer pieces, but Mike and I took pride in our simple possessions — the sagging futon, the rickety table, the black-and-white TV with its tinfoil-topped rabbit ears. Our things proved we weren't obsessed with things.

The next pair arrived as we were struggling to wedge a railback chair into the trailer. The woman had long, graying hair. The man was lanky, with a gold cross dangling from one ear. They'd just come from Tennessee looking for work, he said with a twang that proved it, and were setting up a place to live.

"Whatever you don't need, we sure could put to use," he said.

Lamps and tables littered the lawn. Mike repeated what he'd told the first guy, to come back later. But the couple lingered, watching me try to push the wooden chair into a sliver of space.

"Here, let me give it a shot." The woman flipped the chair sideways and slid it neatly into place. She stepped back smiling. "Sometimes all it takes is a fresh pair of eyes."

We all stood there for a moment looking at the chair.

"Never mind," I said. "Let's take it back out. You can have it."

"What? Look, it fits right in there."

"No, really. We've got all this other stuff to get in." I waved toward the piles on the grass.

They loaded the chair into the trunk of their old brown Cadillac and drove off, engine thundering, leaving a puff of blue exhaust.

By late afternoon, our apartment was still strewn with odds and ends. Outside, Mike shifted boxes like puzzle pieces, working to open a few more cubic inches of space. The man from Tennessee returned alone. We let him go upstairs and help himself. He selected an old stereo and speakers, a coffee table with missing legs, a plastic dish rack, a potted plant that needed watering.

"The wife likes a little green around," he said.

After he left, the man on the bike returned. I felt a twinge of guilt; shouldn't he have had first pick? But I hadn't quite believed he'd come back. We gathered objects marked for the trash: a plastic parson's table, a dirty throw rug, the factory-installed car radio that I'd had replaced with a good stereo. The man stacked the items in his handlebar basket. He said little, but seemed ready to accept anything.

"Could you use some milk?" Mike asked. "There's half a gallon upstairs."

The man nodded, and I ran to get it. When I opened the refrigerator, I spied a box of Bisquick, half empty, held shut with a rubber band. I hesitated, thinking it might be an insulting handout. I grabbed it anyway.

"It's probably pretty old," I apologized, showing it to him.

The man reached for the biscuit mix. He fit it into the pile on his bike, nodded thanks and rode off.

Another man was rummaging through a wastebasket we had set on the curb for the garbage collectors. "Man, this all you got?" he complained. But even he didn't leave empty handed. He took the wastebasket itself.

It was early evening when the lawn was finally clear, the apartment empty of all but drifting dust. Mike got into his truck and I climbed into my hatchback. The vehicles were so full we could barely see out the windows. Their sagging undercarriages scraped the pavement as we pulled out of the driveway. We headed toward the interstate, carrying more than I had ever realized we owned.

Chapter Five

Between Innocence and Experience

Finding Your Voice(s)

Back when I began my writing career, one of my teachers told me, "Voice is everything." I knew he was right — but I also knew that my fictional voice, regardless of character or point of view, frequently sounded false and strained. So after those several unfinished novels I told you about, I switched to memoir and finally discovered a voice in which I could tell my own story. Ironically, what I also discovered is that memoir, like fiction, offers a range of possible voices from which to choose. A voice that sounds harmonious in one of your memoirs might sound off-key in another. Not only that, but each memoir itself implements more than one voice.

Knowing this, however, isn't always as easy as actually hearing or finding the authentic voice(s) for any given work. *Love Sick*, for example, took five long years to write because I initially couldn't hear the various voices in order to fully portray myself. I hadn't anticipated that the voices in my first memoir would not work for the second. *Because I Remember Terror, Father, I Remember You* employs a young girl's voice and a more adult narrator who guides the reader through the quagmire of my incestuous family. *Love Sick* also uses two main voices: an addict voice and a sober voice. Whereas the voices in *Terror, Father* sound vulnerable, raw, scared, the voices in *Love Sick* sound tougher, edgier, albeit, in certain places, also scared.

Subsequently, as I've been writing memoir essays, I've learned each requires its own voice and sound as well. Remember that essay I thought would be a simple high school love story — until my grandmother plodded onto the page? In early drafts, when I was under the illusion I was only writing about the love triangle, the voice sounded thin, insipid, juvenile — along the lines of: "Oh my gosh, I think I'm in love!" This is a major reason why the early drafts failed. After my grandmother appeared, however, the voice grew darker, more textured.

> The voice of each piece you write needs its own tone, rhythm, vocabulary, and energy.

Using Multiple Voices

To better understand and differentiate how voice is used in memoir, I've developed two main categories by reimagining phrases originated by the poet William Blake: The Song (or Voice) of Innocence and the Song (or Voice) of Experience.

You can think of the Voice of Innocence much like the horizontal plot line: it's the voice that tells the story of what happened, the events. On the other hand, think of the Voice of Experience like the vertical plot line: it's the voice that interprets or reflects upon the events. In this chapter, then, we're not learning an altogether new idea. Voice, in effect, provides the sound of the plot lines. When the plot shows an action (conflict, motivation), the voice speaks this action using a sound that's compelling. Without dynamic voices, the plot — any plot — would grow boring.

The Voice of Innocence

This voice relates the facts of the story, the surface subject or action. It's the voice that tells us, in effect, "first this happened, and then this next thing happened." What we can now see is that both the horizontal and vertical plot lines contain emotion — after all, to be human is to feel! However, in the horizontal plot, those emotions are new and poorly, if at all, understood. Similarly, the Voice of Innocence reveals the raw, not-yet-understood emotions associated with the story's action by portraying the person you were (and what you felt) when the sequence of events actually took place. Does the voice sound interesting? Funny? Sad? Angry? Intense? Anguished? The Voice of Innocence makes use of one, two, or a whole chorus of sounds, leaving it to the Voice of Experience to sort them all out.

The Voice of Experience

With the Voice of Experience, therefore, we add a more mature voice or persona that, in effect, explains and deepens the Voice of Innocence with metaphor, spirituality, irony, reflection. This voice offers the progression of thought in the memoir by examining what the Voice of Innocence (facts and raw emotions) means. This more complex viewpoint interprets and reflects upon the surface subject.

Say, for example, the Voice of Innocence describes an anxiety attack; then, the Voice of Experience seeks to understand why you had it, what it means. What are the ramifications of past occurrences and behaviors? What are the metaphors that deepen the events? This voice speaks the vertical plot line, offering insight and a fuller awareness of actions. Imagine that you're gazing over the railing of a bridge and, with authorial X-ray vision, you can see below the surface of water, deep into the heart of a river, deep into the metaphorical heart of you. With this voice you transform the lived moment, rather than merely recollecting it or reminiscing.

Instead of using the phrase "different points of view," as in fiction, I use the phrase "different depths of view" when considering these two voices. In this way, a writer maintains a cohesive narrative or story while also journeying into the core of self-discovery.

How do you know when to use one voice, when the other? No hard-and-fast rules apply. These voices are flexible and can be introduced at any time. For example, you don't have to begin the memoir in one voice, say Innocence, before switching to a more authorial voice halfway through. One page, one paragraph, even one sentence might incorporate both. Within one brief section of *Love Sick*, for example, I use these two voices when describing a maroon scarf that once belonged to my married lover, but which he gave to me: "I press the scarf against my nose and mouth. I take a deep breath. The scent is of him — leaves smoldering in autumn dusk — and I believe it is a scent I have always craved, one I will always want. I don't understand why the scent of the scarf . . . seems more knowable, more tangible than the rest of him."

Here, I begin in the Voice of Innocence (addict voice), providing factual and sensory details about the maroon scarf, romanticizing its scent of smoldering dusk. The raw (albeit unexplored) emotion I feel toward this man — who wraps such a magical scarf around my neck — proves this is love. Doesn't it?

"No," the Voice of Experience, the sober me, implies, in that last sentence. Instead, the scarf embodies alienation and loneliness, as well as a need for comfort. I love the scarf because, as an addict, I don't know how to love the man — or, more importantly, myself. This sober, authorial voice guides the reader through the confusion of the addiction, depicting, over the course of the memoir, why I have self-destructive affairs with dangerous men.

In short, the Voice of Innocence conveys what happened: *I pressed the scarf to my face, inhaling autumn dusk.* The Voice of Experience examines what the author, sitting at her desk writing, understands about events now: *The scarf was more knowable than the man.* Ultimately, a writer's exploration is more interesting than just the facts by themselves.

These two voices, working together, mirror the conflict inherent in plot as well. Throughout *Love Sick*, for example, the Voice of Innocence (the addict persona) fights to act out with dangerous men. At the same time, the Voice of Experience (the persona seeking sobriety) fights to walk away from these men. These voices, tugging in opposite directions, heighten the two plotlines.

The "I" in memoir is a literary device to both enhance and explore complicated truths. Just as we are complex people in real life, we must be equally complex personas on the page—albeit artistically rendered.

Let's look at how these two voices deepen and define the protagonist in our faux memoir. Earlier, we observed her walking to the drugstore to buy a pregnancy test. Now, at home, the scared Voice of Innocence provides the surface facts and the raw, unprocessed emotions of events:

> Sitting alone in my bedroom, I feel as if I'm reduced to one blue dot on this wand. *Pregnant.* I shake the stick, as if I can shake it — my life — loose. This can't happen. How different from that night out behind the baseball field when I felt, well, loved — Adam's mouth sweet and cool as spring grass, yet also insistent with beer . . . his hands loosening all the sadness in my stomach.

The Voice of Experience follows, ruminating, exploring what the surface facts mean:

> But that wasn't love. Why have I followed in my mother's footsteps, pregnant, and not yet out of high school? Is it because I'm also like my father, seeing life through the bottom of an amber-colored bottle? Or am I secretly afraid of leaving this familiar home? Maybe I'm afraid I'll fail at my dreams if I go to New York. Alone. Would I actually be lonelier there, in that cement and steel city, than here among linden and spruce? Maybe I got pregnant as a way to hold me — my true self — here, so I'll never be alone, never leave home at all.

As these voices speak, do you also see plots unfolding? Here, the author ruminates about the motivation for her actions: she's following in her parents' footsteps.

Though both voices are important, sometimes it's easier to hear the Voice of Innocence. You already know this story — the one you've lived. But what did you learn from the living? To find out, you reflect upon events as shown in the final sentences in the above passage. Reflection is more than simply recollecting or remembering the past. It's a search to see our stories in a new and metaphoric light. Whereas in the Voice of Innocence you're writing the thing itself ("what happened to me"), the reflective voice presents a reconfigured version ("how do these events in the past look to me now?"). At my desk, writing, I ask myself: What are the metaphors that make sense of the narrative? What are the patterns in my life? What does it all mean?

If you don't have all the answers, that's fine. Asking questions is more important than definitively answering them. Conjecture. Allow for ambiguity. Events usually aren't black and white. Even in black-and-white photographs we notice shadows, all the shades of gray. To discover your true self, act like an archaeologist sifting through layers of self and soul.

Without this Voice of Experience, the memoir might address significant events, but it would read more like journalism — timely — whereas it should feel *timeless*. As you write, pretend to toss stones in a pool of water. What do you see? Write the compelling ripples of life you see on the skin of water, not just the smooth surfaces. Let your gaze follow the stone as it slowly sinks. By plumbing these depths, you'll discover what ebbs and flows below.

Your Everyday Voice and Your Literary Voice

In my everyday life, I don't speak in metaphors. Nor do I use artfully crafted language. I'm not particularly careful about word choice. I don't use sensory imagery or many concrete details. Sentences, when spoken to friends, meander and loop all over the place, replete with half-developed ideas and observations, with a bunch of *hmms* and sighs thrown in for good measure. Have you ever taped an interview and later tried to transcribe it? Spoken conversation is full of hesitations, leaps, and gaps. You have to edit it for the page, stitching together connections that aren't immediately apparent. In short, a spoken voice, though it can be breathless or intimate, is rarely as carefully structured, formed, or considered as the written voice.

Let's say, for example, I have to tell my boss an embarrassing reason why I need a month off. After hemming and hawing, I finally blurt out: "My therapist says I have to go into rehab." This brief explanation hardly brings us inside the moment. It provides only minimal information.

Like a spoken voice, a journal or diary can also be intimate, but it, too, usually doesn't shape life into art. For example, here is a diary voice that would more or less represent my real thoughts the day I entered rehab, after having sex with a man named Rick in a motel. "I've been lying to Randy. I've been lying to my husband. I'm a wreck. I feel like I'm dying. I didn't want to meet Rick. I'd promised Randy I'd never have sex with Rick again. I didn't mean to. I didn't want to. I don't know why I keep doing these things. I need help. I really need help. Now. As soon as I see Randy, I'll confess, and plead with him to help me."

These sentences are heartfelt but lack the sensory imagery needed to make a connection with the reader's world. Most of my thoughts are abstract. I sound pathetic and whiny.

When I actually wrote in my memoir about meeting Rick, therefore, I spent about five pages developing the scene. I describe myself dawdling in the parking lot of the Rainbow Motel, where Rick's car is parked, Rick himself, already checked into room #213, waiting for me. I wrote, in part:

> I should leave. I should leave here now. I should drive home and rinse pink gloss from my lips, wipe mascara from my lashes, change out of my too-short skirt and too-tight black lace blouse.
>
> Pausing outside the door of room #213, I hear the television: a car crash, urgent voices. I turn the knob and lock it behind me. Rick lies on the sheet smoking a cigarette, the remote beside him. He inhales. Exhales. Smoke swirls. I watch it disperse. An ash drifts onto the pillowcase. He doesn't notice. He hasn't stopped watching me since I entered.

In my real life, I never thought about this experience using this kind of language or detail. I simply don't think or speak like this. I never used this kind of imagery when I finally confessed to my therapist. However, while the voice in the scene isn't my everyday speaking voice, the scene, ironically, is more truthful — more the way it really happened — as I try to bring the reader inside the actual, tangible, imagistic moment.

So who is this person narrating your memoir? It's both you and not you. It's an artistically created "you": the Voice of Innocence and the Voice of Experience working together. This memoir voice sounds more textured than that abstract way I actually speak; it artistically crafts what I've lived. It can take a while for you to hear this voice, but keep writing until you find the right voice for any given story.

Contrast the above passage from *Love Sick* with the following clinical description from the Web site of the Society for the Advancement of Sexual Health:

> The idea of being "love addicted" may be preferred by sexually addicted women because it fits the romantic, nurturer model of woman, whereas the term "sex addict" connotes an image of "nymphomaniac," "slut," or "whore." The "love" that these women describe is often an addiction to the yearning or euphoria of romance, but has little to do with love.

While the voice in this article provides interesting information, it doesn't invite the reader into a personal story. You could learn something about sexual addiction by studying a manual, but in a memoir a reader learns how it *feels*.

And that's the key: to discover an intimate voice that will invite the reader into your story. Remember how eighteenth-century novelists addressed readers directly: "Dear Reader" or "Gentle Reader"? Such salutations sound as if authors are whispering their private secrets to you and only you, Gentle Reader. And while contemporary memoirists don't directly address readers in these terms, they seem to through the confessional sound of their voices. We write as if to sympathetic confidants.

Guiding Voices

The Voice of Innocence guides the reader through the event itself: *This is my story. Let me tell you what happened to me.* The Voice of Experience, on the other hand, blazes a trail through tangles of conflicting and confusing feelings. By questing and questioning, by reflecting, by providing metaphors for events, the Voice of Experience ultimately offers insight to the reader: *This is what the lived moment means.* If both these guides are trustworthy, sympathetic, urgent, complex, and interesting, then the reader willingly follows these voices through the maze's twists and turns. So, by the end, the reader will have gained insight into the beautiful — if sometimes wrenching — pattern to it all.

WRITING EXERCISES

The following exercises will help you discover the various voices you'll need to explore your stories in all their complexities. As you work on these exercises, note how these twined voices also enhance the two plotlines, horizontal and vertical, discussed in the previous chapter.

1. Recall a photograph from childhood, or dig one out of an old album. Write a paragraph about it using the voice and sensibility of who you were when the photograph was taken. Then, write a paragraph about it through the voice and sensibility of who you are now. Next, write a third paragraph that combines the perspectives of the first two: a paragraph that speaks in both the Voice of Innocence and the Voice of Experience.

2. Imagine a room from your house when you were young, say your kitchen. Write a paragraph describing the kitchen as if you're a child sitting in it. Then, write a paragraph from the viewpoint of you as an adult, ruminating about it. Next, as with exercise 1, above, write a third paragraph that encompasses the first two.

3. Try to remember your last vacation. Even though you are home now, pretend you're still on that trip, and write a letter describing the trip to your mother. Then, write another letter describing the trip to a spouse or partner, then a sibling, then a best friend. Next, write a paragraph about the trip as if it's a journal entry that no one else will see. Finally, craft the description of the vacation as if preparing it for publication in a magazine. Note how the voice, tone, and details subtly (or not so subtly) shift, depending upon whom you're addressing.

4. This exercise focuses on how the use of voice twines with plot development, or arc (combining what we discussed in chapter 4 with our discoveries in chapter 5).

To begin, make a list that describes where you are from. What are your origins? What concrete details describe you and your family? For example, I spent much of my childhood in the Caribbean, so my list includes the scent of salt water, the rustle of coconut palms, my father's bay rum aftershave, volcanic mountains. (Be sure to slant your details to mirror the emotions of this time in your life.)

Second, make a list (again, using tangible objects) that describes where you are now — who you have become. Since I now live in the Midwest, the colors and scents that surround me seem muted compared to those of the Caribbean: Lake Michigan is scentless. In winter, snow quiets the earth. The sand dunes don't spike the sky like volcanic mountains.

For my exercise, by examining these details, I would understand how my life, now, compares to that of my childhood: it's calmer, less dramatic.

Write these lists quickly. Free associate. What comes to mind, say, when you envision yourself in second grade? Tenth grade? The first time you moved away from your parents' house? What objects and memories define you? What items or events from your past impacted this journey?

These initial lists, as you weave plot with voice, should help you begin to see the arc of the plot in your memoir, and how you're developing yourself into a persona on the page.

5. This extended exercise will take you through five stages of development to show how "you" can evolve into a fully rounded character on the page.

The fiction writer Flannery O'Connor once said, "A story always involves, in a dramatic way, the mystery of personality." Memoir, like fiction, also depicts multiple and mysterious facets of a personality: an authentic "you" developed into a character, someone who resembles or echoes you, but isn't exactly you — and isn't the whole you. More precisely, for each piece of writing, just as events are chosen for specific plots, you explore specific aspects of yourself, selecting only those character traits that best represent your persona in that particular memoir or essay. I wouldn't, for example, show my desire to be a political activist in that essay I wrote about the high school love triangle. That aspect of my personality would be saved for another piece of writing. Ask yourself: Which character traits are necessary in order to best portray myself in this situation? Who is the appropriate self or persona to tell this story?

Once these character traits are determined for any given piece, the author must render her- or himself into a tangible character. Detail by detail, breathe life into this representational "you" until your presence emerges onto a blank piece of paper or computer screen. As these variously shaded and nuanced images appear piece by piece, it's almost as if your persona undergoes developmental stages: The reader learns the color of your hair, where you live, where the story takes place. Over the course of the paragraphs and pages, we discover what you love, what you hate, what scares you, what confuses you. We watch you interact with family and friends. We understand what you want and what you'll do to get it. We learn what motivates you. We examine the metaphors of your narrative.

We've already looked at two broad categories of voice: Innocence and Experience. What are the steps you need to take in order to transport yourself from a state of Innocence to one of Experience? If you begin at point A (Innocence), what is each stage or step you take to reach point B (Experience)? How do you actually develop yourself on the page? Remember how, before digital cameras, photographic film developed in trays of chemicals? Images appeared slowly, detail by detail, until the finished print appeared in all the colors. This is how we create, or re-create ourselves in memoir. Our personas bloom onto the page, image by image.

Below, I'll describe the five stages that move "you," as a character, from Innocence to Experience. For each stage, I'll offer a brief scene or example that unearths these various layers of personality. I invite you to consider your current memoir project and draw (see figures) and write along with me.

Stage 1 of the Voice of Innocence provides rudimentary facts, or facets, surrounding a personality: fairly straightforward exposition to ground your persona in time and place. Even if you don't announce that this is 1998, for example, use details — music playing on the radio, a newscast on the television, etc. — that give the reader a fairly good idea. Let the reader know, if not the specific town or city in which your story takes place, at least what state. Is it summer? Winter? Are you alone? Are you with a lover? Your cat? Have you just graduated from high school? College? What's the most important detail that grounds this particular story? Grounding is crucial in order for the reader to feel your presence in a tangible world, fixed in a particular moment of time, of place.

> In the heat wave of 1998, I swelter through the early months of my teen pregnancy. I hardly leave my house, even to walk the few blocks to Lake Michigan.

Think of this particular voice as a stick figure that has the basic outlines of arms, legs, torso, and head: a simple presence in the world.

Stage 2 is a more observant but still slightly distant personality that introduces a more writerly style, yet is still part of the Voice of Innocence. Here, you provide the reader with an idea of how you observe your world of the senses, a world of carefully selected and slanted sensory details that help portray character, so the person you're creating on the page is tangible, living in an atmospheric milieu. For example, if you're sitting in your bedroom, ecstatic to be pregnant, you would notice how sun glints the window glass like pieces of crystal. If, on the other hand, you're devastated to be pregnant, as is the case with our hapless invented heroine, then the very same details would be slanted

entirely differently. *The sun, reflected in the glass, is hot and blinding. I can barely see.*

The following is how we might find her — after that drizzly April, as spring moves to hot summer — irrevocably closer to her fate.

> Summer humidity seems to drip down the walls and windows. All I taste and breathe is heat, like fluid metal. The mortar of the log cabin in which my family lives is disintegrating, the logs slipping from the frame. I feel as if waves of moisture rise off Lake Michigan and churn through town, down alleys and streets. There's no way to walk through these agitated currents, no way out. Even the glass on the windows is too hot to touch.

Add eyes, nose, mouth, ears, and hands to your stick figure as he or she begins to sense the world.

Stage 3 is a more evolved personality, one with feelings, hovering between Innocence and Experience. You're writing closer to the heart with a sense of urgency and raw emotion. You're *feeling* the facts of the story, how you felt when the events originally occurred. As much as possible, tie feelings to tangible details. Just to tell the reader, say, that you feel sad probably won't cause the reader to feel your sadness. Instead, reveal the sadness to the reader through the use of imagistic details. But don't overdo it. You don't want your persona screaming, crying, and emoting all over the page. Don't drench those pages in tears. The paper will disintegrate! Too much emotion pushes readers away,

doesn't allow room for them to feel what you're feeling. Show your readers emotion without beating them over the head with it.

> I can't protect myself from this endless, endless heat . . . can't protect my unborn baby, either. My father, as usual, returns home drunk every night. My mother screams that I'm careless for getting pregnant, for being like her. I can't talk to Adam. Suppose he wants to marry me? Suppose he doesn't? I curl up in bed, day after day, sweating, too immobilized to wash or even brush my hair.

Draw your stick figure with tangled hair, slumped in a bed. Add sweat and tears. Or draw your own stage 3 figure to inspire a stage 3 paragraph for your memoir.

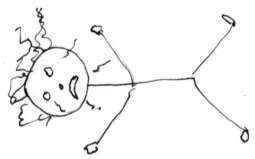

Stage 4 introduces a metaphorically expressed personality and fully brings the reader into the Voice of Experience. This metaphoric voice offers insight into the facts and feelings of stages 1 through 3. Here, for example, it becomes apparent that the "disintegrating" log cabin is a metaphor for the narrator herself. While we'll discuss metaphor in more detail in the next chapter, basically, a metaphor is a comparison that slants sensory details so that they portray, say, a state of being. That sun glinting the bedroom windows, reminding the narrator of crystals, is a metaphor for joy or happiness. Since *our* heroine is scared and sad, however, details and images are slanted to metaphorically depict an unhappy state of mind.

> I feel no protection between me and heat. No protection for this baby. Really, it's my body that's lost its mortar, and the slippage seems to be in my heart.

Add a heart and a brain to your stick figure. Try your hand at crafting some appropriate metaphors for your own persona's state of mind in your memoir.

Stage 5 presents a fully developed, reflective character, one who ruminates and dreams. Metaphor is sustained in order to connect elements and events in the memoir into a cohesive whole. A metaphor, then, isn't only something that's periodically sprinkled into a story; rather, the entire piece has a metaphoric quality — as we'll learn in greater detail in the next chapter. In stage 5 you also consider the past, as well as other people in your life. What do you hope, wish, dream, fear? What are the lessons you've learned? While poets and fiction writers are taught to show, not tell, in memoir it's acceptable to show *and* tell — or, to use terms more relevant for memoir — *reveal* and *state*. But be aware that the "stating" can't arise out of thin air. It must emerge from an action or a tangible image — actions and images you've already established on the horizontal plot line and the Voice of Innocence. If you feel sad, scared, or hopeless, first reveal the origin of these feelings as tangibly as possible, before reflecting upon them.

> When I can no longer stand my screaming mother and drunken father, I drag myself outside to the lake. No wind. No waves. No relief. The gunmetal gray water spreads flat and stagnant before me. Rather than feel hopeful that one day I'll be courageous enough to flee my home and

reach the horizon, now the gray of sky and water merge. No horizon. I feel trapped in sand, as if it's cement, and I'm unable to walk away. Ever.

Who am I now? I've always seen myself as a girl who seeks danger — like my mother? My father? Before, I felt invincible, a girl who loved to have a good time. It's only now that I feel alone, abandoned on this distant shore.

But, no, not alone. This baby. Is it a baby yet? What should I do? Give birth? Or that word — that ugly word I can't even say.

Surround your figure with question marks, exclamation points, metaphoric imagery, symbolic musings, dream icons, etc., so your once-stick figure is now rounded and whole. Thinking of your own memoir project, try a passage that reveals and then states.

While I've drawn a progression from a distant, rather simple voice into one that's more engaged and complex, this doesn't necessarily mean that your memoir must begin at stage 1. Instead, you could begin in the middle of things, at that point of impact we discussed in the chapter on plot, and then use flashbacks, as needed, to fill in necessary backstory.

And even though you, as a character, will evolve and emotionally grow over the course of the memoir (this growth is that vertical plotline twined with the Voice of Experience), you can still weave in and out among the five stages from the first page to the last. You can even use two or more of these voices or stages in a single paragraph or sentence. I've only separated character development into five stages in order to dissect the various ways to build a character, to make this process easier to understand. In actual practice, it's not this rigid. As you write, be aware of how these stages morph, one into the other. In real life, too, our own stages of development are usually subtle, not clearly delineated. At one point (or on one page) in our lives, we believe X to be true; the next year, however (or the next chapter), we believe Y to be true. So even as we're crafting life into art, let's not forget that we're still writing about real people. Real life.

FOR YOUR READING PLEASURE

I admire the way Candance L. Greene portrays the voices of all three women in the essay "The Visit": her own, her mother's, and her grandmother's. Each is distinctly rendered through description and dialogue. Greene, too, implements two distinct voices: Throughout most of the essay she focuses on the Voice of Innocence, describing each moment. Then, in the penultimate sentence, we're invited into the Voice of Experience when she signals her deeper understanding of events, noting that one day she will be taking care of her mother, not her grandmother, in a nursing home.

THE VISIT

We work in silence. I slowly lift one leg, then the other. My mother chooses the more difficult task, and wipes my grandmother's bottom. I feel shame at my unwillingness to do it. My grandmother's face is closed to me. She stares into the distance, occasionally wincing at whatever scene is playing in her mind.

"Grab the Depend," my mother says quietly. Her face is stern. She looks angry. I help her push the diaper up my grandmother's thighs. *I have never seen her thighs,* I think. They are ashen trunks of flesh rippling under the force of the cloth, these Pampers we place on her.

"Help me," my mother says, her eyes pleading, her mouth set. "I'm sorry," I say under my breath. I walk to the head of the bed and gently lift my grandmother's hips in hopes this method will make the job of diapering her easier.

"Mama," my grandmother says in a childlike voice. I stare into her eyes, not knowing what to say. This woman, the very core of our family, grabs my forearm and says, "Mama, I'm so happy to see you."

I look at my own mother. She is wringing her hands. Her eyes fill with tears. She looks at me, urges me to say something, anything worthwhile. I look at my grandmother, smooth her white hair, and wonder why she always kept it hidden under those synthetic wigs, why she never saw its beauty. "It's alright," I tell her. She smiles, and her eyes glaze. The moment is over.

Together, we finish dressing her and place a flannel nightgown over her flaccid body. I watch mom clean my grandmother's fingernails. She makes sure to wash the undersides, massage the cuticles, lovingly lotion her hands as my grandmother sleeps.

We gather our belongings and walk out of the room that is my grandmother's new home. In the car, there is no need to talk. There is no need to mention the fear we both feel thinking that scene will play again in our lives. We just turn on the radio, listen to Stevie Wonder, and hold hands at red lights.

Chapter Six

Mock Moons and Metaphor

Crafting Memoir into Art

One night, unable to sleep, I watch an autumn moon framed in my bedroom window in Michigan. It pauses, large and luminous, as if hovering just on the other side of the glass. I am startled: I haven't noticed the moon for a long time, haven't followed its journey across its home in the night sky. Now seemingly so close, so intimate, I almost believe, if I breathe deeply, I'll be able to smell it. I sense it — cool, heavy — anchoring the sky, anchoring me, with blue dreams of the universe.

But the moon is not blue.

What color, objectively, is it? I wonder. Dark white? Gray white? I try to remember facts about the moon. What information, discovered by NASA scientists and astronauts, have I read in newspapers and magazines? What pictures have I seen beamed from its surface? I think about getting out of bed, switching on my computer, and Googling "moon," to see what data can be retrieved, not from my personal observed space, but from cyberspace.

I do not get out of bed. I don't want objective information about the moon. All that matters at the moment is what the moon means to me. Shouldn't I rely on the observation of my own senses?

Now, as the hour grows later, most of the moon shines in one pane of glass, the remainder in another. In this split image, a glimmer of re-flected light leaks behind the orb, causing a fuzzy boundary, blurring perception, so that I observe one large moon trailed by a smaller one, this slur of moon a mock moon, more enchanting than the moon itself. For it is a *personal* moon that only I can see in the glass of my own window.

I want to feel this moon. I want to touch it. Taste it. Since it is now my personal moon, I imagine it a blueberry-freeze marble or a sweet chunk of rock candy, cool as blue ice. I wonder why, when I see or imagine the moon, my synesthetic heart feels the word "blue"? I allow my mind to unfocus. To drift. To journey where sensory association, personal metaphor, lure me, flowing from image to image: from moon, to heart, to lonely heart, to empty nights, to blue nights, to blue moons. Unfettered, my memory floats to specific moments when the moon and my heart blued.

In this late-night, semi-dream state, it is as if I tumble out my bedroom window here in Michigan, a window of time, to be imaginatively cast into other places. Other times. I travel backward. To childhood. To adolescence. To other nights. I yearn to understand all my moons. I feel a need not only to search for other moons but, more importantly, to discover why a blue moon seems a metaphor that links particular sections of my life together. What does "blue moon" mean to me?

The only way to discover the answer to this question is to write. So I pick up my pad of paper, letting my mind drift. I follow lines of words, luxuriating in billowing strands of connotative memory, as I travel from this moon in Michigan to nights that still linger in shadows of my mind. In order to know what blue moons mean, to understand the importance of this image, to discover the metaphors, I must write and see where I am led.

On Caribbean nights, as a young island girl in the West Indies, I watch the moon darken with arcing branches of royal poinciana and frangipani trees. The Caribbean moon blues with reflected water from the viridian and turquoise sea. My mother, ill, leaves me for hospitalization in the States, far away. Lying in bed in a froth of mosquito netting, in a room with open shutters, the moon seems to watch me — watches over me — through long, blue tropical nights. I reach toward it, imagine I grasp it. I am tugged by it, along with the tides, as if it carries me to my mother on the other side of the sea.

Once bidden, once encouraged, once invited, how swiftly this image evolves as I retrieve the past. Even as I sense the moon outside my bedroom in Michigan, still I search for its personal meaning to me. Now, I see — and write — of a teenager in New Jersey, a girl full of longing for sad, teenage songs. How clearly I now remember dancing across a high school gym to the strains of the song "Blue Moon" with Jamie, my boyfriend. My feet slow to *Blue moon, I saw you standing alone* . . . I smell Jamie's scent of Ivory soap and Aqua Velva, see his short-clipped blond hair, the small overlap of his front teeth. I still remember how blue I feel when, later, he leaves me. That damp night, lilacs drip outside my bedroom window. I am alone with the spring moon, its blue eye still watching me, still guarding the sky.

From the West Indies to New Jersey, I am next tugged by sensual tides of association to Israel, where I am living on a kibbutz during the first moon walk. While Israeli friends gather around a television set for glimpses of Neil Armstrong and his spacecraft, I wander into the dark hush of fields and lie on the ground beside *mish-mish* (apricot) trees. I watch the real moon, not a speck of spacecraft visible, not wanting to see it blemish the moon's cool peace. I watch the moon with the scent of warm apricots in the ancient night. I miss my friends in the States. I miss the familiarity of language and location. I miss a boyfriend from whom I recently parted. Again, I am alone. And blue. Yet not entirely alone, for the constant moon is with me.

The Caribbean. New Jersey. Israel. Three entirely different locations. Three periods of time separated by many years. But as I write these scenes, I see threads, connections. Although in *Romeo and Juliet*, Juliet calls the moon an "inconstant orb," for me it is constant, even as it changes sizes and shapes in its cycles. Whether it's a full moon, an autumn moon, a sickle moon, or even a blue moon, still, it is moon, tugging tides of my heart and memory. So as childhoods fail, as boyfriends abandon, as countries are temporarily discarded and friends lost, it is the moon that remains, that is constant, even as it, and my heart, feel blue.

Before we examine the idea of metaphor in more detail, let me explain how I'm using the term in this chapter. At its most basic level, a metaphor is a literary device that substitutes one thing for another to bring a thought or emotion into clearer focus. We do this all the time without realizing it. If we say someone isn't the sharpest knife in the drawer, we're using a metaphor to make our estimation of that person's lack of awareness visual and concrete. There are many different, specific variations of metaphor. For example, if you use "like" or "as" to make a comparison, that's called a simile, as in T. S. Eliot's famous and strange "The evening is spread out against the sky / Like a patient etherized upon a table." On a broader level, however, metaphor is an associative way of thinking and writing, no matter which specific kind of figurative device is being used.

It is this broader level of metaphor I'm focusing on here, the whole constellation of ways in which we slant specific images so that they re-create with immediacy our own unique emotional perspective.

So the moon, for me, metaphorically signifies safety and constancy, an ongoing life. It does not signify coldness and distance. It is only by writing about the moon that night in Michigan that I reclaim these sensory memories, turn memories into metaphor, sensory descriptions to deepen and organize my writing — even, yes, my life.

When I teach writing, I encounter students who claim they struggle to remember their childhoods, or can't recall details from the past. Or, even if they remember, they tell me they don't know what the events mean, don't understand the connections. I assure them they do have stories, that they will discover them, as well as their metaphors, through smell, taste, touch, sound, sight — all their senses.

In other words, writing our senses helps us remember the past while also allowing us to make sense of it. What do events mean? Why bother writing about a West Indian moon, or the song "Blue Moon," or a moon I watched in an apricot orchard in Israel? I do this in order to understand the connections among events in my life. While writing memoir, I need to do more than merely relate events, more than just tell readers the facts of my life. Finding connections gives writing, gives life, meaning. So, even as I am here in my bedroom in Michigan, I am also, as a writer, back there. Back there in the past where I lived the metaphors, even as it is only now, as a writer, that I am finally able to understand them. So I must gather my sensory details, to organize them. Examine them. For only after details are extracted can they be transformed into metaphor. From these metaphors we will discover fuller understandings of our lives.

Let's see if the moon might pause in the sky for a moment as we briefly consider another image. Remember that maroon scarf I told you about in chapter 5? In that passage, I explored how it's possible to incorporate two voices into one paragraph. Now, let's examine the same maroon scarf as a metaphor.

When writing about the scarf, I had to do more than merely state that my married lover gave me this scarf, which had belonged to him. What did it represent? What did this object (any object or event) mean? By describing the scarf using sensory imagery, I learned, while writing, that this physical object took on almost mythic proportions because, in the sexual addiction, it was more knowable to me than the man who gave it to me. Since I was unable to love, find comfort, or be emotionally intimate with this man, I loved his scarf — an object close to him — instead.

Why is this image important? What does this maroon scarf mean if no one else has one just like mine? How can you, the reader, identify with it? How does metaphor actually work? While you probably don't have your own maroon scarf that played an important role in your life, you almost certainly, at one time or another, longed for comfort. In short, by the way I describe the scarf (slanting its details), it becomes, in this memoir, a metaphor for comfort. And this longing, embodied by the scarf, is the common thread between me, the author, and you, the reader.

You identify with my feelings, longings, and desires if you've felt the same ones. But in order for you to identify with these abstract feelings, I must render them tangibly, through objects (scarf, moon, etc.), so you can actually taste, smell, see, touch, and hear them.

Now, as our blue moon continues across the sky, let's see what else we learn from it.

The song "Blue Moon," written in 1934 by Rodgers and Hart, has been recorded more than 240 times by such diverse artists as Glen Gray & the Casa Loma Orchestra, the Marcels, Frank Sinatra, Plácido Domingo, Olivia Newton-John, Elvis, Charles Mingus, and Ella Fitzgerald. So our blue moon, apparently, speaks to many people. We relate to it — even as each recording artist sings the song in his or her own individual style and rhythm.

By creating images rich with metaphor, writers provide this same kind of universality. Such images bridge our outer and inner spaces, thus allowing readers to enter into our individual lives and experiences. Only metaphor can make my personal maroon scarf universal, my particular view of the moon blue enough for everyone else to see.

As readers ponder our words on the page, what most pulls at their emotions — like the moon pulling the tide — are the associations they contain. These associations imbue words with their own force fields.

Just like the moon.

Finding Your Metaphors

I lead quite an unexamined life until I sit down at my computer or my notebook. When I go for a nighttime walk along the Lake Michigan shore, I don't think, "Oh my gosh, the moon is a metaphor for constancy in my life!" It would never occur to me. Daily, I just bumble along shopping, fixing dinner, doing the laundry, answering e-mails, playing with my cats, playing Scrabble with Marc, watching television, dithering around . . . until I sit down to write.

Maybe I'd find it easier to write if I *were* more aware of the meaning in my day-to-day life. But I'm not. Only when I write do I discover what my story means, what my metaphors are. In college, the maroon scarf was only a scarf! Now, when writing about scarves or moons, I finally understand the power latent within them.

> Don't expect to know your metaphors **before** you begin to write. This is what you'll discover **as** you write.

Robert Frost once said, "No surprise for the writer, no surprise for the reader." To me, what this means is that I solve mysteries about my life only when I write, and then convey the excitement of discovery to the reader. It's strange to think, but I don't fully understand my life until I write it.

Which is a good thing! If we knew all the answers ahead of time, there'd be no reason to write our narratives. Why bother if we already know all the answers? We write to find out what our stories mean — rather than merely stating what we already know. It's not just the event we remember that wants to be set down on paper. More important is the story we haven't yet explored.

Your job as a writer is to take everyday things and slant them in order for them to give up their secrets. Don't use details as if they're mere information. If you simply write "the moon is white," "the scarf is maroon," or "the wand is blue," you're being specific, which is good, but you're not evoking your own symbolic, metaphoric meaning.

The Metaphoric Memoir

It's one thing just to insert an emotionally potent image here and there, sprinkled sporadically throughout a memoir, but quite another thing to write metaphorically as an all-encompassing way to depict the story in its entirety.

Let's say I'm writing a memoir exploring the abstract emotion of loss. I'm struggling with a scene in which I'm dressing for work, because I don't immediately see a way to slant the scene's details to reveal loss. I keep writing. I remember slipping my feet into an old pair of black shoes — the leather cracked, heels worn. This image of worn-down shoes is a metaphor that conveys my sense that life is, literally, down at the heel — filled with loss.

Still, this is only one metaphor, whereas the arc of an entire memoir calls for a range of associations that has an emotional center. What this means is that all the details work together to construct a narrative that advances your plot and theme.

Let's assume that while I'm writing my memoir about loss, you're writing a memoir whose theme is how life is filled with joy. You, too, have an old pair of shoes, but you love how these worn shoes make your feet feel comfortable, how they have conformed to the shape of your feet. Exact same detail, but different slant, different metaphor. As we each continue to write our respective memoirs, we cast about for additional details and images to enhance the overall metaphoric quality of the memoir.

Next, let's suppose we each happen to have a vase with a flower painted on it; the vases have hairline cracks from when they were accidentally dropped. In my memoir about loss, I will focus on the crack. Not only that, the petals on the painted flower will appear wilted. You, on the other hand, writing about how life is joyful, won't even notice the crack. Or, you'll reflect upon how you've been able to face life's misfortunes and repair the damage. The colors on the painted flower may be fading, but look how long they stayed bright!

Let's return to our unwed mother and the pregnancy test wand, which turned so blue that she felt as if she were plunging into an ocean. In that passage, the reader is alerted that the narrator is scared to be pregnant. Suppose, on the other hand, she's overjoyed to be pregnant. How can we take this very same detail and convey a feeling of joy? *The wand turned deep and blue, the color of baby-blue eyes, the color of the lake and sky on the first spring day of the year.* The same detail, slanted differently, creates a different metaphor. The metaphoric world, as it were, is in the details: this pair of shoes, this maroon scarf, this blue wand, that blue moon.

Seemingly mundane details and images, when slanted, coalesce into a metaphoric whole. Now, your story is vivid and immediate, one to which others can relate — which is why writers write, and readers read.

Metaphor: A Window onto the World

Suppose you stare out a darkened nighttime window. What do you see? Initially, you observe a faint, gauzy image of yourself. The longer you gaze, the more your eyes grow accustomed to the dark. You begin to see the world — moon, stars, outlines of trees — more clearly. As you watch and dream — maybe about high school boyfriends or men wearing maroon scarves — you'll soon realize that this window reflecting yourself is actually *superimposed* onto the world.

The next morning, you again glance outside. In daylight, you see the world vibrant with color, landscapes in sharp focus: the first crocus of spring; the Jewish deli across the street from your Manhattan apartment; a haze over Los Angeles. And, as you ponder this landscape, maybe in your mind's eye you see — metaphorically — the promise of renewal; the cultural mosaic of America; nature in peril. The horizon, after all, is limitless. Limitless. Even as, there you are, still framed inside the window.

When writing memoir, it's as if you observe yourself in a window, both during the day as well as at night, in order to see yourself and your world from different perspectives: dark and light; surfaces and interiors. Memoir is not simply a mirrored image of oneself. Rather, you, as a memoirist, examine yourself as if in the glass of a window: yes, you see yourself, but you *also* witness a larger world outside — one that's superimposed over your reflection.

Write as if you're looking not into a mirror but out of a window. If you do, your story, your personal metaphors, will be cast upon a wider world, upon the stories of others. It's as if you are layering the self onto the world — the self onto family, culture, society, history — onto issues larger than just yourself.

> The world both inside and outside your window should be
> illuminated by the light of your story.

With memoir, many kinds of landscapes present themselves outside that window — both physical and metaphorical. For example, your personal story can be framed by nature, as in Terry Tempest Williams's *Refuge: An Unnatural History of Family and Place*. Or perhaps your story sheds light on sexuality and gender, like Rigoberto Gonzalez's *Butterfly Boy: Memories of a Chicano Mariposa*; Barrie Jean Borich's *My Lesbian Husband: Landscapes of a Marriage*; or *What Becomes You*, by Aaron Raz Link and Hilda Raz. Maybe your family story is told against a backdrop of politics and war, like Gail Gilberg's *Snake's Daughter: The Roads in and Out of War*, which explores her relationship with her father, a soldier who died in Vietnam. Or, in contrast, maybe your story is one of a political activist, protesting the war in Vietnam, such as *Fugitive Days* by Bill Ayers. Perhaps your story reflects the landscape of your tribe, where the personal is twined with the cultural, as in Esmeralda Santiago's *When I Was Puerto Rican*; Kate Simon's *Bronx Primitive*; Nahid Rachlin's *Persian Girls*; or Nathan McCall's *Makes Me Wanna Holler: A Young Black Man in America*. Others, like Mary McCarthy (*Memories of a Catholic Girlhood*) and Mark Curtis Anderson (*Jesus Sound Explosion*) write about their religious tribes. Evan Handler, in *Time on Fire: My Comedy of Terrors*, sets his story against a backdrop of physical illness.

In Xu Xi's book *Overleaf Hong Kong: Stories and Essays of the Chinese, Overseas*, the arrival of a telegram, delivered by a "messenger boy," becomes a metaphor for what the young Xu Xi longs for — the whole world outside the window of her family's Hong Kong apartment.

> Should Mum be home, there follows a commotion of rummaging in her handbag for a tip. Twenty Hong Kong cents, a virtually worthless amount today, was enough for the dark-skinned "messenger boy," or . . . that was what my mother said. They were almost always dark-skinned Chinese, these suntanned men who were hardly young, but robust and hardy enough to bicycle through the roads of Kowloon . . . to bring us

those white envelopes . . . enclosing urgent missives from Jakarta or Tokyo or London . . . that larger, unknown world.

About signing for the telegram, Xu Xi writes, "It was a moment that felt adult, important, as if my signature on that line conferred on me a knowledge of that larger world, making it tangible, palpably real." What she implies as well is that the messenger won't escape his life. Thus, through metaphor, this personal story of Xu Xi expands to include a broader context concerned with race and socioeconomic status.

Domestic landscapes can likewise be fully realized by observing images of oneself reflected in that glass window. Karen Salyer McElmurray, in her book *Surrendered Child: A Birth Mother's Journey*, writes about the wrenching personal act of placing a baby up for adoption; more broadly, she's also addressing the nature of loss and grief. In memoirs such as these, as well as those about domestic violence or child abuse, the personal and particular also depict wider social and cultural issues. According to Vivian Gornick, "The subject of autobiography is always self-definition, but it cannot be self-definition in the void. The memoirist, like the poet and novelist, must engage with the world, because engagement makes experience, experience makes wisdom, and finally it's the wisdom — or rather the movement toward it — that counts."

Even though our individual stories are different, we communicate through the common language of metaphor by embodying our ideas in images and details. By ruminating upon ourselves, we also conjure stories of others. By this acknowledgment of others' experiences, we address a whole range of social, political, and cultural issues.

It's impossible to live every life, fight every war, battle every illness, belong to every tribe, believe in every religion. The only way we come close to the whole experience is by embracing what we see both inside and outside the window of the page.

WRITING EXERCISE

Tell the story of your life in a short-short memoir (about 600 words) by following one type of image that recurs in three or so different stages (or episodes) of your life. Examples could be individual songs, pieces of furniture, books, clothes, hairstyles, kinds of food, cars, flowers . . . or the moon!

The essay should show a progression from paragraph to paragraph. What do you learn? The idea is to discover some insight about yourself that you don't have at the beginning.

For example, let's say you portray your life through music. What kind of music did you like as a kid? As a teenager? As an adult? Show how your taste in music changed depending upon events in your life, or how music was representative of various episodes or times.

Or, another example: maybe you want to examine your life through details in a fast-food restaurant. How do the golden arches of McDonald's appear to you at sixteen if you're depressed? Garish, harshly lit. For the second paragraph, say you're now twenty and happy, so the exact same golden arches now appear sunny. For the third paragraph, say you're a mother and taking your child to McDonald's. How do these arches appear to you now? The same image, slanted differently, conveys a new or different feeling.

Find those details, slant them metaphorically, and other people will relate to your story.

FOR YOUR READING PLEASURE

In her essay, "Tetanus, You Understand?" Ellen Morris Prewitt crafts individual sections with metaphors as she builds toward the final, stunning metaphor: tetanus. Here are a few images and specific details that function as metaphors: "a mattress-less bed"; the way the hallway in the courthouse cuts off the sun; the various black-and-white images in the Grand Canal section dated August 30, 1993.

Can you find more? The essay itself is metaphoric as Prewitt realizes, at the end, through a chance encounter with a stranger, how her husband's insecurity about wealth, like tetanus, is a toxin.

In an e-mail exchange with Prewitt, I asked her about the interesting structure she chose for her essay. She wrote back: "The images from Italy were from my travel journal; the first entry of the essay is an actual journal entry. So the journal form was a natural. The difficulty for me was in connecting the two halves of the essay. Finding the hinge in the middle was the key. So it is shaped with the 'Divorce' section; the 'Hinge' section; the 'Italy' section." For each essay she writes, Prewitt says, "It, the essay, has 'to tell me' the form, where, for me, so much of the information for the essay lies — even if the reader doesn't know she is garnering information from it."

TETANUS, YOU UNDERSTAND?

September 2, 1994:
Has anyone ever loved you as much as me?

October 12, 1995:
My possessions thrown into the arms of skeptical moving men, my three tiny dogs snatched and trundled into an apartment with white-painted walls, my mother arrived from North Carolina and sleeping on the floor inside the frame of a mattress-less bed. Fled, while D. was out of town, with fear billowing behind me.

October 17, 1995:
Ensconced with the lawyers, I plead: slice to the bone, quickly, un-cleave what was cleaved; and protect me from the spurt of blood. For in striving toward business success, D. turned himself inside out — personally, financially, sexually — so that I do not know him, and not knowing him, I fear him.

 The petition is filed. The legal gears grind.

October 31, 1995:
I follow my tank of a lawyer into the low-ceilinged courthouse. Seeking the court's ordered protection, we step into the hallway leading to the judge. The downward slope cuts off the sun; the windowless length stretches dark. Against the wall, D. sits on a bench, head bent. Alone.

 He raises his eyes.

 How are the puppies? he whispers.

 And the severed flesh bleeds.

September 25, 1997:
The trial over, the divorce decree entered, the line final.

March 23, 2002:
Time to die to the grief.
  But how?

March 28, 2002
My grief. My guilt. My love.
  Turn from the plaintive, excavate the me into the clear light.
  What do you see?
  I was not the one.
  For D.

August 30, 1993:
D. and I sit on the patio of the Gritti Palace, Venice, Italy. We are on our tenth anniversary trip. So far, we've been down the Amalfi Coast, through Sorrento, around Palermo. Now, we are harbored in the hotel that has housed kings, U.S. presidents, movie stars.

The black water of the Grand Canal slaps against the stone. It is night. Lights on the church across the way turn its marble hard, brilliant, but authentic, so that you can imagine the dents of its porous surface. D. wears a white polo, black and white slacks, black belt and watch. I wear the dress that makes Italian men look.

A waterbus spilling over with people lumbers by.

"What are they doing?" I ask.

They're riding, D. says.

Heads and arms and trunks in stripes and bright colors jut from the windows of the fat-bellied bus.

"Why are they just riding, in that thing?"

D., who grew up with one good pair of shoes, who was rich in his community because his dad took him to the Saturday movies, who was the first in his family to go to college, studies me. They're touring the canal, he says. Look at you, he says, with your ass just off a 130,000 lire gondola ride, your butt sitting on the terrace of the Gritti Palace. D., who'd kissed me in the gondola, his hand trembling as he touched my back, swags his jaw to the side, the way he does when remembering his unmonied past.

And I, whose family has lived in the same white-columned spot for a hundred years, whose great-grandfather was one of the first bankers in the state, whose father wore hand-tailored shirts, sit stunned. For even though my father died when I was three, even though we phoned ahead before visiting the white-columned house, I did expect — to take the gondola, to be sitting on the terrace of the Gritti Palace Hotel.

The waterbus chugs past, continuing on its rounds.

Earlier, at the end of day, I had stood inside an alley that led upwards to a church. Buildings towered overhead, slanted shadows darkened the stones. D., head hanging, trudged up the hill, said, You've just about whipped this puppy.

The alley stones pressed into the papery soles of my sandals. I leaned, slipped off the straps. A woman stopped. Thin but with the ropy muscles of a nurse, her gray hair tucked in a bun, she pointed to my bare feet. "This is dangerous. Tetanus, you understand?"

Tetanus. I did understand: the threat that comes with childhood's rusty nail. Where the toxin gets in, and can't get out.

The woman's black, oversized eyes stared me down.

Later, D. and I would take a watertaxi to the land, a car to the train. Full of my love, I would kiss D. on the back of the neck while we waited on the platform, then we would run to catch Car #4 before the train left the station.

Chapter Seven

Writing in Style

I love red shoes. Always have, always will. I can't remember a time when I didn't own at least one pair — usually more. An early, preschool photograph, taken in Puerto Rico, shows my feet adorned in red strapped sandals. Currently, I count seven pairs in my closet, including red Simple tennis shoes. Another pair, shiny leather huaraches, I ordered from the Sundance catalogue. For my birthday, Marc bought me red Mary Janes with pink polka dots. In winter, I wear red clogs embossed with flowers, or red suede Earth shoes with patent leather toes. For summer, I recently purchased canvas pull-ons featuring a red and pink camouflage design. Years ago I bought fringed red suede boots at Marshalls. I no longer wear them, but I can't bear to throw them away. I wear red shoes regardless of clothing color; I don't care whether I'm color coordinated or not. Doesn't red go with everything, anyway? Red shoes are simply my style.

Your Story, Your Style

As much as we all dress in a style that evinces us, who we are, we also write in individual styles. Style encompasses word choice, sentence structure, phrasing, rhythm. Some writers use a preponderance of sentence fragments, while others wouldn't dream of writing a sentence with anything less than impeccable traditional punctuation and grammar. Some authors use elevated language, requiring some readers to look up words in the dictionary. Others use straightforward, everyday words. Maybe you could say some writers have a red style of writing, their words hot and tortured, singeing the page, seducing readers with emotion. Here is a line from a Carol Guess piece titled (appropriately) "Red": "[In beauty school] when I make up my lips I use a pale, creamy base to destroy their actual shape, so that the face in the classroom mirror has no mouth." Isn't that stunning?

Others write with icy white words, deliberately forcing an emotional distance. For example, Joan Didion, in *The Year of Magical Thinking*, uses relatively spare sentences to enhance the unblinking, distant eye with which she observes her subject matter. Here, even as she's describing the moment just after her husband dies, the language and style are razor sharp:

> I remember trying to straighten out in my mind what would happen next. Since there was an ambulance crew in the living room, the next logical step would be going to the hospital. It occurred to me that the crew could decide very suddenly to go to the hospital and I would not be ready. I would not have in hand what I needed to take. I would waste time, get left behind.

Virginia Woolf's sentences, on the other hand, project a bluish stream of consciousness, words meandering down the page, more closely mimicking how our thoughts move. Contrast the following two sentences from *A Room of One's Own* with Didion's clipped sentences.

> And when the age of faith was over and the age of reason had come, still the same flow of gold and silver went on; fellowships were founded; lectureships endowed; only the gold and silver flowed now, not from the coffers of the king, but from the chests of merchants and manufacturers, from the purses of men who had made, say, a fortune from industry, and returned, in their wills, a bounteous share of it to endow more chairs, more lectureships, more fellowships in the university where they had learnt their craft. Hence the libraries and laboratories; the observatories; the splendid equipment of costly and delicate instruments which now stands on glass shelves, where centuries ago the grasses waved and the swine rootled.

In five sentences Didion uses 73 words, while Woolf uses 123 words in just two.

> Select a style and a vocabulary that enhance the emotion or mood of the scene. You might use red hot words to heighten emotion, icy words to distance, or serene blue words to cool and refresh.

Generally speaking, short sentences or fragments communicate a sense of urgency, so you might use clipped sentences, say, if your persona is walking alone at night: "The sky darkened. No moon. Fog swathed the streetlights. Not a car in sight. No people, either. At least I *hoped* no one followed me."

Longer sentences convey a more relaxed or contemplative mood: "Sunrays glazed my back as the afternoon sizzled, the waves at Asbury Park fizzing up and down the shore, sandpipers skittering in their wake."

Hear how discordant the style would sound if the above were written using short, choppy sentences: "Sunrays glazed my back. The afternoon sizzled. The waves at Asbury Park fizzed. Sandpipers skittered."

There's nothing inherently wrong with these short sentences, but they inject an ominous sense of urgency where none, in the moment itself, exists.

To return to my red-shoe fetish: Not only is it true that red is my favorite color of shoe, I even love all styles of red shoes, a variety. Likewise, in my writing, elements of my style vary depending on the piece at hand. For example, my first memoir has long, flowing sentences that portray the confusion of a young, hurt child, whereas *Love Sick* sounds tougher, using the shorter, harder, edgier sentences of an addict.

Yet both books sound like *me*.

I rely more on sensory imagery than abstract concepts. I tend to embed myself (my persona on the page) in an atmospheric world. I rely on milieux to convey emotion more than dialogue or physical characteristics. When I write I hear a rhythm in my head, almost as if each syllable is a drum beat. I simply hear when any given sentence should stop — or whether a sentence needs one extra beat.

So as you write, listen carefully to your own cadence and beat. Finding a style that fits might take some practice. But keep at it, as you will discover your own style, your own colors, your own vocabulary and rhythms. You'll discover your strengths as a writer as well as (alas) one or two weaknesses. At least that's what happened to me. My weakness is writing dialogue. I'm just not very good at it, so I do everything possible to avoid it! The people, or characters, in my work speak as little as possible. After you discover your strengths, write with them in mind.

Let's examine two contemporary memoirists, who, in these particular works, push the boundaries of style. It helps to see a range of possibilities, even if you tend to write in a more straightforward manner.

In that chapter "Red" from her memoir *Gaslight: One Writer's Ghosts*, Carol Guess uses many sentences that rely on subject-verb-object word order and traditional syntax. The paragraph length, on the other hand, varies. This relatively straightforward syntax, juxtaposed with uneven paragraph length, causes tension in the reader while, at the same time, reflecting the tension within the narrator:

> I am fifteen and I have no name, but I am learning how to get into a car without showing my underwear to the men surrounding me.
>
> A woman is teaching me.
>
> ... There are ten of us in beauty school, ages thirteen to thirty-nine. "Girls, pretend you are surrounded by handsome men. One of them opens the car door for you. How do you enter?"

The writing style should reflect the emotion of the piece. All parts of the memoir—plot, voice, metaphor, style—should work together.

In her essay "How to Meditate," from her collection *Seasons of the Body*, Brenda Miller uses the unusual, second-person "you" point of view (both implied and stated), instead of the memoir's traditional first-person point of view. It works well in this essay since Miller is, in effect, explaining, or giving directions to the reader as to how you (the reader) should meditate. At the same time, of course, the "you" is Miller, the narrator, instructing herself. This adds an ironic twist since she's saying, in effect, "Here I am at the meditation center — probably it's a good thing, but I don't really want to be here."

> On arrival [at the meditation center] huddle in the Volkswagen with your friends and eat all the chocolate in the car. Chocolate chips, old Kit Kats, the tag-end of a Hershey Bar — do not discriminate. Feel deprived, then light up your last Sherman, pass it around. Watch your fellow retreatants flow into the meditation hall. Note how elegant they look, even in sweatpants and black Wellingtons. Wonder where they get such nice sweatpants. Look down at your baggy jeans, your dim T-shirt and say, *I'm not dressed for this, let's go home.*

Most of us typically rely on a more straightforward approach. Straightforward doesn't mean boring or lifeless, however. As you write, remember why you're a writer in the first place! And why you love to read. Don't we love literature because of the beauty of the language — a finely tuned collection of words? Which exact words — which sentence and paragraph length — best convey the emotion, the mood of that particular scene?

The Muscular Sentence

The length of the sentence isn't as important as the words in it. Be sure that each word is significant, that it fully advances the meaning. As you revise, delete all extraneous words: make your writing muscular. Let's look at sentences that go astray and consider ways to revise them. We'll begin with the first two sentences from our own faux memoir in chapter 3.

Original: "According to my parents, there was a terrible blizzard that day in April when I was born, and every day following, too. We lived in the Upper Peninsula of Michigan (what's known as the UP), where it snowed, or could snow, about seven months of the year."

Revised: "A blizzard blanketed the Upper Peninsula that April day I entered the world."

Why are the other words extraneous? It's assumed that the author learns about the blizzard from her parents. It's irrelevant, in this memoir about an unwed mother, that it snows seven months of the year. The words "we lived in" are unnecessary because it's obvious, from the surrounding words. So why use forty-seven words if you can say the same thing, much better, with thirteen?

Here's another example of how to tighten, and heighten, the impact of your prose style.

Original: "A moment later, after the pregnancy wand turns blue, I open the door to my house, step outside, close the door behind me, and I race down the street, and I see my best friend, Jane, riding her broken-down bicycle, her thick, brown, wavy hair flying around her head, and she waves at me to stop."

Revised: "After the pregnancy wand turns blue, I flee my house. Jane, on her rusty bicycle, waves at me to stop, her brown hair floating around her head like a halo."

Here, it isn't necessary to mention the actual word "see," since it's obvious the narrator is doing the seeing. As much as possible, avoid directional details such as "I hear" or "I smell." Instead, present the sound or smell directly: "A church bell chimed" is better than "I heard a church bell chiming." You likewise don't need to write "I opened the door to my house, stepped outside, closed the door behind me." Instead, simply *be* outside. If you need to convey that you've changed location, write something like: "The cold air blistered my cheeks." This is more evocative than "closing the door behind me." There's a difference between movement and action. An action propels the plot. Movement for the sake of movement (I sat, I stood, I walked) bogs down the plot. It's also possible, in the above example, to avoid identifying Jane as a "best friend" because the two wave to each other. The word "halo" also connotes a feeling of friendship.

In order to discover new and fresh words, use a dictionary rather than a thesaurus. A thesaurus, while offering a wide selection, isn't always exact. Or, if you find a word you like in a thesaurus, look it up in a dictionary to ensure it conveys the exact meaning you want. Another way to build your vocabulary is to keep a list of words you discover while reading.

Avoid what I call the "3 As" in writing: adjectives, adverbs, and abstractions. Rely on nouns and active verbs, instead. As much as possible, state the event, the moment, directly. Syntactically, cut to the chase.

Oh, dear: the above sentences themselves could be revised. They could read:

> Avoid the "3 As" in writing: adjectives, adverbs, and abstractions. Rely on nouns and active verbs. State the moment directly. Syntactically, cut to the chase.

Let's look at a new sentence loaded with the 3 As as well as a way to revise it.

Original: "All I think about are all the lonely, sad, never-ending nights I'll spend all by myself, all alone in my own small blue bedroom, living with my parents in their small log cabin, in the middle of nowhere Michigan, watching my pregnant stomach get bigger and bigger."

Revised: "Night wind sweeps the birch and aspen, leaves rustling the windows. The blue walls of my bedroom close in on me as if pressing against my swollen stomach."

Hopefully, in the revision, the images of "night," "walls," and "blue" convey the feeling of loneliness and sadness, so you don't have to use the abstract words themselves.

More Than Just *And*

Use the conjunction *and* sparingly. You can't avoid it altogether, of course, but after you've written a chapter, scan the work to discover every place you use it. Are these sentences more interesting if you substitute another coordinating conjunction, such as *but, so, for,* or *yet*? You might also consider a conjunctive adverb, such as *however, nevertheless, then,* or *therefore*. Or perhaps the idea will be more dynamic as a simple sentence, as opposed to a compound sentence. In this case, you might consider splitting one loose, stringy sentence into two.

What's wrong with *and*? Used as a conjunction, it only connects information in a sentence as if in a list: "this happened to me and then this next thing happened." It prevents you from establishing a more interesting relationship between ideas. If one thing happens and then another thing happens, all you're saying is that one event follows the other. Not usually too exciting. If, however, one event happens, *therefore* another event happens, a relationship is established. Motivation. Cause and effect. Sentence structure itself helps establish causal relationships and motivation when crafting plot and voice as discussed in chapters 4 and 5. Needless to say, everything — plot, voice, metaphor — originates in *sentences*.

Let's practice removing the word *and* from sentences, in order to replace it with something more precise:

Original: "My period is late, and I stop at the drugstore to buy a home pregnancy-test kit."

Revised: "My period is late, so I stop at the drugstore to buy a home pregnancy-test kit."

Original: "I don't want to be pregnant, and I want to be the girl I was last month and still have big plans for my future."

Revised: "If only I weren't pregnant. If only I were still that girl with big plans to move to New York City."

Play around with your sentences. Try revising them first one way then another. Which way sounds smoothest? Which way best articulates the feeling in the sentence? Which sentence energizes the mood, deepens the atmosphere?

Not *To Be*

The verb *to be* is important in the English language, of course. For example, in the above revised sentences about identity ("If only I weren't pregnant. If only I were still that girl with big plans to move to New York City"), the verb *to be* establishes the meaning. That said, we want to avoid it as much as possible. Active verbs provide more energy and vigor: "I cried" is more forceful than "I was crying." See how the revised sentences, below, use a more direct approach by casting verbs in the active voice.

> *Original*: "Finally, I'm on my way to see the baby's father, Adam, to tell him I'm pregnant. I want him to know I'm scared and I'm angry at him, too. I don't know if I'm even in my right mind at this moment. I'm beside myself, more likely."

> *Revised*: "I race to the auto-repair shop where Adam, the baby's father, works. He glances up from a chassis. I open my mouth to speak, but no sound. Nothing. My breath feels icy, the backs of my knees weak."

> *Original*: "How can I tell him that my dreams to move to New York City will always be more important to me than having a baby or getting married? But standing before him, I find myself with my hands resting on my stomach, as if I'm protecting it."

> *Revised*: "Adam knows about my dreams to move to New York City, dreams that don't include marriage or motherhood. Yet, standing before him, I clutch my stomach, protecting it."

Even though the revised passages are shorter, they convey more dynamic, active images.

As you write, always be aware of sentence flow, of punctuation and grammar. To help you, I highly recommend *The Elements of Style*, by Strunk and White. Another book that shows how to achieve simple elegance in sentences is *Artful Sentences: Syntax as Style*, by Virginia

Tufte. How do authors you admire craft sentences that draw you into their world, a world in which you might remain even after you read the last lyrical sentence in the book?

Dialogue in Memoir

Students worried about accuracy in memoir (see chapter 9 for more about truth in memoir) frequently ask me, *How do writers remember what people said? How can I factually represent an encounter with, say, my mother when I was eight years old?* Sometimes we're writing about events that happened ten or twenty years ago.

Well, we can't remember dialogue exactly. I can't even remember the exact words I used ten minutes ago, let alone ten years ago. And no one's going to walk around recording every potentially important conversation in case we might one day write about it. But not to worry. To write an exact line of dialogue, word for word, isn't the goal of memoir, anyway.

Don't you have a sense — if not a factual transcript — as to how various people speak, people important to you such as friends, relatives, your partner, your spouse? Don't you have a sense as to what your mother said that moment she caught you, scissors in hand, whacking off your hair? Don't you have a strong sense of the conversation when you told your boyfriend you were pregnant, or when you told your girlfriend you wanted to marry her?

Let's examine what might have been an "actual" conversation between our unwed pregnant teen and her boyfriend. Then, we'll revise it to better represent the event artfully. Here, I'll omit most gestures and actions, focusing mainly on speech.

> *Original*: "Adam, hi, how are you?"
>
> "Okay, how are you?" He wipes his greasy hands on a rag.
>
> "Fine, I guess, you know."
>
> "You don't look fine," he says.
>
> "Well, maybe I'm not so fine."
>
> "I'm working now." He points his chin toward the chassis. "What's up?"
>
> "I guess I have a problem."

"What kind of problem?" he asks.

"Can we go someplace?" I ask. "I walked all the way over here, and I have something to say, and I think you should listen."

"Maybe later. Like I said, I'm working."

"But it can't wait."

"What can't wait?" he asks.

"Everything. Nothing. It can't wait."

He sighs and walks toward the door of the garage. "Okay, maybe a second."

"Okay," I say. "Thanks."

"So," he says, "what is it?"

"Well, I have a problem."

"What is it?"

"I guess I'm kind of pregnant."

Revised: "What're you doing here?" Adam asks, wiping his greasy hands on a rag.

"I guess I have a problem."

"I'm working." He nods his chin toward the chassis. "What is it?"

"Everything. Nothing. It can't wait."

He sighs and walks toward the door of the garage.

"I guess I'm kind of pregnant," I say.

In all prose, fiction and nonfiction, dialogue works best when it reflects a hint of speech — a suggestion as to how we speak — as opposed to allowing the characters (real or fictional) to give speeches. As with sentences, keep each line of dialogue as tight as possible. Don't spend a lot of time allowing characters to say "Hello," "Good bye," "How are you?" and generally shooting the breeze. As with sentence length, avoid loose, baggy lines of dialogue. Cut to the chase.

If, in reality, it took our narrator in the above scenario a lot of time to "spit it out," as it were, then consider lengthening the time frame by gestures or actions. Maybe she'd manifest her nervousness by picking up Adam's greasy rag. Maybe she gets grease on her hands. Maybe she tries to rub it off. A tangible gesture can sometimes more effectively convey emotion or meaning than several lines of dialogue.

Past or Present Tense?

I'm frequently asked why I decided to write both my memoirs in present tense, rather than past. After all, the events happened in the past. Wouldn't that make more sense? Perhaps, but writing choices aren't strictly logical; they're emotional and intuitive. When I first began to write memoir (and didn't really know what I was doing), I didn't consciously choose present tense. The words simply started flowing — and there I was — the past *was* the present.

Now, thinking back on the process, I have to say that it felt natural to write both books in present tense — as if the experience is ongoing. In many ways, after all, the past does always stay with us, even as we change and grow. It's not as if I feel stuck or trapped in the past. Yet, while writing, I am in that moment, back then, at that time. The Voice of Innocence conveys scenes as if we're living them now. It represents the emotion of those moments.

The Voice of Experience likewise feels more immediate in present tense. After all, this voice is the author-me, sitting at my desk now, trying to figure out what the past meant. Our discoveries and insights about events are imparted by the author writing in the present. We're writing about memory (the act of remembering), the continuous present.

Having said this, though, I don't think there are any inherent disadvantages to past tense. The feeling of omniscience that the past tense allows is appealing, while the emotional immediacy of the present tense helps draw a reader into the action. What feels most comfortable to you, the writer, in any given piece? How does this essay or memoir need to be told? When you begin to write, how do the words flow? In the past? In the present? If you're not sure which sounds best, try a couple of pages in one tense, then switch all the verbs to the other. Which feels more dynamic?

These Boots Are Made for Writing

What's your favorite color shoe? What's your favorite pair of shoes? Are you ready to slip them on and walk to your desk, ready to write?

Or maybe, like me, you write better barefoot. How best do you think, write? Don your most comfortable sweats and T-shirt. Brew a cup of tea. And off you go.

Or, if you need motivation to start writing a memoir (or to revise it, or to send it out to an agent or editor), chapter 9 discusses, among other things, how to overcome fear of writing, the fear of setting that first word down on paper.

What's the fear about? Maybe it's about disclosing family secrets, knowing that our families will finally hear our truths. Maybe the fear is about going public, exposing our emotional souls to the world. Maybe we worry that people close to us might get angry or upset. Or, maybe we're scared of rejection. You're not alone with your fears. They can be daunting. But we must write anyway. As we'll discuss in chapter 9, it's important to confront fear directly — in order to subdue it.

Why even write memoir? Why divulge our secrets in public? Why reveal the most private things that happen to us? Because if we don't, we live a poorer, less examined life, one in which our voices will be lost.

WRITING EXERCISE

Now, sadly, it's almost time to leave our invented narrator — pregnant and alone. I've spent so much time with her, I feel as if she's a friend. I worry about her. What will happen? What will she decide to do? If she were writing her memoir, I wonder how she would define her narrative. What metaphors would she discover? If she's much older now, how would she reflect back on this time?

Well, I must remind myself this is a make-believe memoir! Which means we can choose any ending for her we like. What do you hope happens to her? How about if I provide several options for an ending, but you decide?

For this chapter's exercise, here are several poorly written sentences; you try revising them by tightening, rephrasing, seeking a more exact word. As you revise, also select slanted details to enhance metaphor and theme. Let's see which ending best fits our unwed narrator.

- After I tell Adam about the pregnancy, and I notice his initial reaction, I think that my choice is clear, that there's no way I can have a baby with a sullen, dull, uninteresting man, and be stuck with him — and *it* — that's how I see the baby, for the rest of what will be a wretched life, just like my mother.

- But later that night I hear a knock on my door and, wouldn't you know it, Adam shows up on my doorstep carrying a bouquet of flowers — not that they're a dozen red roses — but flowers, nevertheless. And after he leaves, I'm confused again and I don't know what to do.

- But really, truly, I know he doesn't love me and I don't love him. I mean, flowers or no flowers. And at least I can decide not to marry him, and the only thing (only!), I have to decide now is whether or not I should have the baby and raise *it* as a single mom and I'm scared and don't know what to do.

- I surf the Web and look at all the photos of New York City, all the places to visit, all the activities and things to see and I even check out some real estate listings, which are exorbitant, of course. And then I think that maybe I won't have to actually go all the way to New York City, that I can maybe go to Chicago, which of course is also a terrific city with lots to do, and before I can chicken out, I pick up the phone and call Planned Parenthood, which is the first place I can think of that might give me information about how to, well, get rid of it since I can't see bringing a baby into this world what with me still a kid myself. I'm still a teenager and I know I don't know how to raise a baby, and I'd hate to wreck a kid's life. That's just the way it is.

- Just for the heck of it, I walk through JC Penney and happen to end up in the baby department and I get so scared, at first, seeing all these cute, little, tiny booties in blue, pink, and yellow and then I pick up a pair and slide my finger inside and get, well, a warm, fuzzy feeling and so maybe I can do it? And then, for a moment, I begin to think of *it* as a girl, a little, tiny, cute baby girl.

After you revise the sentences in each section, decide which paragraph best fits the ending for our unwed mother.

FOR YOUR READING PLEASURE

Even though I suggest, in this chapter, that you vary sentence length and structure, and that contemporary writers usually don't write long sentences like Virginia Woolfe's, all rules are meant to be broken, if they're broken well. Here, in "The Man behind the Shower Curtain," Julie Mullany beautifully crafts a one-sentence-long essay that grips the reader's attention with the title, holding our attention through to the end. She does this without extraneous words.

THE MAN BEHIND THE SHOWER CURTAIN

He's our devil in decaying armor, the modern day cannibal, the suspect neighbor, the psycho Santa, the prank caller, the bad cop, the slow-passing car, the 4:00 AM phone call, the disguised cableman, the shadow at the end of the hall, the man on the corner, the man in the alley, the man behind you, the too-friendly landlord, the noise you can't trace, the armed intruder, the unarmed intruder, the gut feeling, the unrecognizable knock, the unashamed eye contact, the uncomfortable silence, the lone swinger in the park, the suit-and-tie man watching on the beach, the touchy priest, the slow-working house painter, the all-too-regular customer, the pushy date, the dark shaded flasher, the soft-spoken child molester, the eyes at the window, the man lying in the back seat of your car, the Boogie man, the one walking in your attic, the unlocked door, the ransacked apartment, the disconnected phone, the fear in your own home, the unfunny clown, the chummy drunk, the coach you couldn't trust, the two-faced stepfather, the jogger following your path, the stranger who knows your name.

Chapter Eight

Marketing Your Memoir

One spring afternoon in 1996, I was sitting at my desk working on a novel (one, to this day, I've never completed), when the phone rang. It was David Fenza, executive director of the Association of Writers and Writing Programs (AWP), notifying me that my memoir had won their Award Series in Creative Nonfiction. The award, he told me, included a cash prize plus publication with the University of Georgia Press.

Me? A winner? There must be a mistake, I thought, someone playing a joke. I don't remember exactly what I said, but I suspect I sounded both overjoyed and demented. I gushed. Even though I submitted the manuscript hoping to win, it never occurred to me I *would* win. A memoir on the topic of incest winning a literary competition? No way. Plus, whereas I had thought my book might appeal only to women readers, the judge, Adam Hochschild, was a *man*!

After I hung up, doubt continued to flood me. I was sure Dave Fenza had called the wrong person; there'd been a mistake. I phoned him back. No mistake.

Getting Started

Submitting your manuscript to a contest is one way to get it published. Yet I consider myself very lucky, since winning one is a long shot. Publishers — even small ones — release multiple books over the course of a year, whereas only one book can win any given contest. Plus, unlike traditional submissions, virtually all contests charge a fee to enter. These fees are used to pay judges and, in some cases, screeners as well. Screeners, who are also writers, read through the enormous pile of manuscript submissions, passing along to the judge their top selections — usually about ten to twenty manuscripts. Basically, the fees cover all of the work involved in the competition. But if you don't mind spending a few dollars, then submit. In addition to the AWP Award Series, a few other contests held for full-length creative nonfiction manuscripts are the *River Teeth* Literary Nonfiction Prize, the Mid-List First Series Award, and the Graywolf Press Nonfiction Prize. (Guidelines for all of these prizes may be found online.) *Poets & Writers* and the AWP's *Writer's Chronicle* are the best periodicals in which to learn about many more contests, both for individual essays and full-length books. After all, you can't win if you don't enter, just as you can't publish in a magazine if you don't submit work.

Publishing Outlets: Pros and Cons of Each

There are three main outlets to get your book into print, each with its own advantages and disadvantages. If you want to try a large for-profit publishing house, the first of these outlets, you need to secure an agent. You can do so based either on a book proposal or with a completed manuscript. Once the agent accepts you as a client, she or he will shop your manuscript around to various publishers, such as Random House, Simon & Schuster, W. W. Norton, and Doubleday.

> **Advantages:** You'll receive the largest amount of money via this route (though very few authors receive six-figure advances). The company is responsible for the considerable outlay of funds to get your book into print, such as cover design, layout, copyediting, printing, and marketing. They handle all distribution, which is how your book actually gets from a warehouse into a bookstore (both brick-and-mortar and online). These large companies offer their authors a great deal of credibility, so you'll also have the opportunity to receive more national coverage and media attention, though nothing is guaranteed.

Disadvantages: From the time your book first gets accepted (never mind how long you waited for the manuscript to actually find a home), it's usually well over a year before the book appears on a shelf in a bookstore. If your book doesn't hit it big almost immediately — selling virtually its complete first printing — these large houses will probably allow your book to go out of print relatively quickly. For-profit companies must pay taxes on books (inventory) stored in their warehouses, and they aren't usually willing to do so for long periods of time while the author hopes the book will one day find a large audience. Also bear in mind that most brick-and-mortar bookstores return unsold inventory to the publisher approximately three months after publication! That's a quick turnaround. Not much time to generate buzz. While there are exceptions, large publishing companies, for the most part, are more interested in earning money than advancing your career.

With small, independent publishers and university presses, a second outlet, you don't necessarily need an agent. You can either submit a book proposal or send a query letter with a sample chapter. (Check the Web site of each individual publisher to determine their submission guidelines.)

Advantages: While you won't receive a large advance (sometimes none), you'll find many similarities with large publishing houses. Reputable independent publishers and university presses cover all costs of producing and distributing the book. An advantage of a smaller press is that you'll usually be able to work more closely with the editorial, design, and marketing staffs. Since nonprofit university presses aren't restricted by the same tax laws as the for-profit publishers, chances are greater that your book will remain in print for a longer period of time. Many of these publishers also tend to care more about your long-term career and will stick by you through the lean years.

Disadvantages: You probably won't earn as much money, even in royalties. While the first print run for a book with a New York publisher (a midlist book not expected to be a blockbuster) might be about ten thousand copies, a typical press run for a small publisher is closer to two or three thousand. It might not be as easy to get national media attention, since their marketing budgets are smaller than a New York publisher. However, all publishers, large and small, now expect authors to do more and more in terms of promoting their own books. Long gone are the days when publishers and publicists handled everything. So be prepared to market and promote, regardless of who publishes your book.

The third outlet, self-publishing, seems to hold less of a stigma than in the past. Whereas once these companies were called "vanity presses," they're now more likely referred to as "print-on-demand publishers."

Advantages: Instant gratification! No waiting around. No rejection letters. Your book is available for purchase just a few months or less after completing the manuscript. No need to worry about that small window of opportunity, as with large publishers, hoping your book will hit it big before it goes out of print. It will never go out of print. You also maintain total control over the "property" itself; you don't need to secure permissions, say, to make it into an audio book or post an excerpt of it on the Web.

You also have total control of your book in terms of selecting the title, book jacket, and design, as well as editing, printing, distributing, and marketing. Of course, depending upon how much work you want to put into it, this control is either good news or bad. That said, most of the print-on-demand publishers offer a team to help guide you through the process — for a fee, of course. Three of the larger self-publishers are AuthorHouse, Xlibris, and iUniverse. Even more print-on-demand companies are sprouting up; a Web search will help you find them. Also, use reviews on the Web to determine the reliability of these various companies.

One of the largest pros is that you keep all the profit. In traditional publishing, you only receive a small percentage from the sale of each book (royalties), maybe anywhere from 7 percent to 10 percent per book. This means that even if your book lists at twenty-five dollars, you only receive a couple of those dollars. The publisher retains the rest. When you self-publish, on the other hand, although you pay all the up-front costs, you keep all profits, about fifteen dollars on a twenty-five dollar book. Big difference.

Disadvantages: You are financially responsible for editing, design, and all other expenses. The self-publishing companies offer some advice in terms of marketing, but you have to pay for ads and promotional materials. Also, a stigma still lingers with self-published books; therefore, it's more difficult to find a distributor and/or get the book reviewed. The good news is that marketing is neither as difficult nor as expensive with the advent of the Web. Just be sure you know what you're getting into before you spend good money. Do as much research as possible. Talk to others who have self-published. (See Lynn C. Tolson's story, "From Process to Product: Using Print-on-Demand to Publish," appendix 2.)

How to Decide What's Best for Your Book

When it's time for you to try to publish your book, ask yourself this: which type of publishing company seems like the best fit? For example, if you feel anxious about the possibility of your book going out of print, then pursue publishing opportunities with a smaller press. Don't get caught up in the lure of Big Time New York publishing if it's just not right for you! If, on the other hand, you're willing to take your chances on the book's longevity, and you want to earn a relatively hefty advance, by all means submit the book to an agent.

The tricky part, of course, is that no one has a crystal ball. No one can predict which book might hit it big and which one won't. Small houses get lucky and publish best sellers, while a large publisher can invest thousands of dollars on marketing a book only to see it tank. It's a tough business. So go with your instincts and pursue the kind of company where, at least, you'll feel most comfortable.

Before deciding, however, do your homework. Obtain as much information as possible about agents and publishing houses. There are many sources available. Libraries usually stock a reference book entitled the *Literary Market Place*, or visit www.literarymarketplace.com. It lists virtually all publishers, large and small, independent and university —

though not print-on-demand. Each entry provides a general description of the kinds of books the company publishes. It also offers information about agents. Another helpful book is *Jeff Herman's Guide to Book Publishers, Editors, and Literary Agents*. Online resources are also available. To help you find an agent, you might visit www.agentresearch.com or www.aar-online.org, which is the Association of Authors' Representatives. The Web site www.writersjournal.com offers additional information on how to get published.

One of the best Web sites for writers interested in independent or university presses is www.newpages.com. You'll find a wealth of material including addresses and the kinds of books each publishes. New Pages also provides information and links to literary magazines, creative writing programs, book reviews, blogs, and interviews. Many independent and university presses specialize in particular subjects (regional, nature studies, women's studies, sports writing, etc.). Only query those that are a good fit for your particular topic.

Here is a list of other informative Web sites that provide advice on writing, publishing, and promoting, as well as additional areas of interest to writers — just a sampling of resources available on the Web:

www.writingitreal.com (online workshops, craft essays, author
    interviews, one-on-one help)
www.absolutewrite.com (classes, forums, agent information)
www.writedirections.com (articles on how to write, contests)
www.writersdigest.com (articles on writing and publishing)
www.writersmanual.com (articles on writing and publishing)
www.writing-world.com (articles on writing and publishing)
www.writermag.com (*The Writer*)
www.bylinemag.com (*Byline Magazine*)
www.communityofwriters.com (general information)
www.writers.net (WritersNet organization, general information)
www.booklocker.com/books/676.html (hundreds of marketing ideas
    from *Buzz Your Book* on how to get buzz for your book online)
www.writersandeditors.com (agent lists, publishing and editing
    information)

www.bksp.org (Backspace: The Writer's Place)

www.bookpromotionnewsletter.com

www.clmp.org (Council of Literary Magazines and Presses)

www.dustbooks.com (a valuable source for small press information)

www.writing.com/main/view_item/item_id/844651 (how to write a
query letter)

www.authorsguild.org (The Authors Guild) and www.nwu.org
(The National Writers Union) offer, among other things, legal and
publishing information to writers. In order to ensure your rights are
protected, be sure to have an attorney or agent review all contracts
before you sign.

The only national writing organization to hold an annual conference
is the Association of Writers and Writing Programs (www.awpwriter
.org), which has 471 institutional members and approximately 28,000
individual members. Its journal, the *Writer's Chronicle*, features excel-
lent craft articles and interviews with authors. In addition, it advertises
contests and lists which journals are seeking essays. *Poets & Writers*
(www.pw.org) is also helpful, given its many articles about publishing
and its classified ads listing magazine calls for submissions.

Promoting Yourself as a Professional Speaker

The afternoon of my very first book reading, at Schuler Books in Grand
Rapids, Michigan, I was so scared I felt ill. It's one thing to sit alone in
a room in your house pouring your heart out — or even to know that
nameless strangers are reading the book in the privacy of their own
homes — but it's another thing altogether to stand before an audience
reading these words in *public*. Ironically, I'd always fantasized about my
first reading at a bookstore with my newly published book. But now,
faced with the prospect, I was horrified.

*Suppose no one shows up . . . Suppose, after the reading, I'm asked rude
or embarrassing questions . . . Suppose the reading itself is a failure, that I
am a failure . . . Suppose, suppose.*

So I prepared. Over-prepared. Daily, I rehearsed my twenty-five-minute reading, speaking the sections aloud to myself. I purchased new clothes: a black dress and black boots. Maybe I'd have felt better if I wore red shoes, but black seemed artistic; I didn't want to appear frivolous.

At the very least, I reassured myself, my friends would attend.

The small space in the bookstore was packed. Sure, my friends attended, but complete strangers also appeared, as if by magic. Men *and* women — though mostly women. Who were these people? Why had they driven to the bookstore to see me?

Afterward, people approached me, one by one, to get signed copies of the book. Several of the women leaned close to whisper: *That happened to me, too.* I spoke with each woman, surprised — yet gratified — that they shared their stories with me. I was reminded of my former student Marci, in Georgia, who once whispered her secret to me — that she loved words.

That evening at the bookstore I first fully realized the true power of language, how deeply our words, our stories, connect us to each other, connect us to our readers.

Then, as if to confirm this realization, another woman approached me, a therapist from a local women's center, who invited me to give a speech at her organization. "Your message will help other women," she said. "Will you do it?"

"Yes," I said, though I'd never given a speech in my life. I'd never even considered being a professional speaker. I was a writer, after all. I figured that the main marketing plan for the book would be to give a few readings in local bookstores before creeping back to my writing desk. And that would be that.

She handed me her card; I gave her my phone number; she said she'd call me to set up a date. What I learned from this encounter and others is that a variety of options exist to spread my message about the damage of child abuse.

These social service organizations, I also learned, prefer an actual speech rather than a literary reading. Writing a speech isn't as daunting as it sounds. Ironically, back when I lived in Washington, D.C., and worked on Capitol Hill, I'd written speeches for congressmen; now, all these years later, I wrote speeches for myself, in my own voice.

I developed four different presentations geared for various kinds of organizations, all of which I could easily edit and revise to best fit the needs of the specific conference or group:

For a general audience, I wrote a speech entitled "Child Abuse Is a Human Rights Issue."

For professional organizations of therapists, I wrote "The Silent Language of Child Sexual Abuse," in which I describe my healing process, in order to help members of the audience work with their own clients. When my second book, about sexual addiction, was published, I changed the title to "The Silent Language of Child Sexual Abuse and Addiction," and revised the speech accordingly.

For Jewish organizations, I wrote a speech entitled "My Jewish Journey Home."

And, for women's groups, I crafted a speech with a feminist slant.

All my speeches incorporate sections of my books, so they're much easier to write than if I had to start from scratch!

Since my first book was published, I've given well over one hundred presentations at conferences on child abuse prevention and sexual addiction, as well as at colleges and universities. I've spoken (for a few examples) at the Coalition for Family and Children Services in Iowa, the Michigan Statewide Conference on Child Abuse and Neglect, the Society for the Advancement of Sexual Health, and the New England Conference on Child Sexual Abuse. I also speak to schools of social work, women's studies departments, and to psychology and sociology majors. While I still get nervous speaking in public, the benefits far outweigh any momentary discomfort. By traveling to conferences and giving interviews, I've met hundreds of wonderful people interested in my story. Plus, imagine standing in front of an audience that applauds after you speak aloud your own words you've written! Very gratifying — especially after the long years spent alone in a room, writing.

I suggest you begin locally, in your home town, developing your reputation where you already have contacts. Local organizations are usually tied to state organizations, which, in turn, are tied to regional and national groups. When I contact these groups, I send them a short query letter, no longer than one page, outlining my qualifications and pertinent background information. I include a list of other organizations where I've spoken, and a list of testimonials to let them know how people responded to my presentations. After you establish yourself, word of mouth will help you line up engagements as well.

Whatever the topic of your memoir, you should be able to promote yourself as a professional speaker. Organizations of social workers and therapists deal with clients struggling with all kinds of issues — not, of course, only recovery from child abuse. If you've written about addiction (food, sex, alcohol, drugs, prescription pain killers); the loss of a loved one; physical illness; mental illness (depression, alienation, loneliness); divorce; adoption; dysfunctional families — any kind of childhood trauma — write a speech. Virtually any story can be crafted into a presentation that would be of interest to mental health professionals. All these organizations hold conferences that need speakers; for the most part, they are eager to invite someone who has written about her or his true life story — *your* life story.

Also, I sell more books at professional gatherings than I do at writers' conferences. Since neither of my memoirs received big-city newspaper book reviews, selling books at conferences goes a long way toward keeping them in print.

So contact associations of psychiatrists, psychologists, social workers, family counselors. Tell them you are available to give a presentation or conduct a seminar to help them better understand their clients who are dealing with child abuse, addiction, grief, dysfunctional families, women's issues, spirituality — whatever your background might be. You've lived through the event and come out the other side. Now, you're able to share your knowledge and expertise with others.

Web Opportunities for Your Memoir

The Web offers limitless opportunities to promote your book. Many of the organizations you contact about giving a presentation also have

Web sites. Many post a section called "true stories" or something similar on their sites; these stories are written in the form of brief articles, in which you can also mention your book. Frequently, these organizations have a virtual bookstore where your book can be listed or reviewed, as well.

How to find these online resources? If you know of an organization that deals with the topic of your book, begin there. For example, if you've written about child abuse, the Childhelp organization at www .childhelp.org would be a good place to start. If you don't know the names of any national organizations, then start Googling. For example, if you do a Google search for the following categories, you get over a million hits for each: "grief" + "support groups"; "divorce" + "support groups"; "sexual health" + "addiction." There are over seventeen million hits for "substance abuse." If you type "National Association of Social Workers" into the Google search engine, you get close to half a million hits! And who doesn't write on a topic of interest to a social worker? Be creative in your Google searches. If you don't immediately discover what you're looking for, keep refining the keywords of your search.

Of course, half a million hits are way too many; this is too broad a category. But if you click on a few of the top hits, such as the National Association of Social Workers itself, you'll discover links to smaller, more targeted groups. Contact them to see if you can post an article on their site. Do they have a conference where you might deliver a presentation? Do they have a virtual bookstore? Do they review books? By following links, you'll find even more sites.

> Through the Web, contact social service organizations both for speaking and book review opportunities, as well as the opportunity to post short articles about your story (a greatly condensed version of your memoir).

My first memoir received more than forty reviews in local and nonmainstream journals and Web sites. In 1997, when *Terror, Father* was published, the Web wasn't as developed as it is today, but I contacted such places as *Contemporary Psychology, Counseling Today, Family Therapy News,* and *The Healing Woman.* Web sites you might find particularly helpful are www.byforandaboutwomen.com, www.womenwriters .net, www.menweb.org, www.bookpleasures.com, www.giftfromwithin .org, www.blogtalkradio.com, www.divineseedsofhope.com, www.meta psychology.mentalhelp.net, and www.recoveryworld.com (which gave *Love Sick* one of its best reviews). The Web, of course, was a much stronger presence in 2001, when *Love Sick* was published, and I spent weeks surfing it and posting information. One site, www.newshe.com (the Web site featuring the work of Drs. Laura and Jennifer Berman, now www.bermansexualhealth.com), asked permission to excerpt the book, and the Bermans subsequently invited me to appear on their nationally syndicated television program on the Discovery Health Channel. You never know where a Web search will lead.

In addition to psychology-based Web sites, I contacted sites geared for women writers. Two of the best such organizations are the International Women's Writing Guild (www.iwwg.com) and the National Association of Women Writers (www.naww.org). The IWWG is more of a physical organization, offering non-virtual workshops and conferences around the country. The NAWW is more of an online organization, with weekly newsletters and online seminars featuring a range of topics (writing, publishing, marketing) for women writers. Yet another Web site, www.boomerwomenspeak.com, hosts an array of online interviews on any number of subjects of interest to women, including authors of books. I participated in a virtual interview and found it to be a wonderful way to meet women and discuss important issues.

Even if major review outlets don't review your book, there's no reason not to take matters into your own hands and market your book yourself! The Web has made it much easier to bypass print newspapers and magazines. Once you write and publish your book, then get your own Web site, and start marketing — whether you're reviewed in the *New York Times* or not.

The Importance of All Our Voices

Most writers, of course, do want to be reviewed in the *Times*, since it offers enormous prestige. Years ago, shortly after I began to write, when I still lived in Texas, I met a woman I'll call "Lisa" at a writers' conference in Houston. She had recently published an autobiographical novel about her autistic son. I was in awe of her. And never mind that I had not a clue how to actually craft a novel at that time, I still had grandiose fantasies of cocktail parties with agents and national reviews. After all, I was putting in four solid hours a day on my old Smith Corona portable typewriter. Back then, though, how quickly I was disillusioned when I learned Lisa's book had not received a *Times* review. She had not flown to New York City to meet the literati. Instead, she described giving a reading at a conference on autism. How touched she was, she told me, to share her story with other parents of autistic children, touched because she'd given voice to their hopes and fears.

What a disappointment, I thought, back then. I went off to schmooze with an agent, determined Lisa's fate would not be my own.

Do I still hope to be reviewed in the *Times*? Sure. But I also know that I, as well as my books, will survive without it. I certainly don't wait around expecting it to happen. More importantly, I'm following in Lisa's strong and steady footsteps. I now understand what she meant when she said how touched she felt to speak at the conference on autism.

After each of my presentations, I offer time for questions and answers: *Did your mother know your father was sexually molesting you? Did your father molest your sister? What were techniques used by your therapist that most helped you in recovery?* The audience cares about my answers because the answers will help others — women and men — struggling with their own damaged backgrounds.

WRITING EXERCISES

1. Make a list of all the general themes and ideas contained in your book (child abuse, women's issues, mental health issues, child rearing, loss, grief, midlife crisis, divorce, the environment, etc.).

2. From this list, select keywords that you'd use to put into Internet search engines. Start Googling!

Begin your search as broadly as possible, then narrow it down. The ideas contained in the memoir will assist you in locating groups who will find your message of interest.

Chapter Nine

Confessional and (Finally) Proud of It

U ntil I write the past it flickers in my mind's eye, ghostly, like an old newsreel. In black-and-white photos of my Russian ancestors — photos that survived a boat trip from the Old Country to the New World — faces fade as if they've aged while sitting in cardboard boxes. Even color Polaroids of volcanic mountains, snapped when I lived in the West Indies, seem cast in a pinkish sheen. As chemicals disintegrate, this part of my life seems tinted by raspberry-colored fingernail polish. I leaf through family albums, but no one appears distinct. No one seems ever to have been fully alive.

For years, my life resembles these snapshots: faded and one-dimensional.

Then, I pick up a pencil. Slowly, I wake. I blink and inhale. Exhale. Finally, I choose to examine my past. Finally, it's more a relief to write my life than ignore it, a relief to develop a clear focus and vision. "To write one's life is to live it twice," Patricia Hampl explains, "and the second living is both spiritual and historical."

The first life isn't fully lived, fully seen or understood, until we write it.

I've been asked: Isn't it painful to write about the past, all those scary childhood memories?

Writing about pain *is* painful — but it's also a profound relief. With every written word the pain lessens. It's as if I extract it, one word at a time. Only through writing, for example, do I finally understand why I craved that maroon scarf, why I coveted it, saved it, for years. To write about that married man in Boston with whom I had an affair, who seduced me, who wrapped his scarf around my neck, was to metaphorically unwrap the scarf . . . *and finally let him go.*

I've been asked: Can't you understand your life just as well through therapy?

Both writing and therapy are ways we interact with — and interpret — our past; both may play a role in helping us make sense of and/or recover from traumatic events. The major difference is that the sole purpose of therapy is to advance our recovery, while writing artfully for an audience requires we make sense of our lives in a way that speaks to others. While therapy helps deepen our understanding of our lives, writing sharpens our senses so that images and details from the past emerge in a new context, one that illuminates events for ourselves as well as for our readers.

While writing isn't a substitute for therapy, informal personal writing can also add to the experience. In journaling, for example, we write solely for ourselves, to explore feelings privately. Or we might compose letters (not necessarily to be sent!) to people who have hurt or abandoned us, affording us an opportunity to express feelings we could never say in person or in public. Freewriting to get our emotions down on the page as fast as possible, with no thought toward rewriting, publishing, or editing, is also a private, yet effective, form of communication to enhance our understanding of ourselves. Whether for an audience of many, or just one, through writing, I tell my story.

Memoir writing, gathering words onto pieces of paper, helps me shape my life to a manageable size. By discovering plot, arc, theme, and metaphor, I offer my life an organization, a frame, which would be otherwise unseen, unknown. Memoir creates a narrative, a life story.

Writing my life is a gift I give to myself. To write is to be constantly reborn. On one page I understand *this* about myself. On the next page, I understand *that.*

Western Civilization in an Eggshell

In college, while having that affair with the maroon-scarf man, I took a course entitled the History of Western Civilization. Even now, just thinking about that dense, heavy textbook, I want to curl up to nap with my cat. It must have been over a thousand musty pages. At least it felt that heavy as I lugged it back and forth between my dorm and class in my green book bag.

I'm surprised I didn't flunk the course. I rarely listened to the professor. I took few notes, daydreaming, instead, about the maroon-scarf man.

All the battles, purges, revolutions, and pogroms remained dull words on pieces of paper. Western civilization read like a grocery list of dates, names, times. Historical documents were rendered as if from afar: lifeless, bloodless. To be honest, assassinations and political coups actually would have been interesting if the descriptions of mayhem were vivid and sensory, if the key players confessed their inner lives. But the powerful don't often show us their true selves; instead, they seem to have relinquished this right and appear as figures frozen in marble or bronze. To really understand the Holocaust, for example, I (much later) read memoirs by "ordinary" people such as Anne Frank, Elie Wiesel, and Primo Levi. Patricia Hampl explains that memoir "reaches deep within the personality as it seeks its narrative form and also grasps the life-of-the-times as no political treatise can."

Reading history books, I never learned, for example, what the American and Russian revolutions tasted like, what they sounded like, how they smelled. I wanted to know the private thoughts and motivations of Czar Nicholas II, his empress, Alexandra, and Anastasia — as well as those of the Russian revolutionary peasants. After all, my own grandfather, when conscripted into the Czar's army, fled Russia. Dodging the draft, he emigrated to America. But these threadbare facts are all I know of his story.

Or, if only my grandmother had kept a diary or written a memoir telling her Great Depression story, a story about an egg, I would have been riveted.

Here are the few details I know about my grandmother's story: During the Depression, my mother's family, like most, had little money. One day, with no food for her five children, my grandmother went door to door until someone gave her one egg. One egg to split among her five children. On the way home, she dropped it. She retrieved a spoon and a cup from her house and, as best she could, scooped it up.

I wanted to know more. Growing up, I asked my mother to repeat the story over and over, hoping she would recall additional details. Was it a white or brown egg? Who gave it to my grandmother? How did she drop it? Did she trip? Did it slip from her fingers? Had she dropped it as she removed it from a pocket, just as she approached the house? What was she wearing that day? Was it winter, summer? How much of the egg did she salvage? Was she able to cook enough to feed my mother, her brothers and sisters? What was my grandmother thinking and feeling the moment the egg slipped from her grasp?

Even listening to my mother's barely remembered version, I was hooked by the sympathetic protagonist. I identified with the sense of loss symbolized by one ruined egg.

The story *moves* me, tells me more about the Great Depression than a facts-only chapter from a dry textbook. As Patricia Hampl says, "No one owns the past." Or, I might add, why doesn't my grandmother own the past as much as a historian? I've always wanted to know the story behind the story — the *real* story — a person's secret, inner life. In school, I was always more curious about voices out in the corridor than what happened in class. Bored, I rested my chin in my palm, ear cocked toward the hallway, wondering about students' whispered confessions just outside the door. I want to know *your* story. And *yours*. It's why I read memoir. How else can I learn about *real* civilization?

The dancer and choreographer Martha Graham said:

There is a vitality, a life-force, an energy, a quickening that is translated through you into action. And because there is only one of you in all time, this expression is unique. And if you block it, it will never exist through any other medium, and be lost. The world will not have it. It is not your business to determine how good it is, nor how valuable, nor how it compares with other expressions. It is your business to keep it yours clearly and directly, to keep the channel open.

When writing, if I forge even one good sentence on any given day, I know I have discovered a kernel of emotional truth. I feel that life-force Graham describes, feel it, like my pulse. Exhilarating.

One Secret, One Word, at a Time

I have a secret to tell you.

Now, by this point, you must think that surely this woman couldn't possibly have any secrets left to tell. Through writing, I've divulged that my father sexually molested me, that my mother didn't protect me, that my sister, to protect herself, abandoned her family as much as possible. In addition to childhood secrets, I've confessed adult secrets as well: unhappy marriages, divorces, infidelities, an eating disorder, and a sexual addiction.

What else can I possibly have to say?

On the face of it, then, this secret I'm now going to tell you may seem mild in comparison, perhaps anticlimactic.

Here it is: I received what surely must be the worst SAT scores in the history of the universe. To compound this embarrassment, I was rejected from every college to which I applied except for a two-year division of Boston University. Even after all these years, this causes me shame.

So why tell *you*?

Or why write about things like incest and sex addiction? Isn't it difficult enough to confide our innermost secrets to a best friend or therapist, let alone complete strangers? To say nothing of risking hostility, ridicule, denial, anger from aunts, uncles, cousins, siblings, grandparents, parents. *What will the neighbors think? What will my mother say?*

Why jeopardize relationships?

Because it's a relief to no longer hide behind a veil of secrets. Growing up, I lived a double life. On the face of it, we seemed like a normal, happy family: My father had an important career, first in government, then in banking. Nice houses. Pretty clothes. But all this seeming perfection was a veneer, a façade, for the *other* life. It masked the reality that my father sexually molested me, a reality never spoken aloud either in private in our house, or in public.

As an adult, I likewise lived a double life. Even after that shaky start with those wretched SAT scores, I did graduate from college. For a while I worked on Capitol Hill. My first husband was an attorney, my second a college professor. Even divorced, I appeared respectable. Yet, as with my childhood, this seeming normalcy masked my messy life. For years, I was an out-of-control addict.

Now, after writing my secrets, the weight of life feels lighter. I step into the world more honestly.

But what about other people involved in my secrets, especially my parents? Aren't I, in my writing, supposed to protect their privacy?

No.

Since my family was involved in the creation of who I am, I feel justified, even obliged, as a writer, to reveal the roles they played. It was *because* my father molested me that I suffered from sex addiction, an eating disorder, even, in part, received bad SATs. You see, the night before the exam, I was kept awake by him. The next morning, staring at all those questions, all those empty, blank circles waiting to be filled, I was numb. Stunned. Drowsy. Dissociated. I felt like a blank, empty circle.

How can I write a life, be a memoirist, without including members of my family? They are woven into the threads of every experience. If I don't write, I will once again be silenced, just like the child-me; in essence, my father, again, will silence me. If I don't write my secrets I will, in effect, still be keeping *his*. Only my own words can finally fill that blank, empty space that once was me.

My main sadness as a writer and as a daughter in my family is that I didn't write these truths while my parents were still alive. Only by telling our family truths could we have been an authentic family. Only by telling my secrets can I be an authentic woman. This is the only way for me to be an authentic writer, as well.

Why didn't I write my first memoir while my parents were still alive? I was in mid-therapy when they died, not yet sure enough of my own woman-power. For years, I remained timid, still trying to be the "good" girl my parents raised, the obedient girl who, as a child, had no choice but to compliantly let my father hurt me without saying a word. Not a whisper. Not a hint. Nothing. Even years after the abuse ended, I remained, emotionally, that wounded little girl. I didn't want to upset anyone. I didn't want to bring attention to scary secrets. I didn't want to anger my father or mother. Well into adulthood, I wanted to maintain the pretense of a perfect family. Before I began therapy, I myself was scared to know the truth — scared to admit to myself that my childhood was a wreck, that my "perfect" family was a lie.

Writing is a way to remove the muzzle and blinders from childhood. Writing is a way to take possession of — fully own — my life. Only I own my memories that dwell in the attic of my mind. As sole possessor of them, I am free to write them.

By doing so, I feel my own power. Through telling my story, listening to the stories of others, I am no longer a timid little girl — even as I still, at times, get scared. But I try not to allow fear to preclude me from writing. After years of silence, I have a voice.

Write anyway! Whatever the roadblock. *Write anyway!*

Word by Word

Most memoirists I know are scared to write their stories, but the point, I think, *is* to write anyway — in our own way, in our own time. As you challenge yourself, you'll feel more courageous every day. On tough days, think of writing just one page at a time. If you need to break it down further, tell yourself you're writing just one sentence at a time. Or, on *very* tough days, one *word* at a time. This may sound obvious, but the only way I know to work through difficult material is to do just that: go through it one word at a time. To learn to sit in the dark places, even knowing the only way through something is, well, through it. To skirt an issue, to sidestep it, is to remain in an emotionally vague or unfeeling place. As Vivian Gornick says in an interview in *Fourth Genre*,

"[Memoirists must] go down to something hard and true beneath the easy surface of sentimental self-regard."

Even if you're scared or leary to push yourself beneath the surface, even if you're reluctant to "go there," *go anyway, write anyway.* When writing memoir I sometimes need to remind myself that I've already lived through, survived, the actual moment, whatever it was. Now (I tell myself) I'm "only" writing about it — figuring out what it meant. In an interview entitled "On Writing through the Hard Place," Mark Doty, author of *Heaven's Coast,* says, "I get tempted to hold back . . . all the time . . . For me this takes the form of . . . finding myself saying, 'Do I have to feel that?' At that point I'd rather stop and, say, take a nap; it's the experience of resistance and avoidance, [but] if I can just stay there, writing . . . through the tension . . . then often I am rewarded." Doty goes on to explain that during the time he wrote about caring for his partner when his partner was dying of AIDS, it helped to also keep a journal. In it, he'd write "about what I plan to do, what resists me . . . It just seems a way to gain a bit of distance, and writing about the writing often points out what I hadn't seen, or need to do next."

Writing memoir requires courage. Doty admits that "it's . . . scary . . . to transform your life . . . into a story; it can make you feel used up . . . Those feelings had more to do with marketing than with writing, really, and they passed."

Sometimes the fear evolves from the material itself; other times it's a fear about what others might think of it. And while we'll look at this second concern more in the following section, for now, if you're struggling just to set words down on paper, try to not even think about others. *Write anyway.* I, at least, pretend to write just for myself, ignoring (as much as possible) the fact that friends, family, even strangers might one day read my story. I pretend *no one else* will ever see my work; in any event, it's my choice whether I'll ultimately share it with anyone or not. I tell myself I'm writing this book, first and foremost, because I *must.* Which is true. The act of writing itself is of primary importance. This is where the spirituality of artistic endeavor resides. Focus on the words themselves during the creation process. Just write your truths without worrying about the reaction of others. In order to be creative and fully engage in the process, writers must give themselves permission to set aside the fear about what the outside world might think. As memoirist James McBride says, "Fear is a killer of good literature."

The Courage to Show This to Your Mother
(Penance Optional)

So how did friends and family react to my memoirs? Well, how did *you* react when I told you I received the worst SAT scores in the history of the universe? Did you think less of me? Did you judge me? Did you assume I must be stupid? If, instead, you understood and accepted why I received these bad scores, then chances are your *real* friends (as well as the readers of your work) won't judge you, either.

But, of course, one's family is of grave concern, and family is what prohibits many people from writing and publishing their work. So let me share three stories about what happened to me when my books were published. With one book I lost someone. With the other, I gained a family. With both my books, the relationship with my sister never changed at all.

While I was married, I only hinted to my husband about the double life I led as a sex addict. After we divorced we remained friends — at least until *Love Sick* was published. The last pleasant phone conversation we had was right before he left for the bookstore.

Then, one day awhile later, I received an angry phone call. He was angry both at the way I'd portrayed him, and because I hadn't been entirely honest with him during the marriage. While I couldn't fix his second concern, I think I was generous in my portrayal of him. After all, I didn't tell *his* secrets, such as . . . (Oh, wait, memoir isn't supposed to be about revenge!) Yes, I portrayed him as emotionally distant — which is how I described *myself* as well. This was our marriage. I had to be honest about it. But I was as gentle toward him (in my opinion) as possible, while still telling my secrets, still writing my story.

I *don't* write out of a sense of revenge. I write to understand my own story. And in *Love Sick* I was as hard, or harder, on myself, than I was on him — or anyone else. My intent wasn't to upset him. My honesty is more important to me than his anger.

But don't assume that your revelations will always result in anger or loss of relationships. You might be surprised. Here is my second story.

I began to write *Because I Remember Terror, Father, I Remember You* about two weeks after my parents died (within six days of each other), so I didn't have to worry about their reaction. I was, however, concerned about my father's large extended family, many of whom lived in Chicago, about three hours from me. But since I barely knew these people, was isolated from them, I decided not to search them out or alert them to the book ahead of time. (I was also scared and really *really* hoped they'd never find out!) I figured I'd let the book go out into the world and see what happened.

Initially, nothing happened. In conjunction with its publication, I even authored an article in the *Chicago Tribune* about the need for child abuse to be seen as a human rights issue. Not a word. The book came out in paperback. Still nothing. Then, about three years later . . .

It was a Friday evening about nine o'clock when the phone rang. A woman identified herself; her name sounded vaguely familiar. A second or third cousin, maybe? She told me she had just finished reading my book.

I barely heard her next words. I sank down on the couch, gripping the phone. I thought I heard the word "sorry." Yes, she was saying she felt so sorry about what happened to me as a child. That *all* the cousins, aunts, uncles had been talking about it the last few weeks, and they were *all* sorry. "No one knew or suspected," she said.

After this initial contact, I received e-mails and phone calls from family members I barely knew existed. Everyone was upset — but *not* that I had told my family secret. Rather, everyone was distressed because of what happened to me, even though my father was always placed on a pedestal by his family. He was a true immigrant success story. He worked his way through the University of Chicago: undergraduate and law school. He held important professional positions. He made the family look good. He had a commanding, successful voice.

Now, all the members of his family heard *my* voice. Really, they heard the voice of a little girl.

I subsequently attended a family reunion to be officially welcomed into the fold.

The third story about my family's reaction concerns my sister. She claims she wasn't abused by our father; yet she never doubted that I was. And when I told her about the upcoming publication of my first book, she took it in stride. Did she wish, instead, one of my novels were being published? Probably. Yet she still told me she was proud. Even so, she hasn't read my books. At first, this upset me. Now, I understand that to read them would be too painful for her. So I simply appreciate that she's supportive. She tells her friends about the books and even buys copies. I feel reassured knowing that they sit in the bookcase in her home.

All memoirists have publishing stories about their family's reactions. Some, like mine, are mixed: positive and negative. Other authors are punished by friends and family, angry that dirty (or even not-so-dirty) laundry is aired in public. Most memoirists continue to write anyway, even as they feel some ambiguity and confusion about the entire process: *I must write this; I'm scared to write this; I should get my family's permission to write this; I won't tell anyone I'm writing this; what happens after I write this; am I a bad person because I wrote this, because I upset my mother?*

When Alison Bechdel, for example, told her mother she was writing *Fun Home: A Family Tragicomic*, she initially believed her mother accepted the news "quite well." In an article in *Slate*, she explains that her mother "didn't quite understand why I wanted to reveal all our sordid family secrets to the general public, but she never tried to talk me out of it." Nevertheless, Bechdel believes that her mother was hurt by the book. "She made that clear, but she also let me know that she grasped the complexity of the situation." Bechdel herself feels equally ambiguous:

I do feel that I robbed my mother in writing this book . . . No matter how responsible you try to be in writing about another person, there's something inherently hostile in the act. You're violating their subjectivity. I thought I could write about my family without hurting anyone, but I was wrong. I probably will do it again. And that's just an uncomfortable fact about myself that I have to live with.

Mindy Lewis, author of *Life Inside,* would probably agree with Bechdel that real stories affect real people. In an interview in *Chronogram,* Lewis explains that during the writing of her memoir, she confronted her mother for confining her, as a teenager, in a mental hospital for twenty-eight months in the 1960s. A terrible fight between mother and daughter ensued, her mother not understanding why, as she put it, Lewis hated her enough to write a book about this incarceration. Afterward, Lewis went into a clinical depression that was "set off by the guilt and terror about writing the book. I felt my values were so screwed up that I'd rather write a book and hurt my mother." It was through the support of others who'd gone through similar situations that she continued writing.

Ironically, it was ultimately the book itself that brought Lewis and her mother close. Lewis sent her mother four chapters-in-progress and received a return letter in which her mother provided her own perspective on events. As the *Chronogram* article goes on to explain, Lewis's mother, by acknowledging her daughter's story, chose "to put her daughter's success and happiness above her own, putting aside her fear and anxiety about being seen as a bad mother." Lewis says, "Our relationship became transformed; I realized how much I love my mother."

Not only did Lewis's relationship with her mother improve as a result of the book, so did her relationships with clients at her freelance graphic-design business. In an e-mail exchange with me, Lewis admits that at first she was worried her clients would judge her, that she'd lose business. Just the opposite happened. "When the book was published, several of my clients attended my readings," Lewis says. "Honestly, sharing my story brought out the human side of business acquaintances, deepened our relationships. I did not lose clients. I gained friends. What an incredible relief not having to hide anymore."

Kim Barnes, author of *In the Wilderness: Coming of Age in Unknown Country*, likewise suggests we not automatically assume that friends — or even close family members — will get angry if we write about them. "If you ... treat [people] with complexity and compassion, sometimes they will feel as though they've been honored, not because they're presented in some ideal way but because they're presented with understanding."

This is not always the case, however. Mark Doty admits that since publishing *Heaven's Coast*, "There are people who *still* don't speak to me ... I learned that I have a certain (probably necessary?) degree of dedication to my own work which allows me not to care about this — at least not to care enough to stop!" He goes on to say that he still finds the form of memoir compelling and complex: "I love how it writes a self into being, but I also think that it's by nature a slippery, troubled thing — it comes with doubt and challenge deeply built in."

Whatever the reaction of family members, our job as writers is still to tell our stories. Our job isn't, after all, to make people feel settled, calm, or comfortable. And even if we ourselves initially feel uncomfortable about shaking things up, we ultimately feel a sense of release and power. If we use this power authentically — if we write to understand our narrative — then we bear witness to honest human experiences and emotions.

Truth and Memory in Memoir

One evening, when my family lived in the West Indies, friends of ours — a mother and her two children — banged on our door. My mother, sister, and I stumbled to the verandah, half-asleep, my father out of town. The friends needed help. The mother, bruised from her husband's beating, planned to flee the island while her drunken husband slept. We collected clothes and money to assist their escape. We drove them down the mountain to the harbor where arrangements were made — I think with the owner of a banana boat — to slip them to another island, where they could catch a plane to the States in the morning.

My sister and I witnessed this event together. I'm sure she recalls it as an exciting adventure. Fleeing! In the dead of night! In her mind's eye she can only, of course, like any of us, see events filtered through her own sensibilities. Growing up, she was fearless. In her tomboy shorts and T-shirts, she tumbled on trampolines. I have a photograph of her swaying from the rigging of the *Danmark*, a square-rigged ship that yearly sailed into Charlotte Amalie. My sister shinnied up palms. She leapt off the high dive of the Virgin Isle Hotel swimming pool.

I, on the other hand, feel a sense of sadness when I think about that family in a boat far out at sea. I recall these events through my own personal filter, profoundly different from my sister's: me, in my neat madras skirt playing the piano, or in my pink tutu dancing ballet. I loved to smell frangipani flowers, but never climbed a tree. As much as my sister flitted around the island, I was encouraged to stay home. My vision of the world was constrained, as if I were shipwrecked on the island with only my parents.

So if my sister were to write a childhood memoir, how disparate it would be from mine! Her memory of that night our friends fled the island would be vastly different, *yet equally true.*

How can I trust even my own memory, my own truth, regardless of my sister's differing recollections? How can I remember with certainty details of events that happened years ago? Did I, for example, really break my collar bone the first day of summer camp after first grade? Maybe it was the second day. I know I broke it, since I have a photograph of myself with white gauze wrapped around my shoulders.

On the other hand, I have no factual proof confirming whether my mother told me, when I was in kindergarten, that a girl in our neighborhood, Penny, was born with a short stub of a tail. I even lack an image of Penny's face, though I suppose, as neighborhood kids, we played together. Yet this story remains embedded in my memory: a girl with a name that smelled like copper. As if that weren't exotic enough, she was born with a stub of a tail. (I always imagine a monkey tail, as opposed to that of a dog or a cat.) I think my mother told me that Penny underwent an operation to remove it, but this part of the story is murkier. Yet, for all time, the words "penny" and "tail" are joined in my mind. I hope the story is true. It *seems* true. If I were to write an essay about Penny, I would present it as what I call "memory-truth." I *feel* this story my mother told me, feel it as strongly as I recall that one night our West Indian friends left the island, feel it as surely as I know that I broke my collar bone in summer camp . . . as loudly as if I still hear the snap.

But if I want documentation that Penny and her tail existed, I'm out of luck.

Well, not really. Because what's most important — both for writers and readers of memoir — is to understand not only what memoir is, but also what it isn't. While it's not acceptable to make up facts willy-nilly when writing about your life, it *is* acceptable to convey your individual version of events — your memory-truth. Readers know that memory is slippery. They know when they sit down to read a memoir that what they are really reading, what the author is really saying, is, "This is how I remember events." Readers know we don't run a video camera 24/7 or record conversations. Intelligent readers know I'm conveying how events *felt* and *seemed* to me, what they mean to me *now*. Memoir is not journalism. It's not supposed to be. When I write memoir, my goal isn't transcription or reportage. Nor do I make stuff up. My interpretation of events forms a reality that is uniquely mine — my truth — how I understand my own life. As Robert Coles writes, memory is "a kind of witness . . . shaped by a moral intelligence . . . Subjectivity and imagination have yet to be declared enemies of what is 'true.' " And what is commonly called "fact" is frequently difficult to pin down in any event. How many eyewitnesses to the same crime provide wildly differing accounts? Events are dynamic. We also rely on *interpretation,* yet interpretation can change with time. Back in college, for example, I thought the fact that the man gave me his maroon scarf was cool. Now, I think the fact that I *needed* the scarf is *sad.* The fact that the scarf exists is factually true, but in one version the scarf is "cool" while, in another, it's "sad." Events are dynamic.

"[Critics are] so assured that there is a thing called a 'fact' and that it can be found like a lost sock, and that once you've found it that's all you've got to do, state a fact. And I think that misrepresents entirely the way the faculty of memory works."—Patricia Hampl, from "We Were Such a Generation"

In a roundtable discussion in *Fourth Genre*, the nonfiction writer Michele Morano, author of *Grammar Lessons: Translating a Life in Spain*, addresses how she handles fact, truth, and memory in her work:

> Occasionally I find a glaring error in my memory that I can't bring myself to correct. The way I remember an incident is too powerful and the emotional truth of the incident is too closely tied to that memory for me to change it. If it's a small matter, I'll let it go. If it's something larger, I'll try to signal to the reader that there's a discrepancy between truth and memory, which in itself can be really interesting. The real messiness of accuracy comes when the experience I'm writing about involves other people, who may not remember things the way I do or who may not want their stories told. This is a perpetual problem for the nonfiction writer, and there's no clear answer for how to deal with it. Writing from personal experience and from memory involves . . . grappling with questions of truth and accuracy and fairness, which is really hard. But the positive side is that tremendous power can come from those negotiations as well.

The subjectivity of truth and the nature of memory are issues that concern most memoirists. As Mary Karr, author of *The Liar's Club*, says, she's sure that she's "forgotten, blurred, or misremembered a zillion events, characters, details large and small." However, she goes on to say, "it's understood that memoir is not an act of history but an act of memory, . . . innately corrupt. That said, I believe a writer makes a contract with the reader to tell the truth."

Yet Karr also acknowledges that, "As soon as you start to leave things out—to shape a tale—you're maneuvering the actual." What she means, I think, is that we can't — nor would we want to — duplicate exact moments in time. Instead, we select which details to include, which to leave out. We manipulate time. All these decisions structure our artistic endeavors. The goal of memoir is less to replicate life and more to craft it into art. We're writing a life, not xeroxing it. If I were to exactly recount any given day, even the most exciting day of my life, the document would be boring. Writing memoir relies on choosing which details to present, which events best represent the particular story I wish to tell.

For example, suppose you write about your marriage over a ten-year period. In one section maybe you describe a party in 1990, when you first realize you no longer love your spouse. The rest of that particular day, leading up to the party, is of no consequence for this narrative. Instead of burdening the work with meaningless details, you juxtapose details of the 1990 party with those, say, of a similar one in 1980, when you first realize you want to marry this person. Details better cohere when following a thematic arc rather than a simple chronological structure. Is this manipulation of time equivalent to lying? No. It's a more honest way to tell your memory-truth; it's the way to craft a life into art.

In other instances, memoirists may not even remember the exact chronology of events. To return to the maroon-scarf man, for example, once I finally wrote about him I no longer recalled on which date he actually gave me the scarf, though I remembered *how* he gave it to me. Does it matter, in terms of the memoir's inherent accuracy, whether he gave me the scarf the first week of October or the last week? Probably not. What I write still represents the lived moment. The maroon scarf itself is the constant fact, the tangible detail through which I enter a portal of memory into the scene, allowing me to explore its metaphoric significance. Memoir relies on twining objective facts with subjective truth. At the same time, it also explores the meaning and the metaphor behind these truths. Metaphoric truth is as important as historical fact. You are exploring your life's narrative — as opposed to a mere listing of it.

Danielle Trussoni explains how these various elements of memoir work in conjunction with each other. While writing her memoir *Falling Through the Earth*, she relied on facts to describe her father crawling through tunnels built by the Vietcong during the Vietnam War. Trussoni researched the culture and military history of Vietnam, even going so far as to visit the tunnels themselves, years later. But once she established this factual side of the story, she "entered into a more imaginative process, where I attempted to reconstruct characters and scenes from my life. I made a conscious decision to rely on memory, keeping all of the nuances and colorations of my point of view."

> Memory itself is a reality. The way that events are tinted through individual experience—like a hand-colored photograph—is one of the great themes of memoir.

A related issue is how to balance the (albeit subjective) truth you want to convey in memoir with the desire to disguise the identity of certain people in order to protect their privacy. Is it a lie or a necessity to use, at times, composite characters or to disguise friends? For most of us, used judiciously, such devices are necessities. In my own work, while each character/persona is based on a specific person, I usually try to protect non-family-members by changing names, perhaps, or hair colors, or professions, or how many children they have; in short, I change a few details. It's possible to protect privacy (as much as possible) in this way, while still capturing the essential truth of that person. A rule of thumb you might follow is, during the writing process, to honor the privacy of friends and family in such a way that allows you to feel most comfortable — knowing that your editor or a publisher's attorney might suggest additional changes later.

If you're using composite characters and/or if you don't have photos, legal documents, or corroborating evidence as to what factually happened, then be honest with your readers. You can always insert a disclaimer in the front of the book simply stating that this is a work of memory, not historical fact. But also understand that memory is neither true nor false. It just *is*. Don't spend months and years doubting your recollection in a way that prevents you from writing. Trust memories. Trust feelings. Write *your* truth, how *you* remember events. Writing, in fact, will bring you *closer* to your truth. I frequently retrieve previously forgotten details once I immerse myself in the senses of the scene, once I develop those shadowy photographs into detailed imagery. I ask myself: *how did that spring evening smell when my high school boyfriend broke up with me?* Of lilacs? Damp lilacs. Yes, now I remember . . . and the scene blossoms onto the page. As Joel Agee says, "The liar steals truth; the artist creates it." Or, to quote Richard Rodriguez, the purpose of "writing is to get us back to the mystery of our lives."

The only thing readers won't forgive is an out-and-out lie. Nor should they. Otherwise, if you write well enough, and authentically enough, readers will know that you're *discovering* your truths, and will be eager to accompany you on the journey.

> Memory is not the history of what happened; memory is the history of our **story** of what happened.

What Readers Understand about Memoirs

One reason for the recent healthy explosion of memoirs, *confessional* memoirs, is because our stories, the stories of "outsiders," people considered "other," people who challenge accepted societal norms, have been silenced for so long. Until relatively recently, we seldom read about the innermost stories of, say, addicts, survivors of troubled childhoods, gays and lesbians, people of color, political subversives. Additionally, until recently, it was considered impolite for *anyone*, regardless of background, ethnicity, religion, or gender, to share intimate secrets in public. Traditionally, there's been a dearth of books written by ordinary people who render their life stories in extraordinary (literary) ways.

But readers *want* confessional stories. Readers better understand their own lives by reading how *you* coped with adversity, what you learned from it. Here are just a few statistics that would seem to reflect what these books would mean to the public.

- One out of four women is sexually molested by the time she is eighteen. Five thousand women died within a seventeen-month period preceding the terrorist attacks of 9/11 (in which 2,948 people perished) — a result of domestic violence.
- According to FBI statistics, of the 9,652 people in the U.S. who were the target of hate crimes in 2006, 52 percent were targeted because of their race. Intriguingly, the state of Alabama reported only a single hate crime, while the state of Mississippi reported none at all.
- According to a John Jay College of Criminal Justice study commissioned by the United States Conference of Catholic Bishops, eleven thousand allegations of sexual abuse were made between 1950 and 2002. Yet 30 percent weren't even investigated because the alleged perpetrator had died, leaving thousands of victims — the majority of them male — without recourse.

Growing up, I spent hours in bookstores and libraries, but memoirs written about any of the above subjects were so rare I never noticed any sitting on the shelves — nor would I have even thought to look. Friends and teachers discussed favorite novels, but I have no recollection of anyone saying, "You've got to read this wonderful new memoir." All the more urgent, then, for us to write and promote our stories. In addition to the obvious importance of good literature for its own sake, readers want to feel connected to — and learn from — others' narratives. After Mark Doty published his memoir about his partner dying of AIDS, after he began to receive letters from others likewise encountering loss, Doty realized, "I began to think about the book as something . . . useful to people who were themselves in a state of new grief, or anticipating grief; I hoped to make my experience in some way of use."

"Let us go forth with fear and courage and rage to save the world."—Grace Paley

Most memoirists I know interact with their readers in ways that novel-ists and poets usually don't. (The ratio of letters written in response to my memoirs, versus my poetry collection, is a few hundred to one!) In my case, people, mainly women, e-mail me or post messages on my Web site to let me know what happened to them — letting me know that I've told their story, too.

As we write, we never tell only our own stories. Even if facts differ, we still respond to commonly felt underlying emotions.

Discover the emotion and depth to *your* story. Write it down. Your readers will feel this urgency, too.

> By reading memoir, we learn more about our own humanity, more about ourselves as well as the world. Readers want to accompany writers on their journeys. Confessional writers are emotional guides.

What the Media Doesn't Understand
about Confessional Stories

What's the first question I'm asked on a live radio-telephone interview shortly after *Love Sick* is published?

"Where's the kinkiest place you've ever had sex?"

I am speechless. I want to hang up the phone. I want to put the male radio host calling from Denver on hold and call my therapist, ask him what I should do. Maybe I should have been prepared, but I am caught off guard. Humiliated. I want to say: *That's not what my memoir is about.* It's about *recovering* from sex addiction. It's about recovering from in-cest. It's about discovering the meaning of this narrative. It's about ex-ploring the language of addiction.

He doesn't ask about that. Instead, since I haven't sensationalized myself in my writing, he does it for me. Since I don't trash myself in my writing, he trashes me. Since I've written no sexually graphic scenes in the memoir, he, in effect, is stealing my story and writing the base scenes himself. One way or another, I *will* be sensationalized. Not by me but by him.

William Kittredge, in *Hole in the Sky*, explores our need to write stories about how "home should be named . . . sacred," how we should "take serious care, making use of the place where we live."

I agree: memoirs about the home front should be considered sacred, as sacred as stories about war, for example. Yet why are members of the media and society, broadly speaking, more likely to honor stories written by hostages, prisoners of war, or soldiers who have fought in foreign, faraway places? Aren't stories about domestic civil wars, stories of abused women and children, domestic POWs and homebound hostages — just as acute? Yet when we write about our wars closer to home, or even *in* the home, we are frequently, and pejoratively, labeled "confessional" writers. Whiny. Michael Skube, for example, writes particularly hostile book reviews in the *Atlanta Journal-Constitution*, proclaiming that Linda Katherine Cutting's incest memoir, *Memory Slips*, is more "therapy . . . than memoir." In another article, he writes, "People are spilling their guts out, confessing the unimaginable and sometimes the purely imaginary. We've gone tabloid. Infidelity, which can at least be interesting, is old hat. Boring. Incest is in — all in the family, you could say."

Contrast this with a *New York Times* review of Senator Bob Dole's memoir, *One Soldier's Story*, in which the reviewer says that "Mr. Dole is not much of a writer . . . he is not introspective, and his natural style is terse. He does not like to dwell on his difficulties . . . But the facts have their own power, and Mr. Dole's habit of understatement works to his advantage." Even though, according to the *Times*, Dole's writing isn't elegant, even though his memoir (which, by definition, requires interior analysis) lacks introspection, and even though he doesn't dwell on difficulty (one of the hallmarks of memoir), the *Times* recommends we read it anyway.

Ironically, when the media glorifies these traditional male roles, it also becomes more difficult for men themselves to break their own stereotypes and write their own books from the home front.

There are men who have, nonetheless, been expanding the genre of memoir by exploring more internal journeys, as evidenced by such authors as Lee Martin (*From Our House*), Richard Hoffman (*Half the House*), Greg Bottoms (*Angelhead: My Brother's Descent into Madness*), Floyd Skloot (*In the Shadow of Memory*), and James McBride (*The Color of Water: A Black Man's Tribute to His White Mother*). And while I hope that one day all books will be judged individually by merit alone — not by genre or subject matter or by the ethnicity or sexual orientation of the author — so far this hasn't happened.

For example, *Newsweek* denigrates memoirs *and* novels about incest by headlining one 1994 review, which focuses on Marilyn French's *Our Father*, "They're Daddy's Little Girls." The message is clear that writers, regardless of genre, should avoid the subject altogether: "Victims, victims everywhere . . ." the article accuses. "It's all part of the culture of victimization." *Esquire*, meanwhile, excerpted *Love Sick*, labeling it "The Least Successful Attempt at Prurience," failing to recognize that the point of the passage was *not* to arouse, but rather to show sex addiction as emotional and spiritual suicide.

This resistance to intimate stories is pervasive. In an article in *Poets & Writers*, Azita Osanloo, a fiction writer, claims that "memoir [has become] the publishing world's version of reality television." She also suggests that memoirists are merely trying to cash in on the fact that they "live more dysfunctionally, more tragically, more multiculturally, more *exotically* than anyone else." Anthony Brandt, the former essay editor for the prestigious Pushcart Prize anthology, states, in an even more disturbing article, that "the genre [creative nonfiction] encourages a certain amount of self-indulgence, if not outright narcissism. What's easier, after all, than writing about yourself? All the facts, the memories, lie before you. You usually don't have to look anything up." What's particularly distressing is that Brandt doesn't understand the most basic tenets of memoir! He even goes on to say that feminist essays rarely have any "literary value."

Let me be sure to acknowledge that many memoirs are, thankfully, embraced by the media — and by our fellow writers. Even Osanloo grudgingly admits that "memoir, in its purest form, enables a writer to uncover those aspects of our culture that have eluded us." The point, though, is that memoir is the only literary form taken to task as an *entire genre*, simply because of the personal, revelatory nature of its subject matter. In a panel presentation at the 2007 NonfictioNow Conference at the University of Iowa, Sonya Huber (author of *Opa Nobody*) asks "whether this phenomenon reflects the frequency with which women and members of other minorities find voice in the genre? Is there a connection between these 'outsider' voices and the ease with which this work is dismissed as technically substandard, unworthy, or pandering to public tastes that are assumed to be coarse or base?"

According to Tom Payton, publisher of Hill Street Press, there are "unjustified stigmas attached to books such as Rosemary Daniell's *Fatal Flowers: On Sin, Sex, and Suicide in the Deep South* — and those about child abuse — within the mainstream media." Payton believes that book reviewers need to realize that, "While their mission is not one of social activism (arguably, that is the author's role), nevertheless, burying these important stories is a life and death matter." Payton, in an e-mail interview with me, explained, "Writing can save lives, a message the mainstream media tends to ignore." Sonya Huber, during the above-mentioned panel, addressed this tendency of critics to minimize the lives of the disenfranchised:

> The question for me is: what deep and underlying cultural currents are these critics giving voice to? Let's turn away from the memoirs to think about the critics and these statements. There are certain interesting strains that run through their dismissal of memoir. The first, to generalize, is that if it's about "bad" sex — rape, sexual dysfunction, the end of a sexual relationship, incest, non-heterosexual — it's over-sharing. If the information fits with cultural expectations of sex as bliss and euphoria, the framing is individually liberating.

Rita Felski, a professor at the University of Virginia, offers additional insight as to why critics seem to take the disenfranchised to task. In her article "On Confession," published in the anthology *Women, Autobiography, and Theory*, she writes, "The recognition that women's lives are not private but communal is perhaps the most fundamental message underlying feminist confession." What this means, she explains, is that whereas some men view confession as "degeneration of the public realm into an unseemly obsession with private affairs," a woman's perspective is just the opposite.

In academia, where we would expect a broader perspective, I've even found some uneasiness in terms of writing about personal experience. The authors of the article "The Ethics of Requiring Students to Write about Their Personal Lives" try to dissuade English professors from assigning the writing of essays about traumatic childhood events, such as incest and child abuse, fearing students might feel undue distress; additionally, the authors worry that teachers will inflate grades, given the "emotionally charged" content. The article goes on to claim that "students who rely on their own knowledge and perceptions for writing assignments are not asked to engage in the rigorous thinking required to grapple with a world outside their immediate ken."

Dr. Gail Griffin, professor of English at Kalamazoo College (author of *Calling: Essays on Teaching in the Mother Tongue*), disagrees. In an e-mail interview with me, Griffin asserts that "whether it be student papers or professional writing, good autobiography is the opposite of navel-gazing and narcissism. Instead, it draws the path from the self to the world and describes the constant circle of energy between the self and its contexts — family, culture, society, history."

The authors of the above-mentioned article (who mainly, but not solely, refer to undergraduates in composition classes) also deem it unwise to ask working-class students or students of color to write their stories, fearing they might feel "shame" when asked to bring attention to their ethnicities or underprivileged backgrounds. However, as Dr. John Price, professor of English at the University of Nebraska, Omaha (and author of the memoir *Man Killed by Pheasant and Other Kinships*) notes in an e-mail interview with me, "When I assign this article in my creative nonfiction classes, which include experienced and inexperienced writers of many different ages, ethnicities, and class backgrounds, they usually pick up on this condescension immediately — 'Who are they to tell me I can't write about my life?'" Price sums up his — and his students' — reactions to this article by observing that "what appears to be an attempt to protect students, ultimately becomes a mandate to silence them."

Students ultimately, of course, have the choice to reveal as much or as little as they want — on any topic. How I wish one of my college professors had encouraged me to write about myself. I might have understood the truth of my life years earlier.

Why do narratives by those of us labeled — or *mis*labeled — "other" elicit such negative reactions? Perhaps we've hit raw, wounded nerves. After all, if I confront my demons, am I not (covertly) asking you to confront yours?

A Hysterical [*sic*] History of Criticism

Memoir, or literary nonfiction, is not just a contemporary art form — far from it. Montaigne, the acknowledged "Godfather" of nonfiction, popularized the personal essay in the sixteenth century. Even though no woman has officially been anointed God*mother* of memoir or nonfiction, I would point to Anne Frank, who, in *The Diary of Anne Frank*, richly twines the personal story of a young woman coming of age with the horrific backdrop of the Holocaust. In short, even though the form only recently underwent a revolution in terms of subject matter, it evolves from a long literary tradition in terms of its writing and its critiquing. Ben Yagoda, in an article in *Slate*, "A Brief History of Memoir-Bashing: It's Almost as Old as the Memoir Itself," provides interesting examples of the love-hate relationship between critics and the memoir.

For example, Samuel Johnson said in 1759 that autobiographies, where "the writer tells his own story," provide a "certainty of knowledge [that] not only excludes mistake, but fortifies veracity." According to Yagoda, the memoir's fortunes changed in 1825, when Henry Mackenzie wrote that "the confession of a person to himself instead of the priest — generally gets absolution too easily."

The pendulum swung from hate back to love when literary critic Leslie Stephen (1832–1907) proclaimed, "Autobiography . . . is so generally interesting, that I have frequently thought ... it should be considered as a duty by all eminent men; and, indeed, by men not so eminent." While he rightly understands that memoir is a democratic domain for seemingly "ordinary" men (not just kings, prime ministers, or presidents), he discounts women. Ironically, his own daughter, Virginia Woolf, would later break new ground in both fiction and memoir. William Dean Howells (1837–1920) advocates that even more voices should be heard, stating his "wish that more women would write their own lives ... [and] not restrict autobiography to any age or sex, creed, class or color."

But just when you think it's safe to write memoir, William Gass, according to Yagoda, violently turns against it in a 1994 article in *Harper's*: "Are there any motives for the enterprise that aren't tainted with conceit or a desire for revenge or a wish for justification? To halo a sinner's head? To puff an ego already inflated past safety?"

From here, the pendulum seems stuck in the "hate" position. Yagoda's article tells us that, in 1996, James Atlas proclaims: "Why this pull toward the anatomy of self? In part it reflects a phenomenon pervasive in our culture — people confessing in public to an audience of voyeurs." Atlas is followed by *Vanity Fair* writer James Wolcott, who labels memoirists as "navel-gazers," going on to say that the genre is "a big earnest blob of me-first sensibility." Next to weigh in (according to Yagoda) is Daphne Merkin who, in 1998, states that "ours is a culture addicted to exposure, to 'outing' ourselves and others." Michiko Kakutani, book reviewer of the *New York Times*, follows, and while acknowledging that some memoirs are "genuinely moving accounts," most, according to her, are "ridiculously exhibitionistic monologues that like to use the word 'survivor' (a word once reserved for individuals who had lived through wars or famines or the Holocaust) to describe people coping with weight problems or bad credit."

Equally incomprehensible is the view of New Journalism author Tom Wolfe, who likewise takes potshots at memoirists for not using the rigid research techniques he claims to employ in such books as *The Right Stuff*. "A memoir today is like Wikipedia: it is possible that parts of it are actually true," he snarkily writes in a letter to the editor in *Harper's*.

Another critic who truly doesn't get it is *Washington Monthly* writer Lorraine Adams who, in 2002, attacked "the rise of the 'nobody' memoir." The gist of her argument questions the entire genre of memoir written by "'nobodies,' those who are neither generals, statesmen, celebrities nor their kin." What Ms. Adams implies, in effect, is that unless you're famous, there's not much point in writing your story. According to her, your *own life* is out-of-bounds, unimportant — even if crafted into literature. Her embrace of the "eminent" author is a quaint, old-fashioned, undemocratic notion that would dismiss, among others, slave narratives such as *Incidents in the Life of a Slave Girl* by Harriet Ann Jacobs.

So, **are** there bad memoirs? Of course. But aren't there bad poetry collections and novels, too? Yes—though I'm not aware of critics attacking the entire genre of either.

In short, there appears to be a direct correlation between the popularity of memoir and the vitriolic attack of it; the more we tell our stories, the more some critics want us to stop. And while it is true that all memoirs aren't created equal — some *are* sensational or poorly written — still, in a broader sense, I feel that the above critics fail to understand the importance of everyday people finding significance in an otherwise ordinary life. The vast majority of us aren't writing stories ripped from the headlines, to be discarded with yesterday's newspaper.

While Gass, Atlas, Wolcott, Kakutani, Adams, and Wolfe would seem to discredit both men's and women's memoirs, nevertheless, in the current climate, it seems that women's stories remain the most misunderstand and marginalized. For example, Carol Hebald, poet and author of the memoir *The Heart Too Long Suppressed*, about childhood sexual and emotional abuse, receives a fairly solid review in *Publishers Weekly*, but then the reviewer ends by saying that the work "combines solid prose with an Oprah-esque saga of overcoming adversity." But "author publicity will help this book, especially given its inspirational ending." In the mouth of *Publishers Weekly*, "inspirational" makes Hebald's book sound unliterary, as if it is a lesser work. Contrast this with a review of Brian Keenan's *An Evil Cradling: The Five-year Ordeal of a Hostage*, about Keenan's time in Beirut, teaching at the American University, when he was kidnapped by fundamentalist Shiite militiamen and held hostage. *Publishers Weekly* calls it "a riveting and terrifying read that finally ends with the exhilaration of Keenan's inexplicable release."

Don't get me wrong: men writing of war deserve to be heard. It's tragic that Keenan was held hostage, that Bob Dole suffered a wartime injury. But aren't children who are raped and hurt by parents, or wives beaten by husbands, also injured, also held captive, also tortured? Aren't their stories equally important? Shouldn't their lives be written, their books taken seriously and not belittled? As Adrienne Rich said, "Women have been driven mad . . . for centuries by the refutation of our experience and our instincts in a culture which validates only male experience." When we learn more about the human heart in *all* its complexity, we better understand the world.

> "Some people think of autobiographical writing as the precious occupation of the unusually self-absorbed. Couldn't the same accusation be hurled at a lyric poet, at a novelist— at anyone with the audacity to present the personal point of view? True memoir is written, like all literature, in an attempt to find not only a self but a world. The self-absorption that seems to be the impetus and embarrassment of autobiography turns into . . . a hunger for the world."
> —Patricia Hampl

Because I, too, believe that memoirs from the home front feed our hunger for knowledge about our world, I have finally decided to embrace the words "inspirational" and "confessional," in order to own them. So when Tom Wolfe writes that "the only thing that can be said for memoirs is that readers have loved them for at least five centuries," I choose to see in his attempt at dismissiveness an acknowledgment of the power and tradition of the memoir.

So I am now proud to call myself a writer of confessional literature —*fearless* literature. I embrace the "confessional" label because, even though some critics refuse to judge our work by its literary merits, even though some in the literary world do not take our stories seriously, we ourselves must never overlook the equally important and much more heartfelt responses we receive.

After I completed a reading at a library in Athens, Georgia, one woman waited until everyone else had departed. Approaching me, she was so scared she began to cry. She confided that I was the first person she'd told that her father had molested her. She was too traumatized even to tell a therapist. Why did she confide in me, trust me? Maybe because we both survived the war on the home front — without commendations, without purple hearts. Just hearts that are human and, therefore, heroic.

WRITING EXERCISES

The following exercises are designed to help writers overcome their fear of revealing secrets, fear within themselves as well as concern with what others might think.

1. Write a short paragraph about the thing you were most afraid to tell your mother growing up, or the thing that you're still most afraid to tell her now.

2. Make a list of the reasons why you're scared to write secrets. Then, make a second list enumerating why you think it would be a good decision to tell these secrets anyway. Which list, in balance, makes the stronger argument?

3. Who is the person whose potential reaction to your memoir most scares you? Write him/her a letter, whether you send it or not. Tell this person all the reasons why you must write your story, why your story

is important, why your voice must be heard and not forgotten . . . why you must write anyway.

4. Mark Doty says that after his memoir was published,

> I learned that people were hugely grateful for directness, for the portrayal of struggle. I felt less alone in the world. I felt that writing had a practical kind of agency — that is, that it mattered to people and that people *used* it . . . I was hugely grateful for this. I got amazing letters from people who had experienced every sort of loss you can imagine, and they were remarkably heartfelt and powerful.

Write a long paragraph that explores why you think you will feel less alone after writing your memoir. Why do you think your memoir will be of use to others?

The Meandering River

An Overview of the Subgenres
of Creative Nonfiction

The genre of creative nonfiction is a long river with many moods and currents. And even though it traverses waterscapes as diverse as the Mississippi, the Amazon, and the Nile, there are seven basic forms — or ports of call, if you will — which we might explore. At the head of the river lie the categories of biography and autobiography. From here, we flow on to immersion writing (or other forms of New Journalism) in which the author immerses him- or herself in an experience, before traveling on to memoir, to personal essay (including nature and travel writing), to the meditative essay, finally spilling into the lyric essay. In brief, then, the river flows from a relatively exterior focus to an intensely interior one, from a focus on actions and events to one on ideas and emotions. While we begin with a fairly straightforward narrative, we end with one that's diminished or fractured. Yet because this river is a continuum, we'll also find that the ports of call are sometimes so close together that it's difficult to tell where one ends and the other starts.

Let's begin the journey.

Port of Call 1: Biography

A case could be made that biography and autobiography shouldn't be included in the genre of *creative* nonfiction; rather, that they are (or should be) strictly nonfiction, in the same tributary as academic and scholarly writing or journalism. However, given the inevitable subjectivity of the author toward his or her subject, as well as the fact that these two forms have such a long literary tradition, it would be difficult to begin our journey elsewhere.

Biography is a fairly consistent, factual rendering of someone's life, usually a chronological account of "first this happened and then this next thing happened." The author is *supposed* to be objective — although this isn't really possible. While being objective can be a worthy goal, it's a chimera, a necessary fiction. Lawrence Thompson's three-volume biography of Robert Frost is a good example of this subjectivity.

Thompson, Frost's authorized biographer, grew to dislike his subject, and allowed his aversion to become part of the text. Especially in the final volume of the biography, Thompson paints Frost as a man who, among other foibles, sees himself as a poet whose gifts to the world aren't fully appreciated. "He wanted the consultantship [in poetry to the Library of Congress] to be treated as an office in which his views would be listened to by the men who were running the country, and in which he could achieve significant results for his 'cause': poetry, the arts — and (not inconsequentially) his own reputation." The quotation marks around *cause* and the parenthetical insertion of "not inconsequentially" reveal Thompson's changed feelings toward Frost.

More recently, the poet and novelist Jay Parini released his own Frost biography, with its own subjective elements, albeit different from Thompson's. Indeed, according to reviewer Melanie Kirkpatrick, "Parini is a fan of Frost's, and seeks, in *Robert Frost: A Life*, to dispel the mythos created by Thompson." I doubt Parini would disagree with that characterization, even though it suggests he, too, has an agenda.

In an interview with Paul Holler in the online journal *Bookslut*, Parini talks about his own expansive view of biography:

> I make few distinctions between straight biographies and novels. They both are works of fiction. Fiction means "shaping" in Latin. I shape reality in both genres. There are demands that come from the genre itself: You can't really change points of view in a biography, and you can't make things up; but I think these are small considerations, and that in general they both involve creating narratives, and narrative is what I like: telling a story.

Although Parini doesn't go so far as to actually "make things up," other biographers do. The most famous example is Edmund Morris's *Dutch: A Memoir of Ronald Reagan*, in which Morris writes himself as a character into scenes where he was not present. Even though the reader knows Morris isn't physically present, nevertheless, wouldn't it be more honest for Morris to admit up front that objectivity is impossible to achieve? Have Morris, on the one hand (by reimagining events in order to make elements of Reagan's life more immediate), and Parini and Thompson on the other (by having a subjective point of view), subverted the whole notion of nonfiction?

What's real, what's fact — what, in effect, nonfiction *is* — is a question our metaphorical river runs into again and again.

Port of Call 2: Autobiography

Autobiography is likewise, theoretically at least, a factual retelling of events. Like biography, autobiography is celebrity oriented (Elizabeth Taylor writes an autobiography; Ms. Ordinary Woman writes a memoir), based on the subject's "life of action," and thus told more historically than impressionistically — unlike a memoir. The contract with the reader in the case of autobiography is that the historical facts, at least, are true. For example, when President Clinton writes in his autobiography *My Life* that, after his reelection, the United States stopped enforcing the arms embargo in Bosnia, we believe him. Likewise, when he writes about his Middle Class Bill of Rights, we believe the particulars of the bill. After all, we could check these facts in newspapers. Where the book's assertions might be debatable, however, is when Clinton *subjectively* analyzes the successes (or failures) of his policies in order to enhance his presidential legacy.

Unlike biography, autobiography allows some room for personal reflection. In fact, when the private, personal life intrudes upon the public persona, autobiography hovers closer to memoir — for example, when Clinton depicts, albeit in very general terms, his affair with Monica Lewinsky. Yet even as he allows the reader a glimpse of the personal man, the glimpse is just that: there's little reflection or psychological analysis. Instead, he uses generic terms such as "inappropriate encounter" and "selfish stupidity." His deepest exploration of a connection between the affair and a troubled childhood — which would be a gold mine for a memoirist — is his mention that, by keeping the affair secret, he once again lived parallel lives, much as he had as a teenager when his alcoholic stepfather abused his mother.

Since autobiography relies on a retelling of events as they happened, the Lewinsky affair is merely one stop along the way of the written life. In the paragraph following his relatively brief discussion about the affair, Clinton describes a meeting with Prime Minister Netanyahu, saying, in effect: *I had an inappropriate encounter with Monica Lewinsky. I met with Netanyahu. I addressed Congress. I flew to Ireland.* Autobiography — unlike memoir, as we will see — tends toward both a certain documentary sensibility and a well-defined chronological structure. Also, since the goal of the celebrity autobiographer is usually to place him- or herself in a positive light, it's frequently not a search for moral or emotional truths or psychological insight. Autobiographers aren't "likely to explore or to reveal painful and intimate memories," notes critic Estelle Jelinek.

Port of Call 3: Immersion

In the immersion essay or book, the author, as the name implies, *immerses* him- or herself in an experience typically outside of his or her familiar milieu. Immersion writers use the voice of an engaged participant, one who writes in first person, sets scenes, employs sensory description, structures the work with an arc — as opposed to the flatter, more linear voice of a journalist who covers a story with the sole aim of objectivity.

There are two basic ways to approach the immersion book or essay. In the first, the author is the protagonist, thus maintaining a strong, consistent "I" throughout, as in Barbara Ehrenreich's *Nickel and Dimed: On (Not) Getting by in America.* Ehrenreich investigates how the working class survives on the minimum wage, or worse. Rather than rely on interviews, research, labor reports, and statistics — as a journalist would — she herself works such low-paying jobs as waitress and cleaning woman. She is *in* the story; she's part of it. She writes of her experiences with direct and intimate knowledge.

In the second method, the author also writes in the first-person point of view, but isn't as literally a participant in the story. Instead, the author deals with a broader context or more distant experience. For example, in *King Leopold's Ghost: A Story of Greed, Terror, and Heroism in Colonial Africa*, Adam Hochschild obviously couldn't participate in colonial events that subjugated the Belgian Congo. Nevertheless, through documents, research, interviews, and trips to the area, he immerses his emotional and psychic self into the events as much as possible. He writes with a clearly subjective regard for the events, as opposed to the dispassionate voice of an academic or journalist, or the more objective view of a biographer. Hear his voice when he first learns of the Congo's "killing fields" in a book he just happened to be reading: "Why were these deaths not mentioned in the standard litany of . . . horrors? And why had I never heard of them? I had been writing about human rights for years." It was an "atrocious scandal," Hochschild continues, using language such as "blood spilled in anger" and "torn flesh." Just as Ehrenreich empathizes with those who struggle to survive on the minimum wage, so does Hochschild feel immersed in the terror of King Leopold's reign.

In the following section from Hochschild's essay "Isle of Flowers, House of Slaves," we see how, through careful selection of detail as well as the first-person point of view, he manages to immerse both himself and the reader in the action.

These days few spots are purely in the Third World or the First. In Dakar, Senegal, the sun-drenched, crumbling one-time colonial capital of French West Africa, bits of Europe are scattered . . . like an archipelago. The First World islands are sleek [with] high-rise resort hotels . . . Virtually all the guests are white. In . . . bars . . . a liter bottle of Vittel mineral water costs the equivalent of several days' wages for a Senegalese laborer . . .

Farther down [the] road, iron fences have gaps in them; coils of

barbed wire on top have half rusted away . . . As I jog along the road
early one morning, men are urinating in the street, getting up after
sleeping the night in the ruins of buildings.

Even though this essay is more about Dakar than about Hochschild
—he doesn't refer to himself until the second paragraph, more or less in
passing: "As I jog along . . ."—his presence, nevertheless, is felt throughout. He is the guide between these two worlds. His slant on the details
reveals as much about *his* sensibilities as it does about Dakar. It's wrong
for some to have so much while others have so little, he implies. Therefore, compared to biography or autobiography, an immersion essay or
book gives the reader access to a deeper, more emotionally authentic
exploration of the author's subject. This isn't a straight, factual recounting as with a journalist's "who, what, when, where, and why?" questions,
either. The immersion writer guides the reader on an emotional as well
as factual journey.

It is also worth noting the distinction between immersion writing
and personal essays. In the latter, authors *don't* tend to stray far from
their own habitats or familiar emotional landscapes. In immersion
writing, as shown, the author usually immerses him- or herself in an
environment quite distinct from his or her "normal" life: Ehrenreich is
not a minimum-wage worker; Hochschild examines the Belgian Congo
from the vantage point of another century. One of the early works of
New Journalism is *Paper Lion: Confessions of a Last-String Quarterback*
by George Plimpton, who "joined" the Detroit Lions football team to
discover what it was like to be a professional football player — and then
write about it. In short, unlike the personal essayist (whom we'll explore in a moment), the author immerses him- or herself in "events"
solely to write about them.

Port of Call 4: Memoir

Midpoint on our figurative river is the memoir, the subgenre most
people associate with creative nonfiction, since it most obviously employs many of the same techniques we encounter in fiction: dialogue,

setting, character development, plot, and metaphor. In the forms already explored, the text generally follows a relatively straightforward, chronological recounting of events; here, however, the story begins to find a more personal, emotional arc to follow. Unlike biography and autobiography, a memoir isn't about a whole life but, rather, one aspect of it. It's imperative that the author establish her or his clearly defined theme and focus.

What also distinguishes memoir from autobiography is the use of at least two "voices" to tell the story, to explore the depth of events: one I call an "innocent" voice, the other an "experienced" voice. The innocent voice relates the facts of the story, the surface subject, the action — not altogether unlike autobiography. It conveys the experience of the relatively unaware persona the author was when the events actually happened. Whether the events are loosely connected by chronology or not, this voice gives the story a sense of "this happened, and then this happened, and then this next thing happened." It is the action, the external part of the story.

The experienced voice, on the other hand, plunges us deeper into the story by employing metaphor, irony, and reflection to reveal the author's progression of thought and emotion. It reveals what the facts *mean*, both intellectually and emotionally. Reflection is not just looking back, recollecting or remembering the past. It's a search to see past events or relationships in a new light. The experienced voice conveys a more complex viewpoint, one that interprets and reflects upon the surface subject.

Whether the memoir is essay- or book-length, both voices are crucial: one thrusts the story forward; the other plunges the reader into the real heart of the matter. As these voices intersect throughout the memoir, the author reveals the true nature of the journey.

Lisa D. Chavez's essay, "Independence Day, Manley Hot Springs, Alaska," begins with the innocent voice — the narrator describing how, in 1975, she and her mother depart Southern California for Alaska, seeking a new life. This voice describes the wonders of Manley Hot Springs as seen through the eyes of a twelve-year-old girl:

Instantly I am occupied, walking our dog, wetting the toes of my canvas tennis shoes in the silty current, kicking sprays of gravel into the air. I narrate the scene to myself, add it to the elaborate and constant story I whisper of my adventures in Alaska.

Interspersed with the ongoing story is the experienced voice, the adult author-persona who *now* understands: "I do not see what is in front of me: a shabby small town where people stare openly at that frivolous car — bright orange and marked by its out-of-state plates — and the young woman in white, high-heeled sandals and her daughter that have emerged from it." In addition to the "experienced" voice that can describe the car as "frivolous," Chavez employs subtle metaphorical imagery here as well. By including the detail of the bright orange car, she implicitly compares it to the clothing hunters wear. However, as she goes on to show, *she* is the hunted, not the hunter. She is, as she so accurately says, "marked." She, like the car, is *other*.

This is clearly revealed when the narrator's young self experiences racial hatred. Late one evening, Lisa's mother asks her to walk the dog, and as she leaves their rented room above a bar, she is confronted by a man on the landing pointing a gun at her. " 'I told all you goddamn Indians to get the fuck out of my bar,' he says."

In the following paragraphs, the two voices twine together, the innocent voice narrating how she escapes the man, and the experienced voice reflecting upon the event: "I thought [racism] was something else, people who called black people bad names, people who snickered when they heard my last name. *Mexican*, they'd sneer." Chavez, the author-narrator, deepens the moment even more: "And now I have been shaken into a world I don't understand, a cold, foreign world, where men I don't know can hate me for the way I look." This voice of experience continues to explore her place in the world when she reflects how, in California, her darker skin was envied. There, she even secretly felt "superior." In Alaska, however, "brown skin did not mean beach and health, but it meant something . . . shameful . . . Native . . . I would discover how that word could be spit out with as much disgust as any racial slur."

Because memoir is an examination of self, Chavez's persona at the end of the essay is different from her persona at the beginning. By the end, Chavez comes to understand fear; she sees herself and her world through less innocent eyes. "In just a few years . . . I would learn to put a name to what was happening to me, and learn to be angry . . . Even later, I would learn to mold my anger into something I could use."

The lessons learned in memoir aren't as evident in autobiography. In autobiography the author may no longer be president of the United States or a box-office attraction, yet emotionally, he or she hasn't necessarily changed — at least on the page. With rare exceptions, autobiography isn't about exploring the subject's psyche. Memoir is. Autobiography isn't about turning a life into art. Memoir is. The autobiographer justifies "mistakes." The memoirist explores them. The autobiographer focuses on success while the memoirist tries to decipher how or why life events often go wrong. Memoir, therefore, is not a simple narcissistic examination of self — as some critics claim. By employing many of the same techniques as fiction, poetry, and belles lettres, memoir achieves universality.

Also unlike autobiography, memoir relies almost solely on memory. Memoirists may research old letters, conduct interviews with family members, examine family documents and photographs, but the reliance on one's subjective perceptions of the past is at the heart of memoir. Whereas autobiography tells the story of "what happened" based on historical facts, memoir examines *why* it happened, what the story means.

In terms of memoir, the reader understands and accepts this tacit contract that retrieving "facts" from memory is both a selective and subjective business. Yet, at the same time, a reader *doesn't* "allow" the memoirist to lie or make up facts willy-nilly. As Patricia Hampl says about critics' reactions to memoirs, "They're so assured that there is a thing called a 'fact' and that it can be found like a lost sock, and that once you've found it that's all you've got to do, state a fact. I think that misrepresents entirely the way the faculty of memory works." In short, subjective memory is acceptable, while pure invention isn't.

Port of Call 5: Personal Essay

Whereas memoir is a "slice of a life," the author of a personal essay examines an even slimmer piece of that life or, if you will, one bend in the river. Personal essays encompass such topics as nature and travel, or social and political issues. (To travel to another country as a tourist, without immersing yourself in that country's culture, would lead to a personal essay, as opposed to immersion writing.) Whereas memoir is an exploration of the past, personal essays can explore contemporary — even future — events. Instead of the memoirist's thorough examination of self, soul, or psyche, the personal essayist usually explores one facet of the self within a larger social context.

Memoirs and personal essays do have some things in common, however. In both genres, the author imbues his or her work with a strong personal point of view. In addition, personal essayists, like memoirists, usually don't stray far afield from their own habitats or ways of life. Unlike immersion essayists, who seek to immerse themselves in unfamiliar subject matter, personal essayists tend to write about what they already know well. Annie Dillard, for example, writes about Tinker Creek, close to her home in Virginia, a habitat she knows intimately. Dillard, like many nature writers such as Edward Abbey, Farley Mowat, and Terry Tempest Williams, is already a naturalist and environmentalist by inclination.

In her essay "The Molino," Melani Martinez explores her culture, her way of life, by focusing on the molino — a machine that grinds corn for tamales — as the embodiment of her cultural world. We read three long paragraphs about this "grinder in the back of this old worn-down garage turned kitchen" before we directly meet the narrator herself. We smell and hear the machine and understand its impact on her particular world.

> It fills the room with its smell. A burning cloud. A grinding stone. It eats corn . . . It gobbles it and changes it to something else. To money, to food, to questions and lifestyles. It prepares children for the rest of what will come . . . It is a father. It is a dirty smelly father that works and works and pushes and shoves out the meat of little kernels of corn.

When the narrator finally appears, we learn it is *her* father who owns and operates the molino; this is her environment: "I watched it all," she writes. "The lime-covered caldron of boiling nixtamal and the oar he stirred it with were even older than him . . . All the food and all the people and time that went by in that little garage kitchen." This kitchen is a neighborhood gathering place, where news and gossip are exchanged. In addition, most of the extended family works at the molino, including the author as a child. "My father subjected [me] to child labor before [I] knew how to spell it." By focusing on the molino, Martinez crafts it as a metaphor for the grind of eking out a living in the tamale business in a particular culture and time.

Of course, as Martinez explores the molino and what it represents, we have a strong sense of the author's personal sensibilities: "We [Martinez and her brother] paced the floor of that old garage dreaming of school days as the bottom of our tennis shoes stuck to the grime. Other than the corn, everything was black and filmed with . . . fat . . . It was hot, it was humid, and for us there was no greater hell." As in a memoir, therefore, a personal essay reflects upon the author's experiences. Yet, instead of examining solely herself, Martinez allows the molino, as object and as metaphor, to reveal the secrets it holds for her family as well as for her culture.

Port of Call 6: Meditative Essay

A meditative essay, as the name suggests, explores or meditates upon an emotion or idea by drawing upon a range of experience. It's a contemplation. Unlike the previous forms, the meditative essay is not necessarily triggered by a specific event. For example, Hochschild's essay begins when he visits Dakar; Chavez's essay starts with the move to Alaska. Such events aren't necessary in meditative essays. Instead, an image or an idea may propel it into being.

There are two ways to approach a meditative essay. The first way is to examine an idea or emotion by embodying it, making it physical. Let's say someone you love has just died. The loss seems so big that you want to explore the whole notion of "loss" — not just one specific loss. In order to do so, you must discover objects that embody an otherwise abstract emotion. The abstractions must be rendered tangibly. You must discover images or metaphors to embody the ineffable.

The second way to approach a meditative essay is to begin at the opposite end of the spectrum, with the tangible thing itself. But to consider a physical object deeply one must uncover hidden properties *within* the object. Consider a jar of peanut butter. You might begin by describing the label. But then, as you continue writing, you will open the jar, tangibly and metaphorically, to discover what's inside. It's like unwrapping a present. What do you find inside? Peanut butter, of course! But to meditate upon an object, you must discover *more*, something suggested by the object, something that's not just personal experience, rather, some existential or cultural or social or political insight about peanut butter. John Updike does this in his essay "Beer Can," which is a funny, insightful meditation on the often maddeningly impersonal onslaught of "progress."

Robert Vivian's essay "Light Calling to Other Light" provides another example. It begins with a physical candle, before journeying into the abstract notions of joy and belonging. He writes,

Lately, I have started to push a wide, yellow candle into sunlight . . . I move it . . . to capture the light and to hold it for a while. Then its entire fat body glows from within in a rich, mellow flame, like an improbable Buddha who is dining on the universe. Aglow on the table, it is an homage to light for light's sake.

By the end, he writes of the metaphorical warmth of a candle holding him "in a calm embrace in the duration of the sun passing from morning into darkness." The reader sees that the tangible quality of "light," within the "improbable Buddha," is, metaphorically, the discovery of joy within gloom, which is the theme of this meditation.

In short, the abstract idea needs a tangible body; the tangible object needs a soul. In the meditative essay, we see the ascendancy of the *narrative of image* over the *narrative of action* — a trend that has its roots in the personal essay (think of the imagistic metaphor of Martinez's molino). Here it is the image that drives the work, creating meaning and forming the narrative arc.

Port of Call 7: Lyric Essay

In the lyric essay, as in the meditative essay, the writer is not constrained by a narrative of action; the movement is from image to image, not from event to event. Here, the psyche works more in the mode of poets who "let what will stick to them like burrs where they walk in the fields," to quote Robert Frost. (Parini's good poet, not Thompson's bad one.)

In John D'Agata's "Hall of Fame of Us/Hall of Fame of Them," the very arrangement of words on the page suggests poetry:

> Ergo the town.
> Ergo, also, the fence.
> Most of Rachel, Nevada, lives near this fence.
> Come dusk, at the Little Ale'Inn, the town gets drunk on talk about
>   the fence.

The images propel the essay forward, moving from the town, to the fence, to the people, to talk about the fence. The rhythm of this movement, a rhythm created by the short paragraphs and the elliptical storyline, make the essay seem more poetry than prose. In fact, one reason writers use this form is to explore the boundary between essay and lyric poetry. As D'Agata himself writes in the *Seneca Review*, lyric essays, like poems, "require us to complete their meaning . . . The lyric essay doesn't care about figuring out why papa lost the farm, or why mama took to drink. It's more interested in replicating the feeling of that experience."

In this kind of elliptical writing, not all facts are neatly spelled out, understood, or resolved. The reader is required to fill in the blanks as much as possible while, at the same time, accepting that much will remain mysterious. As with poetry, the reader accepts the emotion of the piece itself as the essential "fact." The accumulation of images forms an emotional whole, if not a traditionally essayistic one.

Toward the Sea

Creative nonfiction is all of the above, and more. Elements of two or more of the subgenres discussed can be combined to create "hybrid" genres as well. In many ways, for example, "The Molino," while at heart a personal essay, also includes elements of memoir in the way the author notes the impact of the molino on her life. At the same time, long passages about the molino itself are reminiscent of a meditative chant.

Myriad experimental structures exist in creative nonfiction as well. For the adventurous, anything goes. Memoirs and essays can be written as montages or mosaics. Harvey Pekar's *American Splendor* series of "graphic memoirs" helps redefine "comic books," while the film version of his life uses documentary to deconstruct the usual Hollywood clichés. In *Nola: A Memoir of Faith, Art, and Madness*, Robin Hemley incorporates short stories both by himself and his mother, as well as his sister's letters and artwork, into his own creative nonfiction text.

Pat Mora, in *House of Houses*, relies on poetic language and magical realism. Reading her work, we feel as if every member of her family, alive and dead, are all present, talking together. Marjane Satrapi, in *Persepolis: The Story of a Childhood*, tells her story about growing up in Iran during the Islamic Revolution through a series of black-and-white illustrations, while Lawrence Sutin, in *A Postcard Memoir*, uses postcards, reproduced in the text, as portals into memory.

Waters Ebb and Flow

So, you're in the middle of writing *something*, but you don't know what. Is it memoir? A meditative piece? "How do I decide?" you ask.

Just as bodies of water all have a common element, so it is with creative nonfiction. As we have seen, the distinctions among these subgenres frequently blur. Therefore, the differences are more in terms of degree than kind. For example, memoirs, personal essays, and meditations can all contain similar elements such as employing one voice that relates the action of the story, and another voice to deepen it metaphorically.

Yet, as with water — some being fresh, some salty — there are differences in creative nonfiction. In autobiography, immersion essays, memoirs, and personal narratives, *action* drives the work. The arc is that of you, your persona, seeking to understand this action. This kind of essay flows in a *current of action*, a series of events you're following on a map of a river.

In a meditative or lyric essay, on the other hand, an *idea* or *emotion* drives the work. You seek to give shape to a thought or idea, making the intangible tangible. These essays flow more in a *current of contemplation*. So while you may not be moving forward in time, you're moving deeper into the metaphorical river.

Whatever port of the river you decide to explore, I hope you'll enjoy the journey.

Three Confessional Essays

These short essays on the writer's process were written especially to share with you, readers of this book: Lynn C. Tolson: "From Process to Product: Using Print-on-Demand to Publish"; Karen Salyer McElmurray: "Gazing: Writing from the Womb"; Michelle Otero: "The Weight of a Word."

In "From Process to Product: Using Print-on-Demand to Publish," Lynn C. Tolson shares with us the important, albeit circuitous, journey she took to write and publish *Beyond the Tears: A True Survivor's Story* (AuthorHouse). Faced with breast cancer, she felt she had to publish her memoir *now*. After initial rejection, she decided to take matters into her own hands and publish the memoir herself. It's a forceful book, one that has helped many other women. Today, more than five years since publishing it, Lynn is doing fine. I had the honor of meeting her at a conference where I conducted a memoir-writing workshop. She's at work on a second memoir. The following is her story about publishing her first one.

From Process to Product: Using Print-on-Demand to Publish
Lynn C. Tolson

You have a story to tell, you've written the book, and you want to see your memoir in print. Herein lies the conundrum: a publisher wants a writer to have a literary agent; an agent wants an author who has already been published. The odds are against the writer because a major publishing house may receive ten thousand submissions per year, yet only 1 percent get published. Even if your book is accepted, it may take years to receive the final product. How does a writer overcome these odds and solve the publishing puzzle? Print-on-demand, a form of self-publishing, may be the right answer. Print-on-demand uses digital technology and the Internet to provide a professional copy of your book.

My memoir, *Beyond the Tears: A True Survivor's Story*, took nearly twenty years from conception to completion. In my twenties, after my suicide attempt, my therapist told me that I had a life story that would serve others. However, the whole story was frozen in solid writer's block. I could not tell of the trauma that led to the suicide attempt because the same family that victimized me had conditioned me to keep secrets. Yet I knew that ultimately I had a story of hope and healing. In my forties, I was hit with a diagnosis of breast cancer. Ironically, that broke the ice. I literally had a deadline to complete my story of childhood trauma and subsequent recovery. My mission was to develop my rough-draft manuscript into a book in mere months.

I researched the methods for finding a publisher and/or agent. I sent numerous carefully crafted query letters to agents and publishers, only to receive rejection slips. Finally, I was invited to publish with a traditional house. But I could not bear the publisher's suggested changes, which bordered on fiction. (My narrative was creative non-fiction.) I was also pursued by a "vanity press" (also known as "subsidy press"). In a face-to-face meeting with the publisher, he informed me that he could provide five thousand cover-to-cover copies if I could pay his fifteen thousand dollar fee. When I balked, the publisher suggested that I put a second mortgage on my house to pay the fees. I continued to research other methods of publishing.

Meanwhile, I protected my work-in-progress by submitting for a copyright. This was an easy and inexpensive task. I paid thirty-five dollars to register the copyright for my material by directly connecting to the Library of Congress Web site and following the instructions.

(Prices and procedures may have changed.) A publishing company may also arrange the copyright for the author. It is up to the writer to decide if she wants to copyright all of her material.

While reading periodicals related to writers, such as *Poets & Writers*, I learned about the print-on-demand publishing companies. I researched AuthorHouse (then known as 1stBooks), Xlibris, and iUniverse. Even more print-on-demand companies are now available for a new author's consideration and comparison. Most print-on-demand publishers can make the book available in three months from the time the author sends the manuscript. Once the book is available, a book can be printed and delivered to a customer in three days. Most of my questions were already answered in a FAQ (frequently asked questions) page at the publisher's Web site. Some questions I had not thought of were also answered, such as how to obtain the ISBN (International Standard Book Number), which is required for sales. The low total cost, about 10 percent of the vanity press fees, was the factor that led me to further investigate print-on-demand.

Each company had marketing representatives accessible through a toll-free phone number. I made several calls to the representatives of these three print-on-demand companies. No one company receptionist and/or representative was more or less friendly than the others. In the three years since my book has been published, my publisher, Author-House, has provided me with courteous and effective responses to all of my e-mail and phone inquiries.

Some self-publishing companies provide editing services for additional fees, but I'd already found an editor independent of a publishing company. Having a book professionally edited is an important element. Editing assures the author of a concise story that flows and copy that is virtually free from grammatical error. Hiring an editor is well worth the cost. If I had a single sentence of advice for the writer considering self-publishing, it would be this: use an editor before submitting your manuscript!

When using print-on-demand publishing, the writer e-mails the text via attachment or provides a CD to the company. Then, there will be more decisions: does the author prefer hardback or paperback? (Paperback is more affordable for the consumer.) The publisher will offer de-sign suggestions for the cover, including picture, color, and font. Once the author signs an approval and a release, the publisher proceeds to print.

Speaking of printing, a benefit with print-on-demand publishing is that your book will not go out of print, whereas a traditional publisher may not keep a slow-selling book in print. As long as an author can dis-cover venues for sales, the book will be available to the consumer. For retail sales online, the print-on-demand publisher prints and sends the copies to the online retailer, who passes the copy on to the consumer. A customer may also have an actual bookstore special order from the print-on-demand publisher. This can all be accomplished in a matter of days.

The publishing company will send the author the royalties of the sales on a quarterly basis. However, it is hard to track the sales. If ten consumers purchased a book online, how does an author know that she has received the royalties from all ten readers? In other words, if the pub-lisher sold fifty copies to Amazon, and Amazon, in turn, sold fifty copies to online customers — but the author receives a royalty check stating that only ten copies were sold — there would be no way to track this. Basically, you have to trust that all parties are acting in good faith. This is an obstacle of print-on-demand retailing that I've yet to overcome.

The author must also decide whether or not to purchase additional products for additional fees, such as advertisements and press releases. The publisher I used offered cover-coordinated bookmarks, business cards, and postcards. I wrote the script for these products within the printer's parameters (twenty-five words or less to describe a book on a business card) and the publisher produced the marketing material. These were regrettable costs because none of the methods were effec-tive for gaining readers. Out of 250 press releases sent directly from the print-on-demand publisher to the media, I did not receive a single re-sponse. I learned after the fact that media outlets receive thousands of faxed press releases daily, and mine did not stand out! Nor did anyone comment on the pretty postcards I addressed by hand, stamped, and mailed. Purchasing print products was not the best investment.

A writer's investment dollars are better spent on a Web presence. Most print-on-demand publishers will provide the writer with a brief author's site that is within the publisher's main site. Additionally, an author should have a professionally designed Web site with search engine optimization.

Whether you use traditional publishing or self-publishing, the burden of marketing the product is on the author. Unless the writer is a proven revenue-producing commodity for the publisher (such as a celebrity), the author *must* self-promote. *Beyond the Tears* is in libraries (including the National Domestic Violence Resource Library) based on my efforts to make the acquiring librarians aware of its existence.

The author must find venues in which to sell the book, schedule readings, estimate the number of copies to bring to each speaking event, and prepare to present on the book's topic(s). Unless she has a publicist, the author herself will make the inquiries to increase the book's exposure. There are business consultants that set up marketing plans specifically for authors, for a fee, of course.

Marketing a book is like having a business, and most businesses fail due to not having a plan. At the time of this writing, I have not hired a publicist. Therefore, it is my job to keep my book on the market. In order to do that, I need to keep the main topics of *Beyond the Tears* in mind, and search for relevant Web sites to link to, like-minded authors to associate with, and live events to be present at. For example, my memoir discusses sexual assault, domestic violence, and suicide. Therefore, I have aligned myself with local and regional coalitions that will offer me speaking engagements and/or book signings.

I've had book signings sponsored by brick-and-mortar bookstores, but these are rare. The retailers are concerned about ordering from the publisher and selling copies to the consumer, only to have the books returned. Print-on-demand published copies cannot be returned by the bookstore to the publisher because there is no warehouse to send the returned copies to. I accomplish these signings by purchasing the copies wholesale from my publisher, then selling them myself for retail at the bookstore. For example, I did a presentation on self-publishing to a writer's group that met regularly at a bookstore. The bookstore allowed me to sell my books at the event, and the store got its pre-arranged portion.

However, the sales numbers are not recorded when an author buys direct and wholesale from the publisher. The dollar amounts that create the category "best seller" are measured by retail sales. If an author sells five hundred books on her own that are not tracked by retailers, then those books do not count toward best seller status.

Most independent publishers offer an "affiliates" program, which means that an established writer who has used their services can refer new authors to the publishing company. If the new author tells the publisher that she learned of the publishing company via one of its authors/books, the referring author can receive a referral fee. Once the new author has published with the same print-on-demand company, the established author receives a referral check. AuthorHouse has such a program. I am always pleased to receive the referral payment from AuthorHouse because it means that someone ordered a copy of my book, liked its professional appearance, and has been encouraged to tell her story, too.

Overall, I had a positive experience with the print-on-demand form of self-publishing. However, I have spent thousands of dollars in editing fees, Web site design, and start-up costs. I am working on a memoir about my breast cancer. I'd prefer to have an agent sell my proposal to a publishing house. I'd prefer to receive an advance. But some goals cannot be measured in dollars and cents, especially if time is of the essence. If need be, I'll use print-on-demand publishing again.

Karen Salyer McElmurray wrote the following short essay, "Gazing: Writing from the Womb," at my invitation. In it, she shares with us her journey that moved her to write and publish her memoir, *Surrendered Child: A Birth Mother's Journey.* While, on the face of it, the memoir examines the wrenching act of putting her baby up for adoption, this intensely personal story is superimposed upon larger societal issues that teenage or unwed mothers face: Birth? Adoption? Abortion? Marriage? Whatever our own journeys, we relate to Karen's experience: at one time in our own lives, we've likewise felt loss and grief—regardless of what caused them. This commonality of emotions affords us the opportunity to identify with the writer and her story. Here, in the following pages, you will learn how Karen came to write this memoir; she also reveals the life-changing events that occurred as a result of sharing her story with the world.

Gazing: Writing from the Womb
Karen Salyer McElmurray

I

In 1980, when I was a student at Berea, a small Kentucky college, I took my first Modern Poetry class. The class met on the screened porch at the home of Dr. Bobby Fong, a kind man who served us tea, and it was there that I fell in love, for the first time, with poems. Here's a pastiche of phrases from our studies that I circled, recopied, marked with hearts and stars in the margins of my book. *Inebriate of air. An agony of flame. Downward to darkness on extended wings. Night's moonlight lake . . . neither water nor air.* I also wrote my own poems in those days, ones about ordinary women, most of them stand-ins for myself. I wrote poems about my experiences as a birth mother, but I was careful, as Emily Dickinson says, to tell my story slant.

The poem I loved most of all that semester was "Unknown Girl in the Maternity Ward," by Anne Sexton. Here is part of it:

Child, the current of your breath is six days long . . .
moving to my touch. You sense the way we belong.
But this is an institution bed.
You will not know me very long.

The truth is I was that girl, or I had been her, about six years earlier, when I'd surrendered my son to state-supported adoption. I knew in my gut that sense of touch between mother and child, the ultimate sorrow when, in the poem, the speaker describes "handing her baby off . . . trembling the selves lost."

Myself and two other young women in the class loved not only Sexton, but Marge Piercy, Sylvia Plath, June Jordan. Why, my friend Ney-lan wanted to know, were we only spending one night on these poets, and weeks on all the others? These poets, we were told, were merely confessional. They were self-indulgent, personal, not a basis for longer, more intensive study. Ashamed, I renewed my efforts toward under-standing the real thing: serious poetry. In the margins of my textbook I can still find this phrase underlined several times: *look for essence.*

II

It would take me years to discover that particular part of my own es-sence called *loss.* I joined groups for childhood trauma and sought therapy through the counseling offices at a series of universities where I studied literature and creative writing. At night I had dreams of ba-bies born like the Buddha from my side, dreamed of cellars and crying babies I couldn't see. I woke with my sheets wet from my own body's sweat and a scent like afterbirth. I dreamed of my lost son at night while by day I pretended he never existed at all.

In a summer poetry workshop I learned that my intensely personal poems were way too narrative, in need of a "larger forum." I gave up po-etry. In a fiction workshop I wrote about a pregnant girl who ran away from home. I wrote about a young woman who had lost a child at birth and couldn't stop dreaming about dolls without heads and birth-giving from her side. Don't, I was told, write dreams. And my stories, I was also told, were not yet fiction. They were too autobiographical. Once again, the words *self-absorption* and *self-indulgence* lingered in the air. What I was writing was somewhere between fact and fiction, somewhere be-tween story and confession, between truth and some other essence I wanted to write, and write with authority. Just whose authority, I didn't know. In none of the stories did I name myself at all.

III

"Memoir is a journey," Patricia Hampl tells us in "Memory and Imagi-nation." The memoirist, she says, "is the traveler who goes on foot, liv-ing [this] journey, taking on mountains, enduring deserts, marveling at the lush green places. Moving through it all faithfully, not so much a survivor with a harrowing tale to tell as a pilgrim, seeking, wondering." My own journey toward my sometimes difficult heart has been a road map of lessons, some of them I have had to unlearn and even to discard.

By the late 1990's I was teaching fiction and composition in a college in south-central Virginia. I'd written and published a novel by then and I had also begun to write small snippets of "something or other" in a journal I often shared with one or two other women friends. In one such snippet, I told the story of sleeping out at night on a beach in Greece and dreaming about my long-lost son. What you need, my friend Wendy told me, is tell your truths. She gave me my first ever copy of *Fourth Genre: Contemporary Writers of/on Creative Nonfiction*. She even wrote a poem for me. "Let your voice blossom," she wrote. "Let it become a wicked and terrible bloom."

But though I wanted to experience a flowering of difficult questions asked and answered and answered again, I approached memoir with trepidation. What was mere confession? Was there social relevance to a personal, and indeed a deeply intimate history? Were shadows and dark truth more socially relevant than a recitation of times and places and all things lost? I came back to that line of Wallace Stevens's poetry I'd copied in my college textbook. *Downward to darkness on extended wings.* And that's just the memoir I wrote, as intimate as I could get, a kind of a trial by fire. A testimony to the darkness I'd always felt inside myself.

It is with this summoning of darkness that I believe I began to reach understanding, that self beyond self. Take the word "womb," for example. "Womb" appears more than fifty times, in various guises, in the pages of my book. During labor I feel "small feet pointing, small, curved arms." And when he leaves my body? "My son, leaving me and me leaving him is the opening to a womb that is now shut, a door to a tomb."

My own journey with memoir has been one through the womb itself, through the dark woods, through my own wounds and my capacity to wound others. Creative nonfiction, far from a mere recitation of events, far from mere self-aggrandizement, has the power to question "truth" and impart to events the magic of possibility. The power of memoir, as I have come to understand it, is a coming to consciousness, a meditation on the past that allows us to say, "I experienced this journey, I have sat with this experience, I have attempted an understanding of it and this is what I now know." The journey in my memoir is not an easy one.

IV

When my memoir was to be published in early 2001, I was ecstatic. I had at last looked inward, told my own story, named myself. *Birth-mother.* And, beyond imagining, a miracle happened at the same time. My son's then-girlfriend, while searching on the Internet for writings by women from Kentucky, found a photograph of me. She searched more. She found a selection of my memoir on a Web site, a chapter title. *June 23, 1973.* The same date my son was born and placed for adoption in a small hospital in Frankfort, Kentucky. My son, Andrew George Cox, and I met at last. We talked, ate at a restaurant, drank too much wine. I asked his forgiveness and held him in my arms.

And yet, in the months that followed, with delays in publishing and, at last, a book I could touch and see, I was once again privy to a variety of responses to personal writing. One of my first two reviews told me just what I would want to hear. *That McElmurray reached the self-awareness to birth this remarkable memoir is a gift both to her son and to readers.* But another review left me spinning. *Labored womb-gazing,* the critic said. I felt as exposed as one day at the office when I found menstrual blood on the back of my skirt. I sat looking at the review for awhile, feeling as ashamed as that.

In the days that followed, I wrote to friends trying to understand the womb-gazing reference. What I finally tracked down on Google was the term "navel-gazing," from a 1997 *Vanity Fair* article by James Wolcott. He had this to say about memoir in general: "Creative writing and creative nonfiction are coming together, I fear, to form a big earnest blob of me-first sensibility." Wolcott further called the memoir a "sickly transfusion, whereby the weakling personal voice of sensitive fiction is inserted into the beery carcass of nonfiction." As Lee Gutkind, the editor of the journal *Creative Nonfiction* says, "Wolcott boils down all

creative nonfiction into what he calls 'confessional writing' and takes
to task as 'navel gazers' nearly any writer who had been the least bit self-
revelatory in their work."

Womb-gazing. Navel-gazing. Gazing, in general, in an inward direction. I had seen a face, my son's. I had done more than gaze.

When women write, critic Marguerite Duras says in an essay, they
translate from darkness, from the unknown, from selves they do not
know. Darkness? Shadows of memory and their fruitful potential to
blossom, become understanding. Memoir? A wild, unknown country
that is the past, the present, an unfolding of the future. Memoirs, memories, the bends and twists of them, a Gordian knot waiting to be un-
tangled. Memoir, marking a journey toward truths as yet unwritten.

V

I am still blessed, a few years after my memoir's publication, to do readings of my book at schools, conferences, and occasionally with small
groups of women, some of them mothers who surrendered their children at birth. They ask me questions as if I am wise, these women, as
if I know answers. *Tell me,* they ask, *how to search for my daughter.* Or
this question: *My brother and I were both adopted when we five years old.
I have begun to search for my parents, but he has not. He is angry. He is
violent. He loathes himself most of all. What should I do?* Or that one: *Isn't
it better to leave the past alone? I have parents, those, the ones right there in
front of me. What good would it do to search? To remember?* And sometimes the questions, the hardest ones of all, are about me and my own
story, all those years ago. *Why,* they want to know. *Why did you give your
son away?* It's easier sometimes if I answer these questions in the voice
of others, references from outside myself. *This book,* a review from an
adoption network said, *is a wonderful place to come to understand what
choice might mean in adoption. What are the effects on a mother who loses
her child, even via choice? And what are gifts, what are strengths in the lives
of women, despite losses?*

As with Karen McElmurray, Michelle Otero wrote the following short essay, "The Weight of a Word," at my invitation, because I wanted her to share her experience about writing and publishing her essay chapbook *Malinche's Daughter*. In *Malinche's Daughter*, Michelle, a Fulbright Fellow, moves from New Mexico to Oaxaca, Mexico, to conduct writing workshops for women survivors of sexual assault. Hear her gentle, yet insightful and authorial, Voice of Experience as she describes what her work means:

> I am like an abortion doctor pre–*Roe v. Wade*. I don't advertise. Women find me. *She's Michelle. She helps women who suffer from violence.* Women who suffer from violence. We say it like it's a disease. *She suffers from violence...* A stranger in a grocery store parking lot, a boyfriend, a father... This is Rita. This is Malinche. This is Teresa, Lucia... We suffer from violence... I'm not a therapist or a doctor. I am a writer... We write to heal our wounds.

Michelle writes to heal her own wounds, too. Later in her chapbook, she explores, through the Voice of Innocence, her own trauma of sexual abuse perpetrated years ago by her brother. Through the use of these two voices, coupled with those of the other women in Oaxaca (who tell Michelle their stories), she creates a chorus of women's voices to deepen the experience. In the pages that follow, not only does Michelle tell us how she came to write the essay collection, she also shares with us the aftermath — how publishing her work affected her and her family. You'll find lovely words at the end of this piece as she encourages *you* to write your stories, too.

The Weight of a Word
Michelle Otero

"My brother is heavy."

The word "brother" kept me from writing, sometimes for hours, sometimes weeks. After completing the final draft of *Malinche's Daughter*, an essay collection based on my work with sexual assault survivors in Oaxaca, Mexico, I stopped sleeping through the night. The word "brother" twisted my stomach in knots that my boyfriend at the time would massage until his hands cramped.

"He is heavy."

I wrote my brother out of early drafts, hoping to hide behind the other women in my book. The reader would know that I was five when someone abused me in my home, that it happened once. That I forgave him. No one would have to know *he* was my brother.

In that time when I was neither writing nor sleeping well, I'd picture myself taking questions at a reading. In my imaginings, someone — always a woman — asked who *he* was, why I didn't name him. She was never angry. Just puzzled.

I could never answer her questions.

I tried.

Answer 1: *Who did it is not important. I forgave him. It's done.*

But who did it is important because, for most of my life, it shaped my place in the family and in the world.

I do not need to blame my brother or my family. When we write out of blame or revenge, our stories suffer, and so do our souls. Telling the truth, asking others to take responsibility for their actions or inaction, is not the same as blaming.

When a woman or girl is violated, our very language works against her, focusing the act on the victim, rather than on the one who hurt her. *She was raped. She was abused.* As if sexual violence were a lightning strike or a house fire. Telling the truth puts things where they belong. It lifts the heavy weight a survivor carries on her back and redistributes it amongst her family and community.

I don't have a need to expose my brother. Telling my story, turning my life into literature, is not the same as "going public."

I wrote *Malinche's Daughter* partly to understand the ways that being abused by my brother shaped my life, my writing, and my work in Oaxaca. I wanted others who had been abused by siblings to know that they were not alone. And I needed to remember that the abuse was part of my life, not all of it.

The published book feels almost weightless compared to my life as a whole. *Malinche's Daughter* is fifty pages. The abuse is one scene. For years it felt like the only scene that mattered, the only significant detail in my life. Not the Harvard degree, the two years I lived in Belize, not my singing voice or sense of humor. Just this stain. Writing alone did not save me. But writing, in combination with an amazing therapist, yoga, meditation, *curanderismo*, and family and friends who reminded me who I am the many times I forgot, helped me integrate the abuse into my life and to move from victim to survivor to advocate.

Answer 2: *I don't want to hurt my family.*

In telling our stories, in telling difficult truths, we might feel we are betraying the people closest to us. In Mexico, a woman who betrays her people is *una Malinche* or *malinchista*. Malinche was a teenager and a slave when the Spaniards invaded Mexico in 1519. The conquistador Hernán Cortés made her his concubine and interpreter. She inspires fascination, for little is known about her, and inspires contempt for leading the Spaniards into the heart of the Aztec world. I followed Malinche because I identified with her. A woman who speaks is a traitor. Yet without Malinche's voice, Cortés could not have negotiated with the Aztecs. Because she spoke, thousands of lives were spared.

In writing memoir, in releasing family secrets, we are saving lives. We rewrite our family trees. I don't have children. I don't know if I will. But I do know that *Malinche's Daughter* is now part of my family, and because I wrote it, our burdens will be lighter in this life, my brothers' children will carry one less secret into the next generation. We walk a little lighter in the world.

In remaining silent, we only protect our shame. Shame has enough protection. It does not need our help.

Writing your story might mean that the people closest to you fall away. Since *Malinche's Daughter* was published, my relationships with my brothers have been uncomfortable, at best. Two of them avoid me. Another said, "If you had the guts to write the book, you should have the guts to stand by what you wrote." Despite this, I consider myself fortunate. Nobody denied the abuse. Nobody said I was wrong for writing the book.

I have not lost my brothers. I have asked them to help me carry a load that never belonged to me. I have asked them the best way I know, through the word. In doing so, I have changed the nature of our relationships. Losing the comfortable and familiar stripped me. For a time, I felt I had no skin. But skin, like relationships and love and support, regenerates, and when it does, it protects us again.

Answer 3: *I didn't want to go through all that again.*

A few months after the book release, I attended the Macondo Writers' Workshop in San Antonio. I had submitted to Sandra Cisneros's workshop a series of highly stylized prose poems based on my grandpa's service in World War II and his subsequent depression and posttraumatic stress disorder.

Sandra said, "I'm on your porch admiring the filigree. But you won't let me in the house. And you won't go to the basement."

I cried. She was right. I had spent the last few months in the basement — leaving Oaxaca, returning to the States, finishing grad school, confronting my family with the book. The year before, I had lived in the basement with *Malinche's Daughter*. All that, and look where I am, I thought. Unemployed and practically orphaned.

"I can't," I said.

Sandra said, "Right now you're a full glass of water. Someone bumps you and you spill over. Write from that place. It's the best place to be because your heart is open."

We need community to keep our hearts open. So much in this world tells us that what we have to say does not matter. We need to remember that it does, and that we are the only ones to say it. When relationships in my family of origin shifted, it created space in my life to build my own family. I didn't marry or have children. I began reaching out to other writers, being honest about my fears, asking them about their struggles, telling them what I need — a text message in the morning reminding me to get up and write, someone to read my work on occasion, someone to call from a distant airport when I am traveling. Today I am a sister to four fellow Macondistas scattered throughout the U.S. We share work, send each other daily text messages, and maintain a private blog.

I do go to the basement now. I go alone. After all, I am the only one who can write my story. But these days, I post trusted friends at the door. They wait for me at the top of the stairs and help carry my books as I step back into the world.

Answer 4: *I couldn't remember everything.*

I was five when my brother abused me. I remembered scant details — the afternoon light sifting across the room, and a boy I trusted asking, "Can you feel me?" I wrote the essay "Moving Pictures" around the light and my brother's words. These two details were all I needed to convey the sense of wanting to leave my body and being yanked back into it each time those words were repeated.

The details — images, smells, bodily sensations, sounds, and tastes — we cannot forget are the important ones, the anchors grounding us to truth. What we do not remember is also important. The blurs in our memory are often clues to silence and secrets. We can write into those spaces, exploring their meaning, and releasing them in the process.

I wish I could promise each woman who writes her story that she will get all the support and love she deserves. I wish I could promise that the people who hurt us will return to us in love and kindness. I do promise that if you write honestly and consistently, you will remove the weight from your back and put it where it belongs — in the metaphor, in the image, on the page.

For Your Reading Pleasure
Four Full-Length Essays

As you read the following essays, consider how these authors implement the various craft elements discussed in *Fearless Confessions*. For example, list some of the sensory descriptions that most bring you into any given scene. Which images are particularly potent? Why?

What is the theme of each essay? Can you state, in one sentence, what that essay means to you?

In "Independence Day, Manley Hot Springs, Alaska," what's the motivation for Lisa D. Chavez's love/hate relationship with Alaska? What's the motivation, in Harrison Candelaria Fletcher's "The Beautiful City of Tirzah," that causes the family to adopt stray animals? In "After the Dash," why does Michael Hemery have conflicted feelings about the feather-button? What do you think the last sentence of the essay means, and how does the title reflect the theme?

In Chavez's essay, the State of Alaska itself is a metaphor. For what? In "After the Dash," the feather-button represents something. What? In "The Beautiful City of Tirzah," what larger issues does the owl evoke? How is Pat Boone himself a metaphor in "The Pat Boone Fan Club"? Why is he more than just a singer?

In each essay, underline places where the author segues from straightforward action into the vertical plot line. Likewise, underline sentences where the author deepens the essay with the Voice of Experience.

In each essay, what do you think the author comes to understand about him- or herself at the end? In what way(s) do you think the author is different at the end of the essay from the beginning? What new insight has each achieved either about him- or herself, or about the world?

Perhaps most important, what parts of these essays most move you? Why? For this question, especially, there are no wrong answers!

Independence Day, Manley Hot Springs, Alaska
Lisa D. Chavez

Independence Day, 1975. I was twelve. A little more than a month before, my mother had withdrawn me from school early, loaded up our car — a flashy but impractical Camaro with dual side-pipes — and headed north for Alaska. She brought with her everything she thought essential: daughter; dog; photos of the family she was leaving behind; a haphazard scattering of household goods; and two army surplus sleeping bags, purchased especially for the trip. What she was traveling towards was uncertain but full of promise — a mysterious box, beguilingly wrapped.

What she was leaving behind was certain; perhaps that is why she was so eager to go. A narrow rented house in Southern California; a steady, if boring, secretarial job; a marriage proposal from a man she didn't love. What she was leaving behind were her everyday fears: her route to work through Watts, a place blighted and dangerous even then. The muggings in the company parking lot. The fear of being a young woman alone with her child in a decaying neighborhood, a derelict factory looming across the street. The fear, perhaps, of succumbing to a loveless marriage for the security it offered.

I was too young to really understand my mother's concerns, but I felt her tension. My mother and her women friends wore their fears like perfume, like the lingering scent of smoke from the erupting fires of those violent days. I remember the things my mother's friends talked about: the Manson murders; the serial killer who left body parts scattered on the freeway in trash bags; the man in our own town who killed five people in a movie theater. And the more personal terrors, the ones they alluded to less directly: fear of the arm slipping around the neck from behind, fear of the window breaking in the house in the middle of the night. Fear for their children in a place gone crazy. Or just the fear of being alone. And while my world was a child's world, full of long imaginative games in the park near our house, or afternoons watching

Disney movies at the mall, I also heard my mother and her friends talking about getting out, moving to someplace safe. My mother was looking for sanctuary, and for a new start. She picked Alaska, as far north as she could drive.

Independence Day, 1975. We've been in Alaska less than a month and are still exploring. Now we have driven as far north as the road will take us, landed here, on the banks of the Tanana River. Manley Hot Springs. A town with no function really, except for the raw springs: two pools of hot water bubbling up out of the ground. There's a lodge with a few desultory cabins ringing it. A combination gas station/store. That is all. Down the river a half a dozen miles lies Minto, an Athabascan Indian village. Fairbanks, the biggest city in the interior, swollen to a population of 60,000 by pipeline construction, lies less than a hundred miles south, far enough away — along these rough gravel roads — to be totally insignificant.

And I am twelve. Everything new astounds me, and everything is new. My mother parks near the river and goes to find a place to stay. Instantly I am occupied, walking our dog, wetting the toes of my canvas tennis shoes in the silty current, kicking sprays of gravel into the air. Under my breath a constant stream of conversation. I narrate the scene to myself, add it to the elaborate and constant story I whisper of my adventures in Alaska. Drunk on the stories of Jack London, the poems of Robert Service, I imagine myself a lone adventurer, a sled-dog driver, a saloon girl. I do not see what is in front of me: a shabby small town where people stare openly at that frivolous car — bright orange and marked by its out-of-state plates — and the young woman in white, high-heeled sandals and her daughter that have emerged from it. I do not see the men swigging out of a bottle at the picnic table by the river. I do not see the people getting out of a banged up river-boat, or the beer cans they toss in the current. No. I am in my own Alaska, and it is beautiful. I erase the people, and I am alone in my fantasy of wilderness, only graceful paper birch and the sun turning the river to tinfoil. Even when two men pull a rifle out of the boat, aim it at the sky and shoot, I am unsurprised. Only when my mother hurries me into the car do I understand I should be afraid.

There is only one place to stay, in the hulking log building that serves as a lodge. And there is only one room left, above the bar. We take it, noting the sagging double bed and rust-stained sink. The bathroom is down the hall.

Manley holds few attractions. The hot springs itself—housed in another log structure, this one with steamy windows that gaze at the road like rheumy eyes—is booked out by the hour, and we discover it is rented for the entire evening. We go for a walk with our German shepherd, but we quickly run out of road to walk on. We circle the gas station yet again.

"When does it get dark?" I ask my mother; even though I already know that it does not get dark at night in Fairbanks, I cannot be sure the rules are not different here.

"In August," my mother replies, an answer she has learned from the locals. She looks nervous, walks fast. Finally, I manage to really see around me, to note the people drinking at picnic tables, the hairy-faced men entering the store with guns in holsters. She hustles us back to our little room.

And I continue to ponder the light. If it never gets dark, I wonder, when do kids get to shoot off their fireworks? This year I have no fireworks, no magical cones of cardboard with their heady black smell of powder, cones with names like "Showers of Falling Stars" and "Golden Peacock" that spray the summer night with shivering sparks of sheer delight. Fireworks are illegal here, my mother tells me, and I feel sorely cheated.

All through the sunlit night we hear voices shout and slur from the bar, and outside gunfire and laughter. Years later I will discover that Alaska is not the only place where people discharge guns on holidays, but then I knew only my mother's fear which passed to me like a virus. I lay still on the double bed beside her, pretending to sleep. At five AM a shot in the bar and a shuddering silence. From the car, distant and insistent, our dog's furious barking.

Time passes. I pretend to sleep. The dog barks. My mother nudges me. "Someone needs to walk the dog." That someone is me.

Years later I recount the story. People question me. Why did she send you, a child? What they are asking, what they are telling me, is that my mother was a bad mother. Perhaps. But maybe she thought it was safe; how could she know? And she was tired, and scared herself, and perhaps she thought my childishness would protect me in a way her youth and gender might not protect her.

Perhaps it was a mark of my mother's blind innocence. I like to think that she had some of the indomitable optimism of those who made the same trek before: the stampeders to the gold rush of '98, or the others that came, like we did, lured north by the pipeline boom of '74 and '75. She wanted to believe — like so many did — that Alaska was a land of golden opportunity. Think of what she had done: left a good-paying job and man who wanted to marry her to journey to a place where she knew no one, where she had no prospects at all. For her, I think Alaska represented the possibility of the undiscovered, while California was a territory already mapped with freeways and shopping malls, mile upon mile of housing developments, and the barbed wire threat of barrio and ghetto.

That summer, we were still caught up in the romance of Alaska. We sang Johnny Horton songs on the Alcan Highway: "North to Alaska," and "When It's Springtime in Alaska It's Forty Below." I wrote "Alaska or Bust" with my finger in the dust that caked the car, and my mother smiled and let it stay. She told me that we would have our own house in the country, and I believed her, even though when we got to Fairbanks we lived in a campground next to the fairgrounds, and I stayed there all day exploring muskeg woods behind the camp while my mother worked at Dairy Queen. There were none of the expected high-paying jobs, none of the dream houses that we could afford. We knew no one. But my mother, like me, was lost in her own dream of Alaska, and she refused to be discouraged. So now, when I think back to that time, I try not to judge her too harshly. Alaska was her sanctuary, and she could not imagine, then, that anything could go wrong.

I am a child; I do what she asks. Put on my worn jean jacket. Push my straight dark hair behind my ears, then tie it back with a blue bandana. This is the look I have adopted since I arrived, Indian chic. I do not know what it means, exactly, to dress like this, but I have seen young men and women outfitted in this way — people my mother told me were Indian — and I decide I will dress that way too, because Indians are cool, aren't they? And as I am a bit Indian — a mixture of Chicana and Southwestern Indian and Norwegian that I will much later learn to call Mestiza — I am determined to dress appropriately. My attire adjusted, I move toward the door. Look pleadingly at my mother's blanketed back. I really don't want to go out. Then, in imitation of my mother, I sigh loudly, pick up the keys. Step out into the hall.

Creep down the narrow stairs. Afraid, in my childish way, of strangers, of being where I think I am not supposed to be, up late in a room above a bar. And I see a man on the landing. His back to me. And he whips around and raises a shotgun and aims it at my face. "I told all you goddamn Indians to get the fuck out of my bar."

I am twelve, and I have never seen a gun before. I am twelve, and I come from California, where night follows day in an orderly fashion, where on the Fourth of July I whirl like a comet with sparklers clutched tight in two hands. Where I place black pellets on the pavement to watch them transform into sooty snakes. I am twelve, and I am frozen on the landing of a strange staircase, with a shotgun staring in my face with its one, unblinking eye.

I am usually a silent child, but my fear makes me speak. My mouth opens and out rush words, tumbling over one another like frightened animals. My mother. California. The dog in the car, maybe already peeing on the seat. The dog is like a ship I swim to, desperately. He lowers the gun and I skitter past, fly to the door. Which I cannot open; it is locked. The man raises the latch, shoves me outside.

I stand outside on the cool grass, the early morning bright and exotic around me. I close my eyes for a moment and wish hard for home. Then open them to see revelers sway aimlessly by, laughing, cursing, swigging from bottles. I move toward the safety of the car.

And I am twelve, and I don't know what to do, can't think about what happened to me in any coherent fashion. I do not understand. I know racism exists — though I do not know what it is called — but not like this. I thought it was something else, people who called black people bad names, people who snickered when they heard my last name. *Mexi-*

can, they'd sneer. I knew that. Knew shame, about my last name, which I claimed was Spanish, not Mexican, knowing that to be less shameful, although I didn't know why. But nothing more. Not then. And Indian, what was that to me? An exotic people with feathers, that had some slight relation to my father, to me. But I was not Indian. Nor Mexican. Nor Norwegian. Not really. I am just myself, a quiet girl who liked to read, to write, a girl who had always loved the Fourth of July, the night's rich promise broken by the sizzle and spark of fire.

And now I have been shaken into a world I don't understand, a cold, foreign world, where men I don't know can hate me for the way I look. I don't know what to do, so I take the dog for a walk. She sniffs desultorily, squats on the lawn to pee. I look at the new grass stains on my jeans, souvenirs from the fall I took from the man's push. Two young men pass by, say hello. They have witnessed my ejection from the lodge.

"Did he hurt you?" one asks. They are both Indian; their glossy black hair is tied back with bandanas. They wear T-shirts, jean jackets.

I am afraid to answer, but I shake my head.

"He's an asshole," the other young man says. His words are slow and strangely accented; I will soon learn to recognize this as a village accent. "Fucking white man." He shakes a fist at the lodge.

I try to smile to show my gratefulness, and watch them with head bowed as they walk away. They are drunk; I know that even then, but their words redeem me nonetheless. Later I will understand those words as my introduction into a place I will dwell for all my time in Alaska, those words which delineate me as one of them, as a Native person. For in Alaska, as I would learn, the complexity of my ethnicity was irrelevant; I looked Native, therefore I was.

For a long time I crouch beside the car with my arms around the dog's neck. What will I do? I could sleep in the car, but my mother will be mad. But can I go back in? What if the man won't let me? What if he . . . my thoughts veer away from certain subjects. The dog pulls away, shakes herself. I must go back.

I stand at the door. Through the window I can see the man watching, see the slim shadow of the gun. I am afraid. My legs shake; my hand is weak, but I push the door open.

And the man grabs my shoulder hard. Twists me towards him. Peers down into my face. He is bearded and the hair on his face makes him as frightening as a fierce animal. "All right," he says, though I have no idea what he means. For me, nothing is right. He pushes me toward the stairs and I run up them, breathless, heart somersaulting. I imagine too clearly a sudden crack, a searing pain in my spine. In our room I collapse on the bed as if shot. Tears first, then the story.

My mother waits until the next morning to confront the lodge owner. She gets the story while I mop a pancake around my plate, too scared and shamed to eat. The bearded man is the man who owns the lodge, and he tells his side calmly, reasonably, as if there is nothing unusual about pointing shotguns at twelve-year-olds. Some Indians from Minto were partying in the bar, he tells us, and wouldn't leave at closing time. So he fired a shot of tear gas, cleared the place out. As for me, "She looks like a goddamn Native," he says, and shrugs. And the other guests eating breakfast look at me, nod. There is nothing more to say, no apologies necessary. And my mother's angry words are just irritations, like BBs fired at a grizzly bear.

We left soon after that, and my mother drove as fast as she dared on that gravel road, gripping the steering wheel tight, her hands like fists clenched. I was quiet. I didn't know I should be angry. Didn't know, really, why I felt so ashamed. Even my mother's anger couldn't take that shame away, for under her anger I sensed her own fear of this place she'd brought me to, of these people. Her confusion. She repeated that the man had thought I was Indian, as if somehow that should explain it. But that confused me. Because I *was* Indian, though not Alaskan Indian, and not all Indian. Did that make what the man did excusable? My mother did not explain.

What did it mean to be Indian? Did I put it on with the clothes I wore? Why was my appearance read one way in California and another way in Alaska? In California, where everyone aimed for a tan, my skin color was something to be envied, when it could be separated from the stigma of my Mexican last name. I had grown vain of it, in a childish way. Proud that I often had the best "tan." I secretly looked down on lighter-skinned children, was sure their pink and white skin was ugly, undesirable. Otherwise why would my mother and so many others spend hours roasting themselves brown on the beach? I got it naturally; I must be superior. In Alaska, far from beaches, where the long dark winters bleached skin as pale as the long months of snow, brown skin did not mean beach and health, but it meant something else, something I would understand some people thought shameful. Native. That's what it meant, and I would discover how that word could be spit out with as much disgust as any racial slur.

Manley Hot Springs was a defining moment of my life in Alaska. It was the first time someone mistook me for an Alaskan Native — and one of the most frightening — but it would not be the last. My entire life in Alaska has been shaped by the fact that people — both white and Native — think I am Athabascan or Yupik, Tlingit or Inupiat. I reaped the benefits of that: smiles and conversation from old Yupik women on the bus, an unquestioned acceptance in villages and at Native cultural events. When I taught at the university, I connected easily with Native students. But I also reaped the pain.

When I tell this story to people, there is a coda I usually include. A few years after our trip up to Manley, a similar thing happened; again the lodge owner tried to throw some people out of the bar; again he waved a shotgun. But this time it was not at a child who looked Native. It was at a man — and while I don't know if he was white or Native, I do know he was armed, and he shot first and killed the lodge owner. As vengeful as it sounds, my mother and I were pleased by this, and when I retell it as the logical end to my own story, I smile. He infected me with his hatred, and I was — am — glad he is dead. I like this end because it is satisfying; it gives the story a sort of rough justice. It gives life — so messy and vague — an aesthetically pleasing shape, as neat as fiction. I also like the way I appear in this version: invulnerable, a tough person who can speak of death coolly. Perhaps my liking for this end is leftover from my turbulent adolescence, a time so fraught with pain that my only tool of survival was the tough façade I adopted and my insistence that nothing could hurt me. Perhaps the story, ended this way, is proof of that.

The real end of the story is more complicated. Because of course

I was not untouched. I learned to be afraid, learned that Alaska — as beloved as it would become — was not the sanctuary my mother had hoped for. My mother was able to close her eyes and keep hoping. For me, any possibility of sanctuary was shattered. On the drive back to Fairbanks, I had asked my mother if we could go home. She knew I didn't mean the campground. We live here now, was what she told me, and I remember crying when she said that. I think even then I wondered how I would survive.

In a few years, my mother would have what she dreamed of — the high-paying construction job, her own house. In a few years she would also slam into prejudice and violence on the job, but by then, Alaska was home, so she never seriously considered leaving.

In a few years, I would hear things and learn more: hear the smug tone of the high school counselor as he tried to steer me into the vocational track — despite my good grades; hear, more than once, the anxiety in a white boyfriend's voice as he asked for assurance that I wasn't really Native; hear the nervous laughter at a party when a white man told how he raped "a squaw" in the back of a truck. Hear the silence that followed that laughter. I was spit at in small towns, refused service in bars. In just a few years, I could recite the litany of insults so many people of color know. But I would also learn to put a name to what was happening to me, and learn to be angry. I would learn that what happened to me was not my fault, nor was it unique to Alaska. Even later, I would learn to mold my anger into something I could use.

But I didn't know any of that then. I only knew fear, and shame.

I never wore the bandana or jean jacket again.

After the Dash
Michael Hemery

I doubted the minister's sincerity. "None of us will ever forget Carol," he said at my great-aunt Dottie's funeral. He'd been saying the wrong name for the entire memorial service held next to Dottie's open grave.

"If he says Carol one more time, I'm going to scream," Mom whispered to my dad. But she didn't. None of us did. My great-aunt had no friends that we knew of, so the few immediate family members in attendance twittered among ourselves. My aunt shook her head. My grandfather sighed. Dottie's fifty-year-old son, Jim, kept rising from his seat to snap a picture with a plastic disposable camera. He took pictures of the minister, the wreath of flowers, and several different angles of the casket itself. He'd wind the camera, grinding the gear to advance the film, then return to his seat. The rest of us remained in our folding chairs while the man that none of us had ever met before reminded us of the importance of remembering Carol. He said Carol was a loving mother and aunt. He said she had a fantastic sense of humor. He said she was a valuable member of the spiritual community.

Carol sounded like one hell of a lady.

Dottie was an eccentric who lived a few houses from my grandparents. She didn't drive but rode her bike with the large metal basket to the grocery store, sometimes making several trips a day, bringing home only what the basket could hold. Her plump face pushed her cheekbones up to her eyes, giving the impression they were permanently shut. Until she blinked, which she did incessantly.

Aunt Dottie's house smelled of cat piss. None of the litter boxes were ever changed, so her half-dozen cats urinated on the carpet. She adored cats, referring to them as her babies. But despite her affection, she refused to let them on the furniture. To prevent this, her couch, kitchen table, television, rocking chair, and coffee table were all placed in discarded refrigerator and washing machine boxes, cut unevenly six inches to a foot from the floor. Despite these cardboard moats, the cats slept on the kitchen table and pissed on the couch pillows.

I don't remember many conversations with Dottie, save for the time I was ten and she asked my cousin Mat and me to clean out her garage. When we balked, Aunt Dottie said she'd find something in her purse to make it worth our while. Inside the garage was a large 1950s-era aqua blue car that Mom said Dottie stored for a man she dated after her husband divorced her. The car remained there for twenty-five years. She hadn't spoken to the man since their breakup, but swore he stopped by every few years to check on his car. She'd hear the garage open, the engine turn over. She'd peek out her kitchen window to watch the man run the car up and down the driveway, then quietly disappear.

I pushed a broom in the garage, while Mat slid damp boxes filled with papers and books across the floor. Each time he moved a box, making room for me to sweep, dozens of mice scurried from one location to the next, their feet scrabbling over mounds of old newspapers and magazines. "No matter how much she's going to pay us, this isn't worth it," Mat said. We speculated how much we'd make for the afternoon of work. I thought we'd make at least five bucks each, while Mat claimed we'd end up with nothing.

Mat stacked boxes on top of other boxes, while I moved dirt from one side of the concrete slab to the other. We worked this way for a half an hour, sweeping around the dozens of dead, desiccated mice. When Mat found an old *Playboy* magazine in a pile of garbage, we slipped behind the garage.

The corners of the magazine had been chewed away. When Mat turned the pages, tiny black mouse pellets slipped from between the pages. "These women are probably all old now," Mat said. "Can you picture them naked — their skin all wrinkly? Or maybe they're dead."

I told Mat he was sick for thinking about naked dead women. I said we should get back to work before we were caught. Mat said he was done working, said Aunt Dottie would never know the difference if we cleaned or not, said we might as well collect our money. When we knocked on the screen door after ditching the magazine, Aunt Dottie was listening to the Indians baseball game on her transistor radio. She rocked in her chair, the runners mashing the cardboard of its box lid with each movement. The game was so loud we had to knock twice.

Wordlessly, Dottie opened the door, twisting open the clasp of her change purse. She gestured for us to hold out our hands. In mine she placed a red plastic button. She pressed it hard into my palm, closing my fingers over the gift. Mat closed his eyes and shook his head. I said *Thank you* before my face gave way to disappointment. Mat retracted his hand. He told Aunt Dottie that she didn't have to pay him, that he'd done the work for free. But she insisted. She said she wouldn't let us leave until all of her debts were settled. She fished around in her change purse. Fabric brushed against plastic, a zip of corduroy.

Mat grudgingly held out his hand again. Dottie placed a small feather in his palm, then twisted the clasp of her purse closed. The feather looked like one of the down feathers that sometimes blew out of the tiny hole in my blue winter jacket. Then she took the objects back and wove the feather through three of the button's four holes, tying it off at either end. She handed the feather-button back to me, blinked several times, then returned to her rocker, stepping over the lip of the box.

"I told you she was crazy and we wouldn't get paid," Mat said as we walked back to my grandma's house. I pulled the feather-button from my pocket. It was dull and worn. "Let me have that," Mat said, taking the object from my hand. Then he flicked the feather-button into the road. It skipped across the asphalt until it spun to a stop at the curb.

"We should go get that," I said. "What if she sees it when she's out riding her bike?"

"The crazy old bat can't see anything," Mat insisted. "And even if she does, so what? It's just garbage anyhow."

I began to go back for the feather-button, but Mat pulled my sleeve. "Leave it," he said. "If she does find it, maybe it'll teach her not to be so crazy and cheap."

The family accepted her quirks. For the annual Fourth of July picnics, Aunt Dottie would ride her bike down for hotdogs and potato salad. She'd straddle the bar of her bike, resting the paper plate of food on the handle bars. As soon as she finished eating, she'd pedal back to her house without saying good-bye.

After she died, Mom and Jim were in charge of Dottie's house. While emptying the kitchen Mom screamed when she opened one of the cupboards. On the shelf was a stuffed muskrat. They named it Musky. Before Jim returned home to San Francisco, he sold or threw away all of his mom's belongings — chairs, couches, ceramic knickknacks. The only things worth salvaging were a suitcase full of pictures and the muskrat, which he packed in his carry-on bag.

That's all I know.

Mom says I'm wrong. There were only three cats and one box lid — for the rocker, a gift when she retired from the local college. I didn't know she ever worked. I still believe there were more box lids, but there's no one to arbitrate. When Dottie died, her existence was offered up for interpretation. Slipped memories. Miscounts. Wrong names at the cemetery.

The worst funeral was for Grandpa's brother, Johnny. Grandpa said his brother lost his mind years ago. He believed the FBI had a tap on his phone, so he tore the jack from the wall. Grandpa never visited Johnny. A nurse would stop by his house once a day to clean and feed him. He died during the summer of my sophomore year of college. Mom said I should go to the funeral. She said it would be nice if I came so the living outnumbered the dead.

There were six of us, but my mom and grandfather were the only two who knew Johnny. The minister began the service with a prayer and a call for us to say something personal about the departed. Grandpa said, "He was my brother."

"Is there anything more you'd like to say?" the priest asked.

Grandpa shook his head. The rest of us were quiet.

"Well, as I'm sure you know, Johnny liked good whiskey and to spend his money on dogs at the track," the priest said. "Hopefully God will look past these faults and see the man you knew."

Between the service and the burial, Grandpa invited us to lunch at Olive Garden, his treat. He thanked us for coming, because he said it would have been mighty sad if no one had showed.

"Why the hell did the minister say that about Johnny?" Mom asked.

"Say what?" Grandpa asked.

"The gambling and drinking bit."

"Well, that's what I told him about Johnny," Grandpa said. "I left out the part about how he'd shoot at the neighbor's dogs when they'd go through his garbage or how he'd hang his underwear on the mailbox."

The waitress brought the round of drinks Grandpa ordered for us.

"You could have told him about when you two were kids on the farm."

Grandpa swirled his whiskey and ginger ale. "I can't really remember much anymore," he said. "What does it matter? All this talking is for the living, not the dead." He ordered another round before we even finished the first.

After Johnny's funeral, Grandpa said his first two wives, three brothers, mother, and father were all buried together in this cemetery, in the same block. He said he'd bought a spot for himself next to them, his stone already carved with his name and date of birth. The number after the dash was all that was missing. He said he wanted to find the graves before we left. He wanted to see his mother, see what he'd look like next to her.

We followed him around the graves as he drove up hills and back down. He leaned out his window, shouting it had to be around here somewhere. Finally he parked his car to search on foot. We all helped. The six of us kicked the dirt from toppled headstones, reading the names of people we didn't know. *Loving mother. Caring uncle.*

The pack of us ambled around the cemetery, the alcohol from lunch warming us in the cool summer breeze. After an hour, my grandfather threw up his arms in disgust. He rubbed his right knee. He said it ached, so he was done.

"What's the point, anyhow?" he asked. "When I go, it'll be someone else's problem to find the grave."

"But don't you want to see your folks? To pay your respects?" Mom asked.

Grandpa thought for moment. "Maybe you're right," he said. Finally, we found them.

I've searched for Dottie's feather-button in drawers and boxes in the attic, but I'm sure we left it on the street that afternoon. I thought maybe I went back for it. I would have given it to my son when he was older. I'd press the button into his hand, just like Dottie did to me. I'd tell him this was Aunt Dottie. I'd tell him what I know. We'd make up the rest between us.

The Beautiful City of Tirzah

Harrison Candelaria Fletcher

Animals come after my father dies. Dogs. Cats. Ducks. Geese. A goat. A peacock. They wander to our home several years into his absence, appearing on our doorstep, or catching our eye from feed store cages. Always, we take them in. We line our laundry room floor with bath towels, bed sheets and spare blankets, filling cereal bowls with tap water, and mending cut skin, matted fur, and broken feathers. Then we flick off the light to watch them sleep.

Strays make the best pets, my mother tells us kids. They won't leave.

Beggar's night, 1970. My big brother is late. Again. Our mother has given him permission to play on the ditch bank behind our house and to see if the neighbors will give him Halloween candy a day early, but when I peek out the back window to check on him, the sun has already set and the shadows drip like ink from the cottonwoods. I don't say anything to our mother, who sits stiffly in her antique rocker, tapping a Russian olive switch on the floor. I scoot across the living room on my knees and take my place in front of the TV, where my three sisters watch *Dr. No.* It's a school night. We've changed into our flannel pajamas. Our hair is damp from the bath.

"Mom!"

The back door thuds open. My brother clomps through the kitchen, breathing hard, as if he's been running. Our mother stands, grips the switch and intercepts him in the dining room. The overhead light flicks on, bright as an interrogation lamp.

"Wait," my brother pleads. "I found something. Look!"

I scramble to my feet and jockey for position with my three sisters. Our brother reaches into his corduroy jacket, extracts a small bundle, and opens his hands. A baby bird squints at us.

My mother leans the switch against the wall.

"An owl," she says, kneeling. "It's adorable. Where did you find it?"

My brother had been hurrying home along the ditch when he heard a rustling from the bushes. When he slid down the embankment to investigate, he startled a hatchling that skittered through the dust but couldn't fly. He thought it might have broken its wing, so he scooped it up.

"I looked for the nest but couldn't find it," he says, shifting his weight from one foot to another. "Then I saw the mother by a tree. Someone shot her or something."

Our mother holds the owl to the warmth of her body. It looks up at her, and blinks.

An ornithologist who lives down the street tells my mother we've adopted a screech owl, probably a female, given the description over the phone. Although it's not allowed under city codes, it should be okay for us to nurse the chick until she gets stronger. She's not a danger to us, although we might want to wear gloves when handling her. Feed her bits of stew meat, the ornithologist suggests, and later mice. Within six months, the owl should grow to her full height of five inches. We should keep her in a large cage or an enclosed room. And watch out for our cats.

My mother follows his advice, but vetoes the cage. She wants the owl to fly freely in her home. She retrieves a cardboard box from Safeway, lines it with towels and places a piñon branch inside before setting the carton atop the dining room pottery case where the cats can't easily reach.

The owl is the size and shape of an upside-down pear. Her feathers are gray with black and white speckles. She has two tufts on her head that look like ears, or horns. Her beak is sharp and shiny black and so are her talons. What I like best are her eyes, a piercing yellow, the size of dimes. When she looks at me, it's as if she's reading my mind, or seeing something I can't. One of my aunts can't even meet her gaze. The owl's eyes, she says, are too human.

My mother considers the bird's name carefully. Usually, she names the pets after artists she admires, like Toshiro, the Japanese actor, for the silky black cat. Sometimes, she chooses characters from her favorite films, like Tonya, from *Dr. Zhivago*, for the German shepherd cross. Occasionally, she selects Spanish words that just sound nice, like Sol Pavo, sun bird, for the peacock. When I adopt a mallard duckling from the feed store, I pick Hercules, my favorite matinee hero, and the nickname my father gave me because I was stronger than other newborns in the nursery. For the owl, my mother decides upon Tirzah, after a Hopi basket maker.

"Tirzah," my mother says, savoring the syllables, which break like sunlight through her window crystals, turquoise and yellow.

"What does it mean?" I ask.

"It's an old name," she says. "A religious name. From the Bible."

Later, I look it up in a library dictionary: "Tirzah — A city in Palestine, a beautiful place alluded to in the Songs of Solomon ('You are as beautiful, my darling, as Tirzah')."

During the first few weeks, Tirzah stays put on the pottery case. But as she gains strength, she flutters from her box, hovers a few seconds, and drops to the floor. Worried the owl will break its wings, my mother drapes the box each night with a sheet. But as soon as morning comes, she throws off the cover and sets the container on the dining room table while she makes breakfast, draws in her sketchpad, or pays bills. Tirzah hops out immediately, waddles over, and nibbles her pen. If my mother leaves the room, the owl tries to follow. The only way my mother can finish her household chores is to wrap the owl in a washcloth and tuck her in the breast pocket of her denim work shirt. Tirzah remains there for hours, lulled by my mother's heartbeat.

On Sunday evenings, my grandmother Desolina stops by our house for pot roast with garlic, carrots, and potatoes. Over supper, my grandmother grumbles about her childhood in Corrales, growing up among horses, cows, and chickens, in a drafty adobe where black widow spiders dropped from the rafters into your food. She hated every minute of it, she says, chewing with her mouth open. She hated pumping water by hand and canning apricots and apples and squatting in the dark outhouse, but she learned the old ways despite herself. She knows which herbs make which teas, how to brand cattle and castrate goats, and how to make red wine and corn whiskey. And, she knows about spirits.

While my mother gathers the dishes, I line up my cowboys and Indians on the kitchen table and listen to her and my grandmother whisper in Spanish about dead relatives. When Desolina catches me eavesdropping — and she always catches me — she laughs under her breath and beckons me with an arthritic finger. "Come here, *mí hijito,*" she says, leaning from the edge of her chair, and clutching her shiny black handbag. Then, in a low hoarse voice, she tells me about the fireballs she saw dancing along the Rio Grande bosque, the footsteps dragging down her hallway at midnight, and the hooded crone who transformed into a banshee and chased two of her brothers home one night on the acequia between Alameda and Corrales. "It's true," she says, nodding at my wide eyes, and breaking into a smile of red lipstick and crooked teeth. "Did you go to church like I told you?"

When the owl flutters by, Desolina makes the sign of the cross and squints. Owls are bad omens, she mutters. Navajos consider them evil spirits. *Brujas* use them to deliver messages.

"*Que fea,*" she says, mouth twisted. "Why did you bring that ugly thing into your home?"

My mother shrugs, filling the sink with hot water. "I think she's beautiful."

When Tirzah settles on a chair across from her, Desolina holds the owl's intense gaze. Then, the old woman slips a glow-in-the dark rosary from her purse, turns her head, and spits.

I don't go camping, like the other kids on my block. I don't go fishing, boating, or even to Uncle Cliff's Family Land. My mother doesn't like tourists. She doesn't like to do what everyone else does. On the week-ends, we go exploring. We pile into her metallic green '67 Comet and hit the back roads. We visit churches, graveyards, ranch towns, and adobe ruins, chasing a culture she says is vanishing before our eyes. She talks to old people and collects antique tables and chairs while I run with my siblings through the juniper and ponderosa pine playing *Last of the Mohicans.*

On a Saturday morning washed clean by spring rain, we take my grandfather's pickup north to Truchas, a village so high in the Sangre de Cristos we almost touch the clouds. In a meadow beside the main road, my grandfather Carlos discovers a slice of aspen bark, eight feet long, crescent shaped, with a knothole at one end. My uncle, who's tagged along for the ride, says it looks like a cobra. I see a dragon. My mother says it has character, so we pitch it into the truck.

Before heading back to Albuquerque, we stop at the *tiendita* for gas, chile chips, and root beer. The old man behind the counter tells us the bark was cut by lightning a few nights earlier. He saw the flash and heard the boom. This makes my mother smile. Great symbolism, she says.

Back home, she and my uncle nail the plank across the living room wall as the centerpiece of her artifact collection. Tirzah notices immediately. She flies from the dining room pottery case and claims the perch as her own, sliding into the knothole, watching us through the dragon's eye.

My brother finds most of our strays. Or they find him. He'll see a German shepherd digging in a garbage can, walk right up, and it'll lick his hand, a friend for life. He has a way with animals, who soothe him in a way our mother can't. He was six when our father died. He has the most memories. I was two. I remember almost nothing. We're polar opposites, as our mother likes to say. And she's right. My brother loses his temper like the strike of a match, plays hardball without a glove, and keeps a Mexican switchblade in his drawer. He's always moving, always fidgeting, always running, as if he's afraid to look over his shoulder. I'm steady, docile, and brooding, like my duck, Hercules, with his blunt beak and orange feet, quite happy to never leave his yard.

On weekday afternoons, Tirzah waits by the front window for my brother to return from school. She hoots when he shuffles through the driveway, flies to his room while he changes from school clothes into blue jeans, and perches patiently on his shoulder while our mother tethers them together with a strand of yarn; boy's wrist to owl's leg. Task complete, they step outside to straddle his Stingray bike. I watch from the porch as Tirzah's eyes swallow light and motion; the flashing chrome handlebars, the fluttering cottonwood leaf. "Be careful," our mother says, but my brother ignores her. He stands on his pedals and steers a wide circle under the street lamp, gathering speed for the lap around the block. Tirzah grips his jacket, and leans into the wind.

The owl isn't my pet, although I'd like her to be. She won't come when I call, perch on my finger, or accept stew meat from my hand, as she does with my mother, uncle, or brother. It's not that I'm afraid. It's more that she's too beautiful to touch. When I get nervous, she flies away.

One afternoon, while I'm doing homework, Tirzah flutters down to the dining room table.

"Hi, pretty girl," says my mother, who sits beside me sewing a blouse. "Are you thirsty?"

Tirzah waddles up to me, ignoring the water bowl my mother slides forward.

I tap the pencil eraser on my teeth.

"Go ahead," my mother says. "Pet her. She won't bite."

"I know. She just doesn't like me."

"That's not true. Scratch her head. She loves that. Rub in little circles."

I extend the pencil. Tirzah flinches, eyes wide, preparing to fly.

"See!"

"Just wait. Try again. Slower this time."

I inch the eraser forward until it touches the owl's head. Tirzah squints, but stays put.

"Good," my mother says. "Use your finger. See how funny it feels? Like a ping pong ball?"

Tirzah closes her eyes and leans into the pressure. The more she relaxes, the more I relax.

After a few minutes, the owl curls her toes and rolls onto her side, asleep.

My grandfather Carlos stops by our house sometimes on the way home from his shift on the highway crew. At sixty-five, after raising eight children, picking fruit, and working construction, he insists on holding a job. He nods hello, settles into a corner rocker, hangs his gray fedora on his bony knee, while my mother fetches him a cold Coors longneck. Carlos doesn't talk much. He prefers to watch, listen, and absorb the warmth of a family life he never had as a boy. His father died when he was eight. When his mother remarried, her husband refused to raise another man's son, so she sent him to a boarding school in Santa Fe. He ran away whenever he got the chance, often standing while his family ate supper. Eventually, he left Santa Fe for good, he and a friend, walking a hundred miles through the Rio Puerco badlands to the mining village of Marquez, where he was offered a handyman job. Carlos slept in arroyos, caves, and abandoned barns during that trek through the high desert, bedding down among the range grass, chamisa, and cholla cactus. On those lonely nights, owls watched him from the junipers, bathed in silver moonlight.

On one of his visits to our house, Tirzah flutters to his armrest from her aspen perch. Carlos extends a finger and she hops on. He raises her to his nose, and smiles.

Each winter, our house fills with the sweet scent of piñon. We have no fireplace or wood-burning stove, so my mother sprinkles trading post incense over the steel grate of our living room floor furnace. It reminds her of childhood, she says of the smell, crumbling sawdust sticks between her fingers, then standing back while orange sparks swirl before her eyes. As a girl, she stoked the potbelly stove in her grandmother's kitchen. Piñon reminds her of black coffee in tin cups, thick cotton quilts, and crackling *orno* flames. Piñon takes her back, she tells me.

When my mother leaves to prepare supper, I take her place on the furnace vent, standing in the hot current of air until my blue jeans burn my legs. As Tirzah glides through the room, white smoke curling from her wings, I imagine I'm soaring through the clouds beside her, or drifting like an apparition above the antique tables, the brass lamps, the Navajo rugs and the broken pots, haunting this room forever.

On nights before art show openings, I sleep to the hiss of my uncle's propane torch and the click of his sculptor's tools. He's the baby in my mother's family; fourteen years her junior. He moved in with us four years after my father died because my mother didn't feel safe alone with five children on the rural edge of northwest Albuquerque. She also wanted a male role model for my brother and me, although my uncle was barely out of his teens. He listens to The Doors, Jimi Hendrix, and Country Joe and the Fish, wears a beard and shoulder-length hair, and walks barefoot everywhere, even in the mountains. I think he looks exactly like George Harrison stepping onto the crosswalk of my mother's favorite album, *Abbey Road*, but my grandmother thinks he looks like Jesus. Desolina wants him to be a priest, to help atone for her sins, but instead he becomes an artist. With needle-nose pliers and rods of Pyrex glass, he creates intricate figurines of Hopi eagle dancers, Mexican *vaqueros*, and Navajo shepherds, then he mounts them on driftwood, sandstone, and volcanic rock. I watch him from my pillow with his wizard's hair and welder's glasses, spinning solid into liquid into solid again, crafting icy figures from fire. Tirzah perches above his worktable on these nights, drawn, as I am, to his clear blue flame.

My mother wants to bless our pets. Although she left the Catholic Church some years after my father died, she wants protection for our strays. So, on a warm Sunday in February, we load the ducks, geese, peacock, goat, and owl into our Comet, and attend the outdoor ceremony.

We stand in line behind a dozen puppies, kitties, gerbils, and bunnies. The priest chuckles from the gazebo as he sprinkles holy water. When our turn arrives, he stops midmotion and appraises us behind silver-rimmed eyeglasses. My brother slouches before the dais, arms folded, Tirzah on his shoulder. I kneel beside the black Nubian goat, which suckles noisily from its baby bottle. My oldest sister cradles the peacock, while the other two hold ducks and geese. Our mother lingers on the steps with her eyes hidden behind Jackie O sunglasses. We're longhaired and tie-dyed and proud of it, in full bloom eight years after my father died, surrounded by the animals that brought new life into our home. Parishioners scowl. A poodle yaps. A news photographer snaps our portrait. After a long pause, the priest mumbles a prayer. The next day, we make the front page.

Tirzah surprises us. When one of the dogs slinks through the house, she contracts her feathers, squints, and becomes as thin as a dry branch, camouflaged completely against the gray aspen plank. She changes direction in midflight, too, hovering like a helicopter, swiveling her head, and returning silently the way she came. She's also a hunter. When we place a chunk of stew meat before her, she puffs to twice her normal size, dilates her pupils, and pounces. She thumps the meat hard against the perch, then flings it to the floor. Talons scratching hardwood, yellow eyes blazing, she stalks her meal. Finding it, she stretches her beak wide, and swallows it whole.

During the day, the sun is too bright for the owl's eyes, so she seeks dark corners to sleep. One morning, when the temperature hits eighty-nine, my middle sister reaches into the hall closet to flick on the swamp cooler, but leaves the door ajar. The chain is broken on the overhead bulb, and the closet is always pitch black. Tirzah, gazing toward the opening from her living room perch, flutters atop the closet door. I hold my breath. My sister calls our mother. Normally, the closet is off limits to us kids. We try to shoo Tirzah away, but she won't budge. She will only stare into the cool abyss. After a moment, she lowers her head and hops inside. From then on, the hall closet becomes her sanctuary. To fetch her, I must reach into the darkness, brushing my father's things.

My brother finds another stray, a baby meadowlark that had fallen from a cottonwood into an alfalfa field near his school. He can't find the nest, so he tucks the orphan under his arm and carries it home. Our mother swaddles the chick in a washcloth, fetches some old newspapers, and phones the ornithologist. I watch her fill an eyedropper with water and hold it to the bird's beak. She adores meadowlarks, she says after hanging up. As a girl, while staying with her grandparents in Corrales, she often woke to the song of meadowlarks in the apple orchards across the road.

"It was so beautiful," she tells me, puckering her lips to whistle. "But sad, too."

She retrieves an extra birdcage from the back porch, places the chick inside, and covers the wire dome with a bed sheet, as the ornithologist instructed. Standing on her tiptoes, she sets the bundle atop the pottery case, away from the cats. Tirzah watches from her living room perch.

The next morning, I hear my mother scream. In the dining room, I find her holding the birdcage. In the center lies the meadowlark, wet with blood.

"Poor little thing," she cries, swatting a tabby off the table. "See what you did!"

My uncle steps inside from the back yard, examines the bird, and concludes that its skull has been crushed. He checks the cage for damage. Finding none, he snatches up the cat and holds its paw to the wire bars, but its arm is too thick to fit through. Stumped, he searches the house for clues. On the aspen plank, he discovers bits of wet gray fuzz. After retrieving Tirzah from the closet, he holds her tightly with one hand, then uses the other to extend one of her long bony legs, which slips neatly into the cage, within easy reach of where the meadowlark had slept.

"You dirty rat!" my uncle says, holding the owl to his face. "Did you kill that poor bird?"

Tirzah bites his thumb, wriggles away, and flutters to the living room. She scowls at us the rest of the day. She won't even come to my mother.

I have no bed and no room of my own. For a year I sleep on an aluminum cot beside the antique church pew in our living room. My mother buys me Peanuts sheets to make me feel better but I hate that cot, sliding it down the hall each night. The foam mattress smells like dirty socks. The joints pinch my skin. Be patient, my mother says. For my tenth birthday, she'll restore one of the iron headboards on the back porch. Soon, I'll join my uncle and brother in the boys' room.

When she switches off the floor lamp and the ten o'clock news, I'm alone. I lie back under the silver glow of the curbside street light with the clicks from the vintage clock and the creaks of old walls. From the haze of half sleep, I sense Tirzah awaken. I hear scratching. Feel the weight of eyes. Breathe in the aroma of mothballs and dust. I snap awake and sit up, but there's only a whisper, an echo, a slight disturbance of air.

The longer she stays with us, the more stir-crazy Tirzah becomes. Every few weeks or so, she flies into the broad living room window, unable to see the glass, confused when she can't pass through. My mother draws the curtains, then replaces the drapes with bamboo shades, but whenever a sparrow darts by outside, Tirzah chases after it, straight into the glass. My uncle, fearing the owl will crack her skull or break the window, nails a row of Russian olive branches to the outside of the frame. Tirzah settles on a chair back, gazing through the bars.

One afternoon, the owl goes missing. She's not on her perch, in the closet, or in the back rooms. I search under the beds, behind the bookshelves, inside cabinets. I search with my siblings for nearly an hour but we can't find her. My mother sits in her rocker, jaw muscle flexing.

"She's gone," she mutters. "I know she is. One of you brats must have left the front door open again. How many times have I told you to close that damn door?"

My uncle thumps across the hardwood floor, checking behind chairs and tables. When one of the dogs slinks by, he kicks it. "Where's the flashlight? Who took the flashlight?"

I stand with my sisters in the dining room. I didn't leave the door open. I didn't do anything. But I feel like I did, like I always do when one of the pets is in trouble, like something that happened a long time ago is about to happen again.

"Don't just stand there," my mother says. "Look under the table again."

My little sister starts to cry.

Above the scrape and knock of old wooden chairs, we hear a muffled sound.

"Hoo."

"Hush!" my mother says. "Listen . . ."

"Hoo."

We turn toward the pottery case, to the Pueblo water bowl on a back shelf. Inside it, glaring at us over the rim, is Tirzah. She'd settled inside to sleep, but woke during our commotion.

"There you are!" My mother rushes forward. "My Tirzah . . ."

My sisters gather around her. My uncle snaps a photo.

I hesitate before joining them. I don't like what I see in the owl's eyes. She appears wary, as if she's seeing my family for the first time.

We're late returning home from an outing up north. The horizon burns magenta as we race blue shadows home. We arrive in darkness. My uncle flicks on the house lights while my mother fires the floor furnace. Tirzah, who hasn't eaten since morning, hoots from her perch. My mother squeaks open the refrigerator, scans the shelves, but finds no stew meat, only breakfast steak. She checks the clock. Safeway has just closed. The breakfast steak is fresh, so she chops it for the owl.

The next day, Tirzah won't eat or drink. She barely flies. The ornithologist asks my mother to read the steak label to him over the phone. She does, her voice barely a whisper. The breakfast steak has a chemical protein that stew meat does not, he informs her. Tirzah was poisoned.

My mother paces the living room. My sisters and I pray to St. Francis of Assisi.

The following morning, I find my mother sobbing at the dining room table. She'd woken up early to check on Tirzah and found her motionless in the water bowl. The thirsty owl had leaned over the rim and fallen inside. Too weak to climb out, Tirzah drowned.

My uncle digs deep in the backyard cactus garden, grunting white puffs of steam. My mother stands beside him holding a shoebox. Inside it lies the owl, wrapped in a washcloth. The air is still. The sky is pink and orange. My uncle tosses the shovel aside and it clangs against the cold ground. He and my mother shuffle away, heads down, seeking a hunk of driftwood or a large rock to mark the grave. I stare into the hole, another hole, another absence I will never fill.

After a few minutes, my uncle returns with a piñon branch. Without a word, my mother lowers the shoebox into the fine red sand. We bury Tirzah among the prickly pear, yucca, and chamisa, beside the goat, the peacock, and the mallard duck named Hercules.

The Pat Boone Fan Club
Sue William Silverman

Skimming the *Holland Sentinel*, a local newspaper in West Michigan, I see a man who has haunted me for years. Pat Boone. Once again I gaze at him in alluring black and white, just like the photograph I treasured in ninth grade. According to the article, he will be performing the first Saturday night in May at the Calvary Reformed Church as part of the Tulip Time Festival. I order a ticket immediately.

On the night of the concert, Pat Boone dazzles onto the stage in white bucks, tight white pants, a white jacket emblazoned with red-and-blue-sequined stars across the shoulders. Though he began as a fifties and sixties pop singer, he has aged into a Christian music icon favored by — I'm sure — Republicans. That I am a Jewish atheist liberal Democrat gives me no pause, not even as he performs in this concrete megachurch weighted with massive crosses. In fact, growing up, these very symbols gave me comfort.

I sit in the balcony, seats empty in the side sections. It's hardly a sold-out crowd. While we enthusiastically clap after the opening number, there are no whistles or shrieks from this mostly elderly, sedate audience. There is no dancing in the aisles, no rushing the stage. If a fan swoons from her upholstered pew, it will more likely be from stroke than idolatry. The cool, unscented air in the auditorium feels polite as a Sunday worship service — rather than a Saturday-night-rock-and-roll-swaggering-Mick-Jagger kind of concert.

Yet I am certainly worshipful. Of him. I am transfixed. It's as if his photograph — that paper image — is conjured to life. Through binoculars, breathless, I watch only him, me in my own white jacket, as if I knew we'd match.

I'm not surprised he still affects me. In fact, during the days leading up to tonight, I plotted how I might meet him after the concert, for I must finally tell him what I failed to say last time we met. But in case security guards stop me, I've written a letter that explains the role he played in my life. At the very least I'll ask a guard to hand-deliver my letter. To further prove my loyalty, I've retrieved, from an old scrapbook, my "SUE SILVERMAN IS A MEMBER OF THE PAT BOONE FAN CLUB" card, printed on blue card stock, which I've put in my pocket. But regardless of the letter or fan-club card, I'm determined to get close enough to touch him, the way I once touched that other photograph, years ago. Time collapses as if, even now, it's not too late for him to save me from my Jewish family, save me from a childhood long ended.

I curled up on the baby blue bedspread in my home in Glen Rock, New Jersey, a magnifying glass in my teenage hand. Slowly I scanned the glass across black-and-white photographs of Pat Boone in the latest issue of *Life* magazine. In one, he, his wife Shirley, and four daughters perch on a tandem bicycle in front of their New Jersey home, not many miles from my own. I was particularly drawn to the whiteness of the photos. Pat Boone's white-white teeth beamed at me, his white bucks spotless. I savored each cell of his being, each molecule, as I traced my finger across his magnified image. I believed I felt skin, the pale hairs on his forearms. Only a membrane of paper separated me from a slick fingernail, a perfectly shaped ear, the iris of his eye. Surely the wind gusted his hair, his family's hair, but in the photograph all movement was frozen, the bicycle wheels stationary, never to speed away from me. The family itself was in tandem, legs pumping in perfect, still arcs. It was this crisp, clean, unchanging certainty that I craved.

The hands on his wristwatch were stopped at 3:40. I glanced at my own watch — almost 3:40. I didn't move, waiting for the minute hand to reach the eight, as if I could will time itself to stop, entranced by the notion that we would both endlessly exist in this same segment of time. For even as I tumbled inside the photograph, we remained static on this one particular day, suspended at 3:40 . . .

. . . *trapped together, me on the tandem bike directly behind him, leaning toward him. Now inside the black-and-white photo, I see lilacs, maple trees, shutters on the windows. But I'm never distracted by scents or colors. I never inhale the Ivory soap of his shirt, never sense the warm friction of rubber beneath the wheels of the bike, never have to feel loss or know that seasons change. My ponytail, streaming behind my back, is frozen, captured with him and his family — now my consistent and constantly loving family.*

For hours I fantasized about living inside this black-and-white print, unreachable. This immaculate universe was safe, far away from my father's messy flesh-and-blood hands, hands that hurt me at night.

Through my bedroom window, sun glinted off the glass I held inches from his face. Round magnifier. Beam of light. Halo. I placed my hand, fingers spread, beneath the glass, hovering just above the paper, as if glass, hand, photograph, *him* — all existed in disembodied heavenly light.

As the bus rumbled across the George Washington Bridge, over the Hudson River, I clutched a ticket to his television show in one hand, a copy of his book, *'Twixt Twelve and Twenty*, in the other. Silently, I sang the words, his words, with which he closed his weekly program, "See the USA in your Chevrolet," a show I watched religiously on our black-and-white Zenith. With the darkness of New Jersey behind me, the gleaming lights of Manhattan before me, I felt as if I myself were a photograph slowly being developed into a new life. In just an hour I would see him. I wanted to be with him — be his wife, lover, daughter, houseguest, girlfriend, best friend, pet. Interchangeable. Any one of these relationships would do.

Sitting in the studio during the show, I waited for it to end. Mainly, I waited for the time when we would meet. Yes, I suppose I loved his voice, his music. At least, if asked, I would *claim* to love his songs. What else could I say since there was no language at that moment to specify what I most needed from Pat Boone? How could I explain to him — to anybody — that if I held that magnifying glass over *my* skin, I would see my father's fingerprints? I would see skin stained with shame. I would see a girl who seemed marked by her very Jewishness. Since my Jewish father misloved me, what I needed in order to be saved was an audience with Pat Boone.

Here in *this* audience, I was surrounded by girls crying and screaming his name. But I was different from these fans. Surely he knew this, too, sensed my silent presence, the secret life we shared. Soon, I no longer heard the girls, no longer noticed television cameras, cue cards, musicians. No longer even heard his voice or which song he sang. All I saw was his face suffused in a spotlight, one beam that seemed to emanate from a darkened sky.

After the show, I queued up with other fans outside the stage door. I waited with my Aqua-Net-sprayed flipped hair, Peter Pan collar, circle pin, penny loafers. Slowly the line inched forward, girls seeking autographs.

But when I reached him, I was too startled to speak. Now I faced him in living color. Pink shirt. Brown hair. Suede jacket. His tan hands moved; his brown eyes actually blinked. I could see him *breathe*. I forgot my carefully rehearsed words: "Will you adopt me?"

Besides, if I spoke, I feared he wouldn't even hear me. My voice would be too low, too dim, too insignificant, too tainted. He would know I was too distant to be saved. I felt as if I'd fallen so far from that photograph that my own image was out of focus. I was a blur, a smudged Jewish blur of a girl, mesmerized by a golden cross, an amulet on a chain around his neck. Speechless, I continued to stand, unmoving, holding up the line.

Finally he smiled and asked, "Is that for me?" He gestured toward the book. I held it out to him. Quickly he scrawled his name.

Later, alone in my bedroom, lying on my blue bedspread, I trailed a fingertip over his autograph. I spent days learning to copy his signature. I traced it, duplicated it. Using black India ink, I forged the name "Pat Boone" on my school notebooks. I wrote his name on my white Keds with a ballpoint pen. At the Jersey shore I scrawled my own love letters in the sand. But I had missed my chance to speak to him. For years those words I wanted to say remained unspoken.

Now, watching him through binoculars in the Calvary Reformed Church in Holland, Michigan, I again scan every cell of his face, his neck. I'm sure I can observe individual molecules in his fingers, palms, hands, wrists. He wears a gold pinkie ring, a gold-link bracelet. And a watch! That watch? I wonder if it's the same 3:40 watch. In his presence I am once again tranced — almost as if we've been in a state of suspension together all this time.

He doesn't even appear to have aged — much. Boyish good looks,

brown hair. Yet this grandfather sings his golden oldies, tributes to innocence and teenage love: "Bernadine," "Love Letters in the Sand,"
"Moody River," "Friendly Persuasion," "Tutti Frutti." His newer songs
are about God and country. Well, he sings, after all, to a white Christian audience, mainly elderly church ladies with tight gray curls, pastel
pantsuits, sensible shoes. I know I am the only one here who voted for
President Clinton, who wears open-toed sandals, who doesn't believe
in God. But nothing deters me. I feel almost like that teenage girl yearning to be close to him, closer.

From the piano, he retrieves a bouquet of tulips wrapped in cello-
phane, telling the audience that at each concert he gives flowers to one
young girl. Peering into the darkened auditorium, he asks, half joking,
whether any girls have actually come to the concert. "Have any of you
mothers or grandmothers brought your granddaughter with you?"

I lean forward, looking around. In one section — members of a tour
bus, no doubt — is a group of older women all wearing jaunty red hats.
At least twenty of these hats turn in unison as if searching the audience.
No one else moves. The row in front of me seems to be mother-and-
daughter pairs, but most of the daughters wear bifocals, while some
of the mothers, I noticed earlier, used canes to climb the stairs. After
a moment of silence, Pat Boone, cajoling, lets us know he found one
young girl at his earlier, four o'clock show. He lowers the microphone
to his side, waiting.

Me. I want it to be me.

A girl, her neck bent, silky brown hair shading her face, finally walks
forward from the rear of the auditorium. Pat Boone hurries down the
few steps, greeting her before she reaches the stage. He holds out the
flowers, but she doesn't seem to realize she's supposed to take them.

"What's your name?" he asks.

"Amber." She wears ripped jeans and a faded sweatshirt.

"Here." Again he urges the tulips toward her hands. "These are for a
lovely girl named Amber."

As strains of "April Love" flow from the four-piece band, she finally
takes the flowers. His arm encircles her waist. Facing her, he sings as if
just to her, "April love is for the very young." The spotlight darkens, an

afterglow of sunset. The petals of the tulips, probably placed on stage hours earlier, droop.

After the song, Pat Boone beams at her and asks for a kiss. "On the cheek, of course." He laughs, reassuring the audience, as he points to the spot. The girl doesn't move. "Oh, please, just one little peck." His laugh dwindles to a smile.

I lean back, sliding down in my seat. I lower the binoculars to my lap.

Kiss him, I want to whisper to the girl, not wanting to witness Pat Boone embarrassed or disappointed.

No, walk away from him. Because he's old enough to be your father, your grandfather.

Instead, he leans forward and quickly brushes his lips on her cheek. With the bouquet held awkwardly in her arms, she escapes down the aisle to her seat.

Now his voice needs to rest, perhaps. The lights on stage are extinguished. Images of Pat Boone in the Holy Land flash on two large video screens built into the wall behind the pulpit. The introduction to the theme song from *Exodus* soars across the hushed audience. Atop the desert fortress Masada — the last outpost of Jewish zealots who chose mass suicide rather than Roman capture — a much younger Pat Boone, in tan chinos, arms outstretched, sings, "So take my hand and walk this land with me," lyrics he, himself, wrote. The real Pat Boone sits on a stool watching the video pan to Israeli children wearing kibbutz hats, orchards of fig trees, camels, the Sea of Galilee, Bethlehem, the old city in Jerusalem. The Via Dolorosa. The Wailing Wall. The Dead Sea.

"Until I die, this land is mine."

A final aerial shot circles a sweatless and crisp Pat Boone on Masada. Desert sand swelters in the distance.

This land is mine.

For the first time I wonder what he means by these words he wrote. Does he mean, literally, he thinks the Holy Land is his, that it belongs to Christianity? Or, perhaps, is he momentarily impersonating an Israeli, a Zionist, a Jew? Or maybe this appropriation is just a state of mind.

Pat Boone, Pat Boone. Who are you? I always thought I knew.

The lights flash on. Arising from his stool, Pat Boone is smiling. The band hits the chords as he proclaims we'll all have "A Wonderful Time Up There."

Periodically, growing up, I frequented churches, immersing myself in hymns and votive candles. Once I even owned a cross necklace and a garnet rosary, superficially believing Catholic and Christian amulets offered luck and protection. So I'm more familiar with Christian songs than those of my own religion, even though at one time in my life, in elementary school, I attended Jewish services.

Saturday mornings, when we lived on the island of St. Thomas, my parents and I drove up Synagogue Hill, parking by the wrought-iron gate leading to the temple. We entered the arched stucco door-way, where my father paused to don a yarmulke. Here the air was cool, shaded from tropical sun. In my best madras dress, I trailed behind my parents down the aisle, the floor thick with sand. My feet in my buffalo-hide sandals etched small imprints beside the tracks left by my father's heavy black shoes. I sat between my parents on one of the benches. The rabbi, standing before the mahogany ark containing the six To-rahs, began to pray. I slid from the bench to sit on the sandy floor.

The sand was symbolic in this nineteenth-century synagogue, founded by Sephardic Jews from Spain. During the Spanish Inquisi-tion, Jews, forced to worship in secret, met in cellars where they poured sand on floors to muffle footsteps, mute the sound of prayers. Other-wise, if caught, they would be killed. This was almost all I knew of Juda-ism except stories my mother told me about the Holocaust when bad things happened to Jews—little Jewish girls, too.

Throughout the service, I sprinkled sand over me as if at the beach. I trailed it down my bare legs. I slid off my sandals, submerging my toes beneath grains of coral. Lines of sand streaked the sweaty crooks of my elbows. Small mounds cupped my knees. I even trickled it on my head until it caught in the weave of my braids. I leaned against one of the cool, lime-whitewashed pillars, smudging my dress as well. No one in the congregation, not even my parents, ever seemed to notice. Perhaps they were too engrossed by readings from the Torah to see me . . . while, to me, none of *their* prayerful chants were as lovely as sand. Instead, I watched wands of light beam through arched windows glinting off mica in the sand, off me. I felt as if I, myself, could become one with whitewash, with sand, with light. Then, later that night, home in bed, maybe my father wouldn't find me, wouldn't be able to see or distinguish me. Maybe if I poured enough sand over my body I could discover how to hide all little Jewish girls, make us invisible. Instead, it seemed to be my own father's footsteps that were muffled, for no one in the congregation ever heard or saw him. Not as he really was.

After the concert, I slowly walk through the church lobby, exhausted. At the sales booth, buying a CD, I ask whether Pat Boone will be signing autographs. No one seems to know. A gray-haired man limps past, the word "Security" stenciled on his black T-shirt. The church ladies stream out the door, not seeming to expect anything more of the evening.

I could follow them.

But at the far corner of the lobby is a hallway that seems to lead to the back of the auditorium, behind the stage. It is empty. No one guards the entrance. I turn down its plush, blue-carpeted stillness. My footsteps are silent. It is a hush that might precede a worship service. Solemn, scentless air. Dim sconces line the walls. I had thought there would be a throng of grandmothers lining up for autographs and snapshots. But I am alone gripping his CD in one hand, my letter to him in the other.

At the end of the corridor are two wide doors, shut. I assume they're locked, but as I grasp the knob it turns. Another hallway. I pass another T-shirted guard, this one holding a silent walkie-talkie, his ear plugged with a hearing aid. I assume he'll stop me. But my straight solid footsteps, the determined look on my face, seem to grant me entrance. I must look as if I belong here. I act as if I know what I'm doing.

I *do* belong here. I *do* know what I'm doing.

Beyond another set of doors I reach a small group dressed in Dutch costumes, wooden clogs, including the mayor and his wife, who were on stage earlier to thank Pat Boone for celebrating the Tulip Time Festival. Beside them is another security guard, this one a teenage boy, murmuring into his walkie-talkie. I approach, wanting to ask him where I might find Pat Boone. I decide to throw myself on his mercy. I'm prepared to beg, plead, cry. I will say I've been waiting my whole life. I will say the Voice of God Himself *told* me to speak to Pat Boone.

The guard continues to mumble into his walkie-talkie. For a few more minutes I patiently wait for him to finish, until anxiety floods me. Suppose I miss him? He might be preparing to leave the building right this minute. He'll disappear before I find him.

Then, as if pulled by unseen forces, I turn away from the guard. I retrace my footsteps back through the set of doors.

I glimpse a white shirt. The back of a man's head. Brown hair. *Him.*

He and another man are just opening a door farther down the corridor.

I yell, "Mr. Boone. Pat Boone."

I rush after him, grabbing the door about to shut behind him. We're in a small foyer just behind the stage. Not understanding the force of my need, the other man tries to shoo me away. I ignore him, pleading, "Mr. Boone. I have to speak to you. Just for a minute. I've been waiting. Pat Boone."

I push past the assistant and stand right in front of Pat Boone. His red-and-blue-sequined jacket is off. He's in his white shirt, white pants, white shoes. His face is still in makeup. He has few wrinkles. His eyes are almost expressionless. It's as if his whole life all he's practiced is his public smile, and the rest of his face is frozen — but familiar to me — the way he looked in the photograph. And there they are as he smiles at me, albeit tentatively: his white-white teeth.

My words are garbled, rushed, confused. I don't know how much time I have, when I will be removed. So much to explain. I hardly know where to start. I tell him how much I loved the photograph in *Life* magazine.

"Oh, yes, that tandem bicycle," he says. "I remember that."

"But you saved my life," I say.

I am telling him about my father, what happened with my father, that it was *he*, Pat Boone . . . just knowing he existed kept me going . . . just seeing his photograph helped me stay alive . . . that he represented — what word do I use? "Safety"? "Holiness"? "Purity"?

He has taken a step back, away from me. His smile may have dimmed by one decibel. Am I acting like a crazy woman? Am I the first woman who has ever pursued him to confess that her father once hurt her, and that he, Pat Boone, represented *hope*? Just thinking that one day he might . . . .

"Well, I'm glad to know that I did something good," he says. "That I helped someone."

"Oh, yes," I say. "You were everything. Your family. Your daughters."

"I guess these things happen a lot," he says. "To children. It's terrible."

"Here." I give him the letter. "This will explain how I felt."

He takes the letter, folded in an envelope. That hand — those clean fingers I studied by the hour.

"I'll write back to you," he says. "After I read it."

My audience with him is over. "Thank you," I whisper, turning to leave.

I pause in the parking lot in the damp spring night. The massive walls of the church loom over me. Busloads of grandmothers rumble from the lot.

I was too overwhelmed to tell him about the magnifying glass or his wristwatch. Nor did I say, *I want you to adopt me* — the one thing I've most wanted. Of course, even *I* know how crazy that would sound. Besides, is it even still true?

I get in my car and shut the door. But I continue to watch the church. Maybe I'll catch one last glimpse of him. Him. *Did* he help sustain me all those years? *Did* he offer hope?

Yes. His image. His milky white image.

That sterile pose. I conjured him into the man I needed him to be: a safe father. By my believing in that constant image, he *did* save me, without my being adopted, without my even asking.

At the end of the concert, the mayor of Holland and his wife came on stage to present Pat Boone with a special pair of wooden clogs painted to resemble his trademark bucks. Again, I had to lower the binoculars, embarrassed for him, unable to watch, just as when he gave the tulips to that young girl.

I wonder if anyone else in the audience felt uncomfortable when this father, this grandfather, tried to coerce a kiss from that adolescent girl? Or, did anyone notice *her* embarrassment, her shame? No, that's not a thought that would trouble any of Pat Boone's fans in Calvary. But Calvary doesn't exist for me, cannot be made to exist for me — even by Pat Boone.

Pat Boone! Those two short syllables have stretched the length of my life. So regardless of religion or illusion, his love letters offered me improbable safety — grooved in vinyl, etched in sand.

Reading List of Contemporary Creative Nonfiction

This reading list includes a wide range of contemporary nonfiction works you may want to explore in your journey toward finding your own voice and vision. For periodic updates to the reading list, visit my Web site, www.suewilliamsilverman.com.

Illness, Accident, Grief, Addiction

Isabel Allende, *Paula*

A. Manette Ansay, *Limbo: A Memoir*

Charles Barber, *Songs from the Black Chair: A Memoir of Mental Interiors*

Karen Brennan, *Being with Rachel: A Story of Memory and Survival*

Harold Brodkey, *This Wild Darkness: The Story of My Death*

Anatole Broyard, *Intoxicated by My Illness*

Susan Cheever, *Note Found in a Bottle*

Linda Katherine Cutting, *Memory Slips*

Joan Didion, *The Year of Magical Thinking*

Mark Doty, *Heaven's Coast*

Andre Dubus, *Broken Vessels; Meditations from a Moving Chair*

Hope Edelman, *Motherless Daughters: The Legacy of Loss*

Mary Felstiner, *Out of Joint: A Private and Public Story of Arthritis*

Kenny Fries, *Body, Remember*

Barbara Gordon, *I'm Dancing as Fast as I Can*

Emily Fox Gordon, *The Mockingbird Years: A Life In and Out of Therapy*

Temple Grandin, *Thinking in Pictures: My Life with Autism*

Lucy Grealy, *Autobiography of a Face*

Evan Handler, *Time on Fire: My Comedy of Terrors*

Ann Hood, *Do Not Go Gentle: The Search for Miracles in a Cynical Time*

Portia Iverson, *Strange Son: Two Mothers, Two Sons, and the Quest to Unlock the Hidden World of Autism*

Kay Jamison, *An Unquiet Mind*

Roger Kamenetz, *Terra Infirma*

Susanna Kaysen, *Girl, Interrupted*

Jamaica Kincaid, *My Brother*

Natalie Kusz, *Road Song*

Stephen Kuusisto, *Planet of the Blind*

Mindy Lewis, *Life Inside*

Audre Lorde, *The Cancer Journal*

Nancy Mairs, *Carnal Acts; Waist-High in the World: A Life Among the Nondisabled*

Donald M. Murray, *The Lively Shadow: Living with the Death of a Child*

Christopher Noel, *In the Unlikely Event of a Water Landing: A Geography of Grief*

Reynolds Price, *A Whole New Life*

Alice Sebold, *Lucky*

Allen Shawn, *Wish I Could Be There: Notes from a Phobic Life*

Jay and Sue Shotel, *It's Good to Know a Miracle: Dani's Story, One Family's Struggle with Leukemia*

Sue William Silverman, *Love Sick: One Woman's Journey through Sexual Addiction*

Floyd Skloot, *In the Shadow of Memory*

Susan Sontag, *Illness as Metaphor*

Patricia Stacey, *The Boy Who Loved Windows*

Mary Swander, *Out of This World: A Journey of Healing*

Daniel Tammet, *Born on a Blue Day*

Melanie Thernstrom, *The Dead Girl*

Mark Vonnegut, *The Eden Express: A Memoir of Insanity*

Darcy Wakefield, *I Remember Running: The Year I Got Everything I Wanted — and ALS*

Elizabeth Wurtzel, *Prozac Nation*

Family, Relationships, Friendships, Identity

Laurie Alberts, *Fault Line*

Paul Auster, *The Invention of Solitude*

Peter Balakian, *Black Dog of Fate: An American Son Uncovers His Armenian Past*

Amy Benson, *The Sparkling-Eyed Boy: A Memoir of Love, Grown Up*

Jane Bernstein, *Loving Rachel*

Mary Clearman Blew, *All But the Waltz: Five Generations in the Life of a Montana Family*

Greg Bottoms, *Angelhead: My Brother's Descent into Madness*

John Burnside, *A Lie About My Father*

Mary Cappello, *Night Bloom; Awkward: A Detour*

Susan Cheever, *Home Before Dark*

Joan Connor, *The World Before Mirrors*

Bernard Cooper, *The Bill from My Father; Truth Serum*

Francine Cournos, *City of One*

Laura Cunningham, *Sleeping Arrangements*

John Daniel, *Looking After: A Son's Memoir*

Patty Dann, *The Baby Boat: A Memoir of Adoption*

Debra Dickerson, *An American Story*

John Dickerson, *On Her Trail: My Mother, Nancy Dickerson, TV News' First Woman Star*

Francine du Plessix Gray, *Them: A Memoir of Parents*

Tony Earley, *Somehow Form a Family: Stories That Are Mostly True*

Dave Eggers, *A Heartbreaking Work of Staggering Genius*

Nora Eisenberg, *The War at Home*

Kathleen Finneran, *The Tender Land*

Nick Flynn, *Another Bullshit Night in Suck City*

Patricia Foster, *All the Lost Girls: Confessions of a Southern Daughter*

Paula Fox, *Borrowed Finery*

Dorothy Gallagher, *How I Came into My Inheritance*
Gail Hosking Gilberg, *Snake's Daughter: The Roads In and Out of War*
Rigoberto Gonzalez, *Butterfly Boy: Memories of a Chicano Mariposa*
Mary Gordon, *The Shadow Man: A Daughter's Search for her Father*
Vivian Gornick, *Fierce Attachments*
Kathryn Harrison, *The Kiss*
Carol Hebald, *The Heart Too Long Suppressed*
Michelle Herman, *The Middle of Everything: Memoirs of Motherhood*
Adam Hochschild, *Half the Way Home: A Memoir of Father and Son*
Richard Hoffman, *Half the House*
Sonya Huber, *Opa Nobody*
Susan Jacoby, *Half-Jew*
Brian Jennings, *Mama's Boy, Preacher's Son: Growing Up, Coming Out,
    and Changing America*
Dinah Lenney, *Bigger Than Life: A Murder, A Memoir*
Aaron Raz Link & Hilda Raz, *What Becomes You*
Bret Lott, *Fathers, Sons, Brothers: The Men in My Family*
Lee Martin, *From Our House*
James McBride, *The Color of Water: A Black Man's Tribute to his
    White Mother*
Nathan McCall, *Makes Me Wanna Holler: A Young Black Man in
    America*
Rebecca McClanahan, *The Riddle Song and Other Rememberings*
Karen McElmurray, *Surrendered Child: A Birth Mother's Journey*
Valerie Miner, *The Low Road: A Scottish Family Memoir*
Sharona Ben-Tov Muir, *Tracing the Secrets of My Father's Lives*
Michael Ondaatje, *Running in the Family*
Ann Patchett, *Truth and Beauty*
Molly Peacock, *Paradise, Piece by Piece*
Sandra Scofield, *Occasions of Sin*
Sue William Silverman, *Because I Remember Terror, Father, I
    Remember You*
Deborah Tall, *A Family of Strangers*
Danielle Trussoni, *Falling Through the Earth*
Bruce Weigl, *The Circle of Hanh*

John Edgar Wideman, *Brothers and Keepers*

Gregory Williams, *Life on the Color Line: The True Story of a White Boy Who Discovered He Was Black*

Sean Wilsey, *Oh the Glory of It All*

Edwin John Wintle, *Breakfast With Tiffany: An Uncle's Memoir*

Geoffrey Wolff, *The Duke of Deception: Memories of My Father*

Tobias Wolff, *This Boy's Life*

Mort Zachter, *Dough*

Childhood and Coming of Age

Marvin V. Arnett, *Pieces from Life's Crazy Quilt*

Julene Bair, *One Degree West: Reflections of a Plainsdaughter*

Phyllis Barber, *How I Got Cultured: A Nevada Memoir*

Jo Ann Beard, *The Boys of My Youth*

David Carkeet, *Campus Sexpot: A Memoir*

Jerome Charyn, *The Dark Lady from Belorusse*

J. M. Coetzee, *Boyhood*

Judith Ortiz Cofer, *Silent Dancing: A Partial Remembrance of a Puerto Rican Childhood*

Frank Conroy, *Stop-Time*

Faith Edise, Nina Sichel, eds., *Unrooted Childhoods: Memoirs of Growing Up Global*

James Ellroy, *My Dark Places*

Lucy Ferriss, *Unveiling the Prophet: The Misadventures of a Reluctant Debutante*

Alexandra Fuller: *Don't Let's Go to the Dogs Tonight: An African Childhood*

Helena Ganor, *Four Letters to the Witnesses of My Childhood: One Woman's Childhood in Nazi Occupation*

Henry Louis Gates, *Colored People*

Patricia Hampl, *A Romantic Education*

Heidi Hart, *Grace Notes: The Waking of a Woman's Voice*

Eva Hoffman, *Lost in Translation*

June Jordan, *Soldier: A Poet's Childhood*

Lisa Knopp, *Flight Dreams: A Life in the Midwestern Landscape*
Jennifer Lauck, *Blackbird: A Childhood Lost and Found*
Audre Lorde, *Zami: A New Spelling of My Name*
Debra Marquart, *Growing Up Wild in the Middle of Nowhere*
Mary McCarthy, *Memories of a Catholic Girlhood*
Frank McCourt, *Angela's Ashes*
Paul Monette, *Becoming a Man: Half a Life Story*
Vladimir Nabokov, *Speak Memory*
Bich Minh Nguyen, *Stealing Buddha's Dinner*
Gayle Pemberton, *The Hottest Water in Chicago: Notes of a Native Daughter*
Nahid Rachlin, *Persian Girls*
Alberto Rios, *Capirotadas: A Nogales Memoir*
Richard Rodriguez, *Hunger of Memory: The Education of Richard Rodriguez*
Moses Rosenkranz, *Childhood: An Autobiographical Fragment*
Esmeralda Santiago, *When I Was Puerto Rican*
Lynne Sharon Schwartz, *Ruined by Reading: A Life in Books*
Brenda Serotte, *The Fortune Teller's Kiss*
Kate Simon, *Bronx Primitive: Portraits in a Childhood*
Lori Soderlind, *Chasing Montana: A Love Story*
Ilan Stavans, *On Borrowed Words: A Memoir of Language*
Richard Wright, *Black Boy*

Place, Nature, Science, Travel

Edward Abbey, *Desert Solitaire*
Diane Ackerman, *A Natural History of the Senses*
Susanne Antonetta, *Body Toxic; A Mind Apart*
Kim Barnes, *Hungry for the World*
Rick Bass, *Winter*
Charles Bergman, *Red Delta: Fighting for Life at the End of the Colorado River*
Wendell Berry, *Recollected Essays, 1965–1980*
Jennifer Brice, *The Last Settlers*

Jane Brox, *Here and Nowhere Else: Late Seasons of a Farm and its Family*

Joanna Burger, *The Parrot Who Owns Me*

Franklin Burroughs, *Billy Watson's Croker Sack*

Bruce Chatwin, *In Patagonia*

Allison Adelle Hedge Coke, *Rock, Ghost, Willow, Deer: A Story of Survival*

Jerry Dennis, *A Place on the Water: An Angler's Reflections on Home*

Annie Dillard, *Pilgrim at Tinker Creek: Teaching a Stone to Talk*

Ivan Doig, *This House of Sky*

Ariel Dorfman, *Heading South, Looking North*

Gretel Ehrlich, *The Solace of Open Space*

J. H. Fabre, *Social Life in the Insect World*

Jill Fredston, *Roving to Latitude: Journeys Along the Arctic's Edge*

James Galvin, *The Meadow*

Merrill Joan Gerber, *Botticelli Blue Skies: An American in Florence*

Edward Hoagland, *The Courage of Turtles*

Marybeth Holleman, *The Heart of the Sound: An Alaskan Paradise Found and Nearly Lost*

Garrett Hongo, *Volcano: A Memoir of Hawai'i*

Marcy Houle, *Prairie Keepers*

Cynthia Huntington, *The Salt House: A Summer on the Dunes of Cape Cod*

Barbara Hurd, *Entering the Stones: On Caves and Feeling Through the Dark*

Kathleen Jamie, *Findings: Essays on the Natural and Unnatural World*

Theresa Jordan, *Riding the White Horse Home: A Western Family Album*

William Kittredge, *Hole in the Sky*

Verlyn Klinkenborg, *The Last Fine Time*

Ted Kooser, *Local Wonders: Seasons in the Bohemian Alps*

David Lazar, *The Body of Brooklyn*

William Least Heat Moon, *Blue Highways*

Gretchen Legler, *On the Ice: An Intimate Portrait of Life at McMurdo Station, Antarctica*

Barry Lopez, *Arctic Dreams: Imagination and Desire in Northern Landscape*

Nancy Lord, *Beluga Days*

Norman MacLean, *A River Runs Through It*

Gregory Martin, *Mountain City*

Michael Martone, *The Flatness and Other Landscapes*

Peter Mayle, *A Year in Provence*

John McPhee, *Coming into the Country*

Kent Meyers, *The Witness of Combines*

Harry Middleton, *The Earth Is Enough*

Lawrence Millman, *Our Like Will Not Be There Again: Notes from the West of Ireland*

Kathleen Dean Moore, *Riverwalking: Reflections on Moving Water*

Michele Morano, *Grammar Lessons: Translating a Life in Spain*

Susan Brind Morrow, *The Names of Things*

Kathleen Norris, *Dakota: A Spiritual Geography*

Leila Philip, *A Family Place: A Hudson Valley Farm, Three Centuries, Five Wars, One Family*

Martin Prechtel, *Secrets of the Talking Jaguar: Memoirs from the Living Heart of a Mayan Village*

John Price, *Not Just Any Land: A Personal and Literary Journey into the American Grasslands; Man Killed by Pheasant: And Other Kinships*

Catherine Reid, *Coyote: Seeking the Hunter in Our Midst*

Bill Roorbach, *Temple Stream: A Rural Odyssey*

Dana Sachs, *The House on Dream Street: Memoir of an American Woman in Vietnam*

Alix Kates Shulman, *Drinking the Rain*

Mark Spragg, *When the River Changes Direction*

Robert Stepto, *Blue as the Lake: A Personal Geography*

Celia Thaxter, *An Island Garden*

Paul Theroux, *Old Patagonian Express*

Jim Toner, *Serendib*

Joy Williams, *Ill Nature*

Terry Tempest Williams, *Refuge: An Unnatural History of Family and Place*

Charles Wohlforth, *The Whale and the Supercomputer: On the Northern Front of Climate Change*

Baron Wormser, *The Road Washes Out in Spring*

Paul Zimmer, *After the Fire: A Writer Finds His Place*

New Journalism, Immersion, History, Social Issues, War, Political Issues, Religion, Spirituality, Feminism

Faith Adiele, *Meeting Faith: The Forest Journals of a Black Buddhist Nun*

Ricardo Ainslie, *Long Dark Road*

Steve Almond, *Candyfreak: A Journey through the Chocolate Underbelly of America*

Mark Curtis Anderson, *Jesus Sound Explosion*

Victoria Armour-Hileman, *Singing to the Dead: A Missioner's Life Among Refugees from Burma*

Bill Ayers, *Fugitive Days*

Roland Barthes, *Camera Lucida*

Ishmael Beah, *A Long Way Gone*

Samira Bellil (trans. Lucy R. McNair), *To Hell and Back*

Walter Benjamin, *The Arcades Project*

John Berger, *And Our Faces, My Heart, Brief as Photos*

Ilana M. Blumberg, *Houses of Study: A Jewish Woman Among Books*

Barrie Jean Borich, *My Lesbian Husband: Landscapes of a Marriage*

Lady Borton, *Sensing the Enemy: An American Woman Among the Boat People of Vietnam*

Charles Bowden, *Down by the River: Drugs, Money, Murder, and Family*

C. D. B. Bryan, *Friendly Fire*

Scott Cairns, *Short Trip to the Edge: A Spiritual Memoir*

Truman Capote, *In Cold Blood*

Jung Chang, *Wild Swans: Three Daughters of China*

Dalton Conley, *Honky*

Rosemary Daniell, *Confessions of a (Female) Chauvinist*

Tracy Daugherty, *Five Shades of Shadow*

Joan Didion, *Slouching Toward Bethlehem*

Beverly Donofrio, *Looking for Mary (Or, The Blessed Mother and Me)*

Brian Doyle, *The Wet Engine: Exploring the Mad Wild Miracle of the Heart*

Barbara Ehrenreich, *Nickel and Dimed: On (Not) Getting By in America*

Gretel Ehrlich, *Questions of Heaven: The Chinese Journey of an American Buddhist*

Janet Mason Ellerby, *Following the Tambourine Man: A Birthmother's Memoir*

Eduardo Galeano, *Soccer in Sun and Shadow*

William Gass, *On Being Blue: A Philosophical Inquiry*

Mikal Gilmore, *Shot in the Heart*

Melissa Fay Greene, *Praying for Sheetrock*

David Griffith, *A Good War Is Hard to Find: The Art of Violence in America*

Lee Gutkind, *Almost Human: Making Robots Think*

Sebastian Haffner, *Defying Hitler*

Jim Harrison, *Off to the Side*

Tom Hayden, *Irish on the Inside: In Search of the Soul of Irish America*

Ernestine Hayes, *Blonde Indian*

Robin Hemley, *Invented Eden: The Elusive, Disputed History of the Tasaday; Do-Over!*

John Hersey, *Hiroshima*

Adam Hochschild, *King Leopold's Ghost: Greed, Terror and Heroism in Colonial Africa*

Amy Hoffman, *An Army of Ex-Lovers: My Life at the Gay Community News*

Eva Hoffman, *After Such Knowledge: Memory, History, and the Legacy of the Holocaust*

Samuel Hynes, *Flights of Passage: The Soldiers' Tale*

Joyce Johnson, *Minor Characters: A Beat Memoir*

Sebastian Junger, *A Perfect Storm*

Garrison Keillor, *Homegrown Democrat*

Thomas Keneally, *Schindler's List*

Tracy Kidder, *Among Schoolchildren and House*

Woody Kipp, *Viet Cong at Wounded Knee: The Trial of a Blackfeet Activist*

Arthur Kopecky, *New Buffalo: Journals of a Taos Commune*

Jon Krakauer, *Into Thin Air*

Kazuko Kuramoto, *Manchurian Legacy: Memoirs of a Japanese Colonialist*

Anne Lamott, *Traveling Mercies: Some Thoughts on Faith*

Bernard Lefkowitz, *Our Boys*

Beverly Lowry, *Crossed Over*

Howard Lyman, *Mad Cowboy: Plain Truth from the Cattle Rancher Who Won't Eat Meat*

Joe Mackall, *Plain Secrets: An Outsider Among the Amish*

Norman Mailer, *The Executioner's Song*

Nancy Mairs, *Ordinary Time: Cycles in Marriage, Faith, and Renewal*

Nelson Mandela, *Long Walk to Freedom*

Gabriel García Márquez, *News of a Kidnapping*

Peter Matthiessen, *The Snow Leopard*

Pablo Neruda, *Memoirs*

Kathleen Norris, *The Cloister Walk*

Dan O'Brien, *Buffalo for the Broken Heart: Restoring Life to a Black Hills Ranch*

Tillie Olsen, *Silences*

Mary Rose O'Reilley, *Barn at the End of the World: The Apprenticeship of a Quaker, Buddhist Shepherd*

Susan Orlean, *The Orchid Thief*

Amos Oz, *A Tale of Love and Darkness*

Caryl Phillips, *The Atlantic Sound*

Wang Ping, *Aching for Beauty: Footbinding in China*

Jeff Porter, *Oppenheimer Is Watching Me*

Roberta Price, *Huerfano: A Memoir of Life in the Counterculture*

Slavomir Rawicz, *The Long Walk: The True Story of a Trek to Freedom*

Ishmael Reed, *Blues City: A Walk in Oakland*

Cheri Register, *Packinghouse Daughter: A Memoir*

Richard Rhodes, *The Making of the Atomic Bomb*

Mary Roach, *Stiff: The Curious Lives of Human Cadavers*

Mimi Schwartz, *Good Neighbors, Bad Times: Echoes of My Father's German Village*

Bob Shacochis, *The Immaculate Invasion*

Susan Sheehan, *Is There No Place on Earth for Me?*

Fan Shen, *Gang of One: Memoirs of a Red Guard*

Randy Shilts, *And the Band Played On: Politics, People, and the AIDS Epidemic*

Natalia Rachel Singer, *Scraping By in the Big Eighties*

Eugene Sledge, *With the Old Breed: At Peleliu and Okinawa*

Susan Sontag, *Regarding the Pain of Others*

Brent Staples, *Parallel Times: Growing Up in Black and White*

Leny Mendoza Strobel, *A Book of Her Own: Words and Images to Honor the Babaylan*

Mary Swander, *The Desert Pilgrim: En Route to Mysticism and Miracles*

Hunter S. Thompson, *Fear and Loathing in Las Vegas*

Joyce Thompson, *Sailing the Shoe to Timbuktu: A Woman's Adventurous Search for Family, Spirituality, & Love*

Susan Tiberghien, *Circling to the Center: One Woman's Encounter with Silent Prayer*

Jacobo Timerman, *Prisoner Without a Name, Cell Without a Number*

Studs Terkel, *Working*

Patricia Vidgerman, *The Memory Palace of Isabella Stewart Gardner*

Elie Wiesel, *Night*

Tom Wolfe, *The Right Stuff; The Electric Kool-Aid Acid Test*

Experimental, Montage, Lyric, Hybrid Forms

David B., *Epileptic*

Roland Barthes, *A Lover's Discourse*

Alison Bechdel, *Fun Home: A Family Tragicomic*

Sven Birkerts, *My Sky Blue Trades: Growing Up Counter in a Contrary Time*

Eula Biss, *The Balloonists*

Jenny Boully, *The Body: An Essay*

Italo Calvino, *The Road to San Giovanni*

Elias Canetti, *The Agony of Files: Notes and Notations*

E. M. Cioran, *All Gall Is Divided: Aphorisms*

Inga Clendinnen, *Tiger's Eye*

Richard Cohen, *Sweet and Low*

Dennis and Vicki Covington, *Cleaving: The Story of a Marriage*

John D'Agata, *Halls of Fame*

Seamus Deane, *Reading in the Dark*

Ivan Doig, *Heart Earth*

Albert Goldbarth, *Griffin*

Carla Harryman, *Adorno's Noise*

Robin Hemley, *Nola: A Memoir of Faith, Art, and Madness*

Maxine Hong Kingston, *Woman Warrior: Memoirs of a Girlhood Among Ghosts*

Brian Lennon, *City: An Essay*

Primo Levi, *The Periodic Table*

Daniel Mendelsohn, *The Lost: A Search for Six of Six Million*

Ander Monson, *Neck Deep and Other Predicaments*

Dinty Moore, *Between Panic and Desire: Notes from a Series Projectionist*

Pat Mora, *House of Houses*

Donald Morrill, *The Untouched Minutes*

Tim O'Brien, *The Things They Carried*

Anna Cypra Oliver, *Assembling My Father: A Daughter's Detective Story*

Michelle Otero, *Malinche's Daughter*

Kristin Prevallet, *I, Afterlife: Essay in Mourning Time*

James Richardson, *Vectors: Aphorisms and Ten-Second Essays*

Richard Rodriguez, *Days of Obligation*

Marjane Satrapi, *Persepolis: The Story of a Childhood*; *Embroideries*

W. G. Sebald, *The Emigrants*; *The Rings of Saturn*

Bob Shacochis, *Domesticity: A Gastronomic Interpretation of Love*

David Shields, *Enough About You: Adventures in Autobiography*

Peggy Shumaker, *Just Breathe Normally*

Art Spiegelman, *Maus I: A Survivor's Tale: My Father Bleeds History*
and *Maus II: A Survivor's Tale: And Here My Troubles Began*

Lawrence Sutin, *A Postcard Memoir*

Natasha Tarpley, *Girl in the Mirror: Three Generations of Black Women in Motion*

Peter Trachtenberg, *7 Tattoos: A Memoir in the Flesh*

Xu Xi, *Overleaf Hong Kong: Stories and Essays of the Chinese, Overseas*

Personal Essay, Journals, Anthologies

Faith Adiele, *Coming of Age Around the World*

James Baldwin, *Notes of a Native Son*

Jill Bialofsky and Helen Schulman, eds., *Wanting a Child*

Becky Bradway, ed., *In the Middle of the Middle West: Literary Nonfiction from the Heartland*

Janet Burroway, *Embalming Mom: Essays in Life*

Joshua Casteel, *Letters from Abu Ghraib*

Bernard Cooper, *Maps to Anywhere*

John D'Agata, ed., *The Next American Essay*

Charles D'Ambrosio, *Orphans*

Toi Dericotte, *The Black Notebooks: An Interior Journey*

Mark Doty, ed., *Open House: Writers Redefine Home*

Isabelle Eberhardt, *The Nomad: Diaries of Isabelle Eberhardt*

M. F. K. Fisher, *Among Friends*

Patricia Foster, *Just Beneath My Skin: Autobiography and Self-Discovery*

Daniel Francis, ed., *Imagining Ourselves: Classics of Canadian Non-Fiction*

Anne Frank, *The Diary of Anne Frank*

Ian Frazier, *On the Rez; Gone to New York: Adventures in the City*

Kenny Fries, ed., *Staring Back: The Disability Experience from the Inside Out*

Albert Goldbarth, *Many Circles*

Vivian Gornick, *Approaching Eye Level*

Lee Gutkind, Karen Wolk Feinstein, eds., *Silence Kills: Speaking Out and Saving Lives*

Trudier Harris, *Summer Snow: Reflections from a Black Daughter of the South*

Steve Harvey, *Bound for Shady Grove*

Lillian Hellman, *Pentimento*

Emily Hiestand, *Angela the Upside-down Girl and Other Domestic Travels*

Pico Iyer, *Falling Off the Map*

Genevieve Jurgensen, *The Disappearance: A Primer of Loss*

Judith Kitchen, *Distance and Direction; Short Takes: Brief Encounters with Contemporary Nonfiction*

Carl H. Klaus, *My Vegetable Love: A Journal of a Growing Season*

Ted Kooser, *Local Wonders: Seasons in the Bohemian Alps*

David Lazar, *The Body of Brooklyn*

Phillip Lopate, *Against Joie de Vivre; Portrait of My Body*

John Loughery, ed., *The Eloquent Essay: An Anthology of Classic and Creative Nonfiction*

Rasunah Marsden, *Crisp Blue Edges: Indigenous Creative Non-fiction*

James McKean, *Home Stand*

James Alan McPherson, *A Region Not Home: Reflections from Exile*

Molly McQuade, *The Art of the Word*

Brenda Miller, *Season of the Body*

Tom Montgomery-Fate, *Beyond the White Noise*

Kyoko Mori, *Polite Lies: On Being a Woman Caught Between Cultures*

Naomi Shihab Nye, *Never in a Hurry: Essays on People and Places*

Cynthia Ozick, *Fame & Folly, Quarrel & Quandary, and Metaphor & Memory*

Molly Peacock, ed., *The Private I*

Scott Russell Sanders, *Staying Put*

Marjorie Sandor, *The Night Gardener*

May Sarton, *Journal of a Solitude*

Mimi Schwartz, *Thoughts from a Queen-Sized Bed*

David Sedaris, *Me Talk Pretty One Day*

Rebecca Shannonhouse, ed., *Under the Influence: The Literature of Addiction* (fiction and creative nonfiction)

David Shields, *Remote: Reflections on Life in the Shadow of Celebrity*

Floyd Skloot, *A World of Light*

Tom Sleigh, *Interview With a Ghost*

Larry Smith, ed., *Not Quite What I Was Planning: Six-Word Memoirs by Writers Famous and Obscure*

Ilan Stavans, *Dictionary Days: A Defining Passion*

Michael Steinberg, *Still Pitching*

Gerald Stern, *What I Can't Bear Losing*

Ira Sukrungruang, *Scoot Over Skinny: The Fat Nonfiction Anthology*

Abigail Thomas, *Safekeeping: Some True Stories from a Life*

Anne Truitt, *Prospect: The Journal of an Artist*

Robert Vivian, *Cold Snap as Yearning*

Lawrence Weschler, *Vermeer in Bosnia*

E. B. White, *One Man's Meat*

Edmund White, *My Lives*

S. L. Wisenberg, *Holocaust Girls: History, Memory and Other Obsessions*

Virginia Woolf, *Moments of Being; The Death of the Moth and Other Essays*

Xu Xi, *Evanescent Isles: From My City-Village*

Humor

Stephen Akey, *College*

Max Apple, *Roommates: My Grandfather's Story; I Love Gootie: My Grandmother's Story*

Robert Benchley, *Benchley Beside Himself*

Dinty Moore, *The Accidental Buddhist*

S. J. Perelman, *Most of the Most of S. J. Perelman*

David Sedaris, *Naked*

James Thurber, *My Life and Hard Times*

Rachel Toor, *The Pig and I: How I Learned to Love Men Almost as Much as I Love My Pets*

Occupational Memoirs

Sylvia Ashton-Warner, *Teacher*

Lewis Buzbee, *The Yellow-Lighted Bookshop*

Ted Conover, *Newjack: Guarding Sing-Sing*

Pat Conroy, *The Water Is Wide*

Robert Cowser, *Dream Season: A Professor Joins America's Oldest Semi-Pro Football Team*

Huston Diehl, *Dream Not of Other Worlds: Teaching in a Segregated Elementary School, 1970*

Gail Griffin, *Calling: Essays on Teaching in the Mother Tongue*

Brendan Halpin, *Losing My Faculties: A Teacher's Story*

Ben Hamper, *Rivethead*

Jean Harper, *Rose City: A Memoir of Work*

Thomas Lynch, *The Undertaking: Life Studies from the Dismal Trades*

Frank McCourt, *Teacher Man*

Ann McCutchan, *The Muse That Sings: Composers Speak about the Creative Process*

Susan Neville, *Iconography: A Writer's Meditation*

Don Metz, *Confessions of a Country Architect*

Danielle Ofri, *Singular Intimacies: Becoming a Doctor at Bellevue*

Louise Rafkin, *Other People's Dirt: A Housecleaner's Curious Adventures*

Ruth Reichl, *Tender at the Bone: Growing Up at the Table*

Oliver Sacks, *The Man Who Mistook His Wife for a Hat*

Richard Seltzer, *Mortal Lessons: Notes on the Art of Surgery; Confessions of a Knife*

Frank Vertosick, *Why We Hurt; The Natural History of Pain*

Literary Journals Specifically for Nonfiction

Brevity: A Journal of Concise Literary Nonfiction (750 words or less per piece, an online journal) www.creativenonfiction.org/brevity/

Creative Nonfiction

Fourth Genre: Explorations in Nonfiction

Memoir (and)
River Teeth: A Journal of Nonfiction Narrative
Seneca Review (lyric essays)
Smith Magazine (an online experimental nonfiction journal which
    mixes graphics with text) www.smithmag.net
Tiny Lights: A Journal of Personal Essay
Under the Sun

Works Cited

Adams, Lorraine. "Almost Famous: The Rise of the 'Nobody' Memoir." *Washington Monthly* Apr. 2002. <www.washingtonmonthly.com/features/2001/0204.adams.html>.

Agee, Joel. "A Lie That Tells the Truth: Memoir and the Art of Memory." *Harper's* Nov. 2007: 53–58.

Barnes, Kim. Interview with Robert L. Root. *Fourth Genre* Spring 2000: 170–190.

Bechdel, Alison. "What the Little Old Ladies Feel: How I Told My Mother about My Memoir." *Slate* 27 March 2007 <www.slate.com/id/2162410/>.

Brandt, Anthony. "And the Winner Is: Tips from a Pushcart Prize Editor." *Poets & Writers* Nov.–Dec. 2007: 95–98.

Chavez, Lisa D. "Independence Day, Manley Hot Springs, Alaska." *Fourth Genre* Spring 2000: 71–78.

Clinton, Bill. *My Life*. New York: Vintage Books, 2005.

Coles, Robert. Quoted in Joel Agee's "A Lie That Tells the Truth: Memoir and the Art of Memory." *Harper's* Nov. 2007: 55.

Cox, Hyde, and Edward Connery Lathem, eds. *Selected Prose of Robert Frost*. New York: Collier Books, 1949.

D'Agata, John. "Finding Love at Thirty." *Seneca Review* Spring 2000: 5–11.

———. "Hall of Fame of Us/Hall of Fame of Them." *Fourth Genre* Spring 2000: 31.

DeMille, Agnes. *Martha: The Life and Work of Martha Graham*. New York: Random House, 1991.

Didion, Joan. *The Year of Magical Thinking*. New York: Vintage, 2006.

Doty, Mark. "On Writing through the Hard Place." Interview with Carolyn Walker. *The Writer's Chronicle* Feb. 2005: 48–54.

Ehrenreich, Barbara. *Nickel and Dimed: On (Not) Getting by in America*. New York: Metropolitan Books, 2001.

"The Excerpts: The Best and Worst of Culture This Month." Rev. of *Love Sick*, by Sue William Silverman. *Esquire* Apr. 2001: 44.

Felski, Rita. "On Confession." *Women, Autobiography, and Theory*. Eds. Sidonie A. Smith and Julia Watson. Madison: University of Wisconsin Press, 1998. 83–95.

Fletcher, Harrison Candelaria. "The Beautiful City of Tirzah." *New Letters* Fall 2006: 121–135.

Gornick, Vivian. Interview with Stephanie S. Farber. *Fourth Genre* Fall 2006: 133–149.

———. *The Situation and the Story: The Art of Personal Narrative*. New York: Farrar, Straus and Giroux, 2002.

Greene, Candance L. "The Visit." *Brevity* 21 (2006) <www.creativenonfiction .org/brevity/brev21/greene_visit.htm>.

Griffin, Gail. "Confessional and (Finally) Proud of It." Interview with Sue William Silverman. *The Writer's Chronicle* Special Commemorative Issue 2002: 17.

Grimes, William. "Dole Tells Hero's Tale in His Own Plain Way." Rev. of *One Soldier's Story*, by Bob Dole. *New York Times*. 12 Apr. 2005 <query .nytimes.com/gst/fullpage.html?res=9A00EED7153EF931A25757C0A9639 C8B63&fta=y12>.

Guess, Carol. *Gaslight: One Writer's Ghosts*. Anaheim, CA: Odd Girls Press, 2001.

Hampl, Patricia. *I Could Tell You Stories: Sojourns in the Land of Memory*. New York: W. W. Norton, 1999.

———. "We Were Such a Generation — Memoir, Truthfulness, and History." Interview with Shelle Barton, Sheyene Foster Heller, and Jennifer Henderson. *River Teeth: A Journal of Nonfiction Narrative* Spring 2004: 129–142.

Hemery, Michael. "After the Dash." Printed with permission from the author.

Hochschild, Adam. "Isle of Flowers, House of Slaves." *Finding the Trapdoor*. Syracuse: University of Syracuse Press, 1997: 168.

———. *King Leopold's Ghost: A Story of Greed, Terror, and Heroism in Colonial Africa*. Boston: Houghton Mifflin, 1998.

Huber, Sonya. "Trauma, Truth, and Trash: Public and Critical Takes on Memoir." NonfictioNow Conference. University of Iowa. 1 Nov. 2007.

Jamieson, Katherine. "Rob Me Again." *Brevity* 21 (2006) <www.creativenon fiction.org/brevity/brev21/jame_robme.htm>.

Jelinek, Estelle C. *Women's Autobiography: Essays in Criticism*. Bloomington: Indiana University Press, 1980.

Karr, Mary. "The Liar's Club: How I Told My Friends I Was Writing About My Childhood — and What They Said in Return." *Slate* 27 Mar. 2007 <www.slate.com/id/2162744/>.

Kirkpatrick, Melanie. Rev. of *Robert Frost: A Life*, by Jay Parini. *Pif Magazine* 1 Aug. 1999 <http://www.pifmagazine.com/SID/235/>.

Kittredge, William. *Hole in the Sky*. New York: Vintage, 1993.

Lewis, Mindy. "Mindy Lewis: Inside a Life Inside." Interview with Amanda

Bader. *Chronogram* 11 (2002) <www.chronogram.com/issue/2002/11/feature/index.html>.

Martinez, Melani. "The Molino." *Fourth Genre* Spring 2005: 1–8.

McBride, James. Address. Vermont College of Fine Arts. 29 June 2008.

Miller, Brenda. *Seasons of the Body*. Louisville: Sarabande Books, 2002.

Morano, Michele. "Travel in Nonfiction." *Fourth Genre* Fall 2005: 91.

Morris, Edmund. *Dutch: A Memoir of Ronald Reagan*. New York: Random House, 1999.

Mullany, Julie. "The Man Behind the Shower Curtain." *Brevity* 4 (1999) <www.creativenonfiction.org/brevity/Archives/brev4/mullany.htm>.

O'Connor, Flannery. *Mystery and Manners: Occasional Prose*. New York: Farrar, Straus, and Giroux, 1969.

Osanloo, Azita. "The Pressure to Be Exotic." *Poets & Writers* Sep.–Oct. 2006: 27–30.

Paley, Grace. Accessed 25 Sep. 2008. <www.brainyquote.com/quotes/quotes/g/gracepaley178119.html>.

Panning, Anne. "Candy Cigarettes." *Brevity* 23 (2007) <www.creativenonfiction.org/brevity/brev23/panning_cc.htm>.

Parini, Jay. Interview with Paul Holler. *Bookslut* Apr. 2006 <www.bookslut.com/features/2006_04_008406.php>.

———. *Robert Frost: A Life*. New York: Henry Holt, 1999.

Payton, Tom. "Confessional and (Finally) Proud of It." Interview with Sue William Silverman. *Writer's Chronicle* Special Commemorative Issue 2002: 17.

Prewitt, Ellen Morris. "Tetanus, You Understand?" *Brevity* 14 (2003) <www.creativenonfiction.org/brevity/brev14/prewitt_tetanus.htm>.

Price, John. E-mail interview with Sue William Silverman. 25 Sept. 2008.

Publishers Weekly. Rev. of *The Heart Too Long Suppressed*, by Carol Hebald. Accessed 8 Oct. 2008 <www.amazon.com/Heart-Too-LongSuppressed Chronicle/dp/1555534821/ref=sr_1_1?ie=UTF8&s=books&qid=1222542102 &sr=1–1>.

Publishers Weekly. Rev. of *An Evil Cradling: The Five-year Ordeal of a Hostage*, by Brian Keenan. Accessed 8 Oct. 2008 <www.amazon.com/Evil-Cradling-Five-Year-Ordeal-Hostage/dp/0140236414ref=sr_1_3?ie=UTF8&s=books &qid=1222542306&sr=1–3>.

Read, Katy. "Scavengers." *Brevity* 18 (2005) <www.creativenonfiction.org/brevity/brev18/read_scavengers.htm>.

Rich, Adrienne. *On Lies, Secrets, and Silence: Selected Prose*. W. W. Norton, 1979.

Rodriguez, Richard. "Lunch with Speaker Richard Rodriguez." NonfictioNow Conference. University of Iowa. 3 Nov. 2007.

Sexton, Anne. *To Bedlam and Part Way Back*. Boston: Houghton Mifflin, 1960.

Silverman, Sue William. *Love Sick: One Woman's Journey through Sexual Addiction*. New York: W. W. Norton, 2001.

———. "Mock Moons, Metaphor, and Memory." *Fourth Genre* Fall 2005: 71–75.

———. "The Meandering River: An Overview of the Subgenres of Creative Nonfiction." *The Writer's Chronicle* Sept. 2008: 14–20.

———. "The Pat Boone Fan Club." *Arts & Letters: Journal of Contemporary Culture* Spring 2005: 115–125.

Shapiro, Laura. "They're Daddy's Little Girls." *Newsweek* 24 Jan. 1994: 66.

Skube, Michael. "Dysfunctional Lit Is Where It's At." *The Atlanta Journal-Constitution* 20 Apr. 1997: L10.

———. "Readers Can't Take Any More Catharsis." *The Atlanta Journal-Constitution* 9 Feb. 1997: L10.

Swartzlander, Susan, Diana Pace, and Virginia Lee Stamler. "The Ethics of Requiring Students to Write About Their Personal Lives." *Chronicle of Higher Education* 17 Feb. 1993: B1–B2.

Thompson, Lawrence. *Robert Frost*. New York: Henry Holt, 1966.

Trussoni, Danielle. "In a Land Far, Far Away: How I Wrote a Memoir About My Father." *Slate* 28 Mar. 2007 <www.slate.com/id/2162363/>.

Vivian, Robert. "Light Calling to Other Light." *Cold Snap as Yearning*. Lincoln: University of Nebraska Press, 2001: 105–109.

Wolcott, James. "Me, Myself and I." *Vanity Fair* Oct. 1997: 213–218.

Wolfe, Tom. "Letters." *Harper's* Jan. 2008: 6–7.

Woolf, Virginia. *A Room of One's Own*. New York: Harcourt Brace Jovanovich, 1991.

Xi, Xu. *Overleaf Hong Kong: Stories and Essays of the Chinese, Overseas*. Hong Kong: Chameleon Press, 2004.

Yagoda, Ben. "A Brief History of Memoir-Bashing: It's Almost as Old as the Memoir Itself." *Slate* 30 Mar. 2007 <www.slate.com/id/2162995/>.

Biographical Notes

Lisa D. Chavez has published two books of poetry: *Destruction Bay* (West End Press) and *In an Angry Season* (University of Arizona Press), and has been included in such anthologies as *Floricanto Si: A Collection of Latina Poetry, The Floating Borderlands: 25 Years of U.S. Hispanic Literature,* and *American Poetry: The Next Generation.* Her creative nonfiction has been published in *Fourth Genre, The Clackamas Literary Review,* and in various anthologies. She teaches in the creative writing program at the University of New Mexico and lives in the mountains with two unruly Shiba Inus and a German shepherd.

Harrison Candelaria Fletcher's essays have appeared in *The Touchstone Anthology of Contemporary Creative Nonfiction, Fourth Genre, Puerto del Sol, Cimarron Review, Pilgrimage, Open Windows, The Writer's Chronicle,* and other journals. An essay finalist for the National Magazine Award, his recent honors include a Pushcart Prize Special Mention, *New Letters* Prize for the Essay, *New Letters* Readers' Award, and New Millennium Writers honorable mention. An MFA recipient from the Vermont College of Fine Arts, he teaches creative nonfiction at Lighthouse Writers Workshop in Denver, and is also nonfiction editor at *upstreet.*

Candance L. Greene has an MFA in Creative Nonfiction Writing from Goucher College and has been published in several anthologies and magazines, including *Bittersweet: An Anthology of Contemporary Black Women's Poetry; Southern Breezes: An Anthology of Southern Poets;* and the *Baltimore Urbanite Magazine.* She is a regular contributor to *Channel Magazine,* Baltimore's urban lifestyle magazine. She lives in Baltimore with her husband and two sons.

Michael Hemery is a graduate of the MFA program at Vermont College of Fine Arts (VCFA). He received the 2007 François Camoin Scholarship for "outstanding work in fiction or creative nonfiction" from the VCFA Scholarship Fund as well as two nominations for the Association of Writers and Writing Programs Intro Journals Award. He resides in Cleveland, Ohio, with his wife, the poet Stacie Leatherman, and teaches English at North Royalton High School. "After the Dash" appears for the first time in *Fearless Confessions.*

Katherine Jamieson was an Iowa Arts Fellow in the Nonfiction Writing Program at the University of Iowa from 2005–2007. Her work has been published by *Brevity*, *Sage Magazine*, and *Lonely Planet*, and recently she won the Lantern Books Essay Contest for "Too Much of One Thing Ain't Good for Nothing: Lessons from a Non-Throw Away Society." Currently she is working on a book of stories about her experiences living and working in Guyana, South America.

Karen Salyer McElmurray is currently Assistant Professor of Creative Writing at Georgia College and State University. Her debut novel, *Strange Birds in the Tree of Heaven* (Hill Street Press), received the 2001 Thomas and Lillie D. Chaffin Award for Appalachian Writing. Her memoir, *Surrendered Child: a Birth Mother's Journey* (University of Georgia Press), won the Association of Writers and Writing Programs Award for creative nonfiction and was a 2004 National Book Critics Circle Notable Book.

Julie Mullany has a master's in literature from Creighton University and an MFA from Emerson College in Boston. She has won two first-place prizes and one second-place prize in competitions sponsored by the Academy of American Poets, and has been published in *Natural Bridge* and *Brevity*, and written reviews for both *Nebraska Life* and *Opera News*. Currently, she lives in Chicago and is working on a doctoral degree in Clinical Psychology.

Michelle Otero, as a Fulbright Fellow in Oaxaca, Mexico, taught creative writing workshops for women survivors of domestic violence and sexual assault. *Malinche's Daughter*, her essay collection based on this work, was published by Momotombo Press in 2006. Her work has appeared or is forthcoming in *Puerto del Sol*, *Artful Dodge*, *Border Senses*, and other journals in the U.S. and Mexico. A graduate of Harvard University and the MFA in Writing Program at Vermont College of Fine Arts, she currently resides in Albuquerque, New Mexico.

Anne Panning's short story collection *Super America* (University of Georgia Press) won the 2006 Flannery O'Connor Award for Short Fiction. She has also published the book of short stories *The Price of Eggs* (Coffee House Press), as well as short fiction and nonfiction in places such as the *Bellingham Review*, *Prairie Schooner*, *New Letters*, *Passages North*, *Black Warrior Review*, *Quarterly West*, the *Kenyon Review*, and *Under the Sun*. Her essay "Specs: My Life in Eyeglasses" was listed as a Notable Essay in *The 2006 Best American Essays*; another essay, "Secondhand," was listed as Notable in *The 2007 Best American Essays*. She teaches creative writing at SUNY-Brockport.

Ellen Morris Prewitt was the Peter Taylor Fellow in Nonfiction at the Kenyon Summer Writing Program, 2005. Her nonfiction has appeared in *Alaska Quar-*

terly Review, storySouth, Barrelhouse, The Rambler, River Teeth, Fourth Genre, and the KWG Anthology. She was the 2007 winner of the Tennessee Writers Alliance Nonfiction Contest. A short story received a Special Mention in the Pushcart Prize anthology in 2007. A radio commentary received a PRNDI from NPR.

Katy Read's essays, articles, and book reviews have appeared in *Salon, River Teeth, Literal Latte, Brain Child, Chautauqua Literary Journal, Brevity, Working Mother, Real Simple, More, Minnesota Monthly,* the *Chicago Sun-Times,* the *Minneapolis Star Tribune,* and other publications. She has twice been nominated for a Pushcart Prize and has received awards in a number of literary competitions, including the *Chautauqua Literary Journal* Prize for Prose, the William Faulkner–William Wisdom Creative Writing Competition, the *Literal Latte* Essay Award, and the *Mid-American Review* Creative Nonfiction Competition.

Sue William Silverman's memoir *Love Sick: One Woman's Journey through Sexual Addiction* (W. W. Norton) is also a Lifetime Television original movie. Her first memoir, *Because I Remember Terror, Father, I Remember You* (University of Georgia Press), won the Association of Writers and Writing Programs Award in Creative Nonfiction. Her essay "The Pat Boone Fan Club" appears in *The Touchstone Anthology of Contemporary Nonfiction,* while three other essays won contests with *Hotel Amerika, Mid-American Review,* and *Water~Stone Review.* Her poetry collection is *Hieroglyphics in Neon* (Orchises Press). She is associate editor of *Fourth Genre* and teaches writing in the MFA program at the Vermont College of Fine Arts. Please visit www.suewilliamsilverman.com.

Lynn C. Tolson's memoir, *Beyond the Tears: A True Survivor's Story* (Author-House), illustrates physical, emotional, and spiritual transformation after a childhood with domestic violence and sexual abuse. Please visit www.beyondthetears .com.